Regulating Girls and Women

Regulating Girls and Women:

Sexuality, Family, and the Law in Ontario, 1920–1960

Joan Sangster

OXFORD
UNIVERSITY PRESS

OXFORD

UNIVERSITY PRESS

70 Wynford Drive, Don Mills, Ontario M3C 1J9
www.oupcan.com

Oxford University Press is a department of the University of Oxford.
It furthers the University's objective of excellence in research, scholarship,
and education by publishing worldwide in

Oxford   New York

*Athens   Auckland   Bangkok   Bogotá   Buenos Aires   Cape Town
Chennai   Dar es Salaam   Delhi   Florence   Hong Kong   Istanbul   Karachi
Kolkata   Kuala Lumpur   Madrid   Melbourne   Mexico City   Mumbai   Nairobi
Paris   São Paulo   Shanghai   Singapore   Taipei   Tokyo   Toronto   Warsaw*

with associated companies in *Berlin   Ibadan*

Oxford is a trade mark of Oxford University Press
in the UK and in certain other countries

Published in Canada by Oxford University Press

National Library of Canada Cataloguing in Publication Data

Sangster, Joan, 1952–
Regulating girls and women : sexuality, family, and the law in Ontario, 1920–1960

(Canadian social history series)
Includes bibliographical references and index.
ISBN 0–19–541663–5

1. Sex and law—Ontario—History—20th century.
2. Sex discrimination in justice administration—Canada. 3. Sex discrimination
against women—Law and legislation—Ontario. 4. Women—Legal status, laws, etc.—
Ontario. 5. Sex crimes—Ontario. 6. Women—Crimes against—Ontario.
I. Title. II. Series.

HV6593.C3S26 2001   364'.082'09713   C2001–930626–1

1 2 3 4 — 04 03 02 01

This book is printed on permanent (acid-free) paper ∞.
Printed in Canada

Contents

For Bryan

Acknowledgements

This book was conceived over eight years ago when I co-wrote a play—*Under the Law*—about women in the Peterborough courts; I want to thank my co-authors, Peggy Sample and John Lang, for stimulating my academic interest with their wonderful creative energy and talent. My subsequent research was aided by an SSHRC research grant and a Trent University Research Award. It was also nurtured in the stimulating and supportive intellectual environment, which I have come to value immensely, provided by colleagues in the History Department and Women's Studies Program at Trent University. Faculty members and students in the Frost Centre Graduate Program in Canadian Studies and Native Studies maintained an interest in my work; John Milloy and Peter Kulchyski, from Native Studies, were especially helpful, offering suggestions on sections of the manuscript. Mary-Kathleen Dunn and Ruth Ritchie provided important research aid while they were at Trent, and over the last seven years my administrative life has been eased immeasurably by the kindness and assistance of Carol Little and Judy Pinto.

Staff at the National Archives of Canada, the City of Toronto Archives, and the Ontario Archives provided important advice on sources; archivists working in Access and with Court Records in the Ontario Archives deserve special thanks for their guidance. Colleagues across the country provided help by letting me read their unpublished work, commenting on mine, and showing me the way to new sources. I am especially indebted to Judith Fingard and Tamara Myers, whose examples of personal generosity and scholarly excellence have been and continue to be an inspiration to me. Many years ago Cecilia Morgan provided research aid with the Welland Family

Court research. Thank you also to Connie Backhouse, Robin Brownlie, Dorothy Chunn, Jo-Anne Fiske, Amanda Glasbeek, Mary McDonald, Lorna McLean, Kelly Pineault, Marguerite van Die, and to the women who took part in the Workshop on Women in the Criminal Justice System, held at Trent University in the summer of 1999. Kim Pate, from the Canadian Association of Elizabeth Fry Societies, participated in that workshop; her untiring efforts to change the lives of women in conflict with the law is an example for us all.

Many friends have shared discussions with me about my work and offered timely support when my spirits failed me: thank you to Kathy Arnup, Karen Balcom, Molly Blyth, Lykke de la Cour, Ken Cruikshank, Cecilia Danysk, Frances Early, Janet Guildford, Bernice Kaczynski, Linda Kealey, Suzanne Morton, Jane Parpart, Veronica Strong-Boag, Betsy Struthers, and Karen Teeple. Marg Hobbs generously shared her Whitton files with me. She put me up when I needed a place to stay, and continues to put up with me through thick and thin. Heather Murray did invaluable research in Ottawa, engaging me always with her maverick perspective on academic life. Finally, at Oxford University Press, Laura Macleod, Richard Tallman, and Greg Kealey have been a pleasure to deal with.

As always, the ups and downs of researching and writing a book weigh heaviest on those who are closest to us. My children, Kate, Laura, and Rob, have offered me the benefits and criticisms of 'tough love' over these years, while the teenage girls in our household, Beth, Kate, and Laura, have done their best to keep me grounded in the real world, reminding me that the joys of life go far beyond work and manuscripts. My deepest intellectual and emotional debts are to Bryan Palmer, who debated and discussed my research with me, challenged me with his own political passions, but also encouraged me to assert my own. His loyalty and support have nourished me; his love sustains me. This book is dedicated to him.

1

Introduction

In a rare, public disavowal of the courts, Alberta police and child welfare workers recently decried a judicial decision declaring as unconstitutional a law that allows police to seize and isolate minor prostitutes in 'safe houses' for three days. In the war of words between zealous police and the constitutionally cautious courts, those advocating forced removal of prostitutes from the streets claim the law should be used as a protective measure to forestall the sexual exploitation of young girls.[1] Forty years ago the courts may well have concurred, reflecting the prevailing belief that the law should intervene to protect and reform sexually precocious young females.

To historians, on the other hand, the word 'protection' sets off unsettling alarm bells. Sexual protection applied to girls under the previous Juvenile Delinquents Act (1908–84) often slid into coercive surveillance, even stigmatizing incarceration. The protective impulse, no matter how well intentioned, could not effectively counter the abuse or alienation leading many girls to the streets. Moreover, protection was differentially applied according to social class and it might take on the character of racist paternalism when directed at Aboriginal girls. Protection, then, has a troubled history.

As with many current issues relating to youth crime, however, social and political commentators are unlikely to call on history and more likely to situate their discussion within acutely polarized debates over whether youth crime is escalating, why, and what the response should be: 'boot camps or therapy'.[2] While history does not offer pat solutions to present dilemmas, it may stimulate some sobering second thoughts on current debates—by dissecting the changing definitions of criminality and the process by which law constituted gender, race, and class relations; by mounting a critique of past reform efforts; and, importantly, by suggesting how the law affected the lives of girls and women who came into conflict with it.

Like politicians, historians have recently expressed new interest in the law and criminalization. Working-class history, for instance, has redefined its reach, including more discussion of the so-called 'underclass' that often fell through the cracks of wage work and organized labour. Questions of sexuality and sexual orientation, the regulation and practices of working-class eroticism, have also become more central to its agenda. The discursive construction of both criminality and sexuality (and their connections) and the techniques of disciplinary and penal power are being explored through records of the courts, asylums, prisons, expert discourse on crime, and media accounts of criminal trials.[3]

This shift in historical interest—from earning to stealing, from modes of production to modes of pleasure—is comprehensible in the current political context, not only because of the heightened politicization of sexuality and discussion of the underclass metaphor,[4] but also because the theoretical and political tenor of our times has shifted from Marxist debates to post-structuralist and deconstructionist ones. The latter perspectives may not automatically lead to an emphasis on sexuality, law-breaking, and 'deviance'. Yet, as Terry Eagleton suggests, they redirected our gaze to these issues with Foucauldian eyes focused on the 'margins' and on the construction of sexual subjectivity—or, as Marxist critic Teresa Ebert claims, they have cast our eyes away from the very real issues of racism, 'exploitation, labor and production'.[5]

These debates were an important stimulus to the subject of this book, the sexual and familial regulation of women through the law, with the law representing not one monolithic text but a complex of institutions, codes, practices, and personnel designed to govern, control, and aid women. Admittedly, theft, murder, and other crimes against property and persons are not uncomplicated issues. But the sexual regulation of girls and women is intertwined with so many other histories—of the family, medical and social work practice, working-class culture—as well as with debates about the role of the state, courts, and the law in shaping belief and subjectivity, that it is necessarily highly charged and interpretively contested terrain.

Rather than providing a comprehensive history of all familial and sexual regulation, I concentrate on some key issues that drew women into the courts, as plaintiffs or defendants, exploring how women attempted—not always successfully—to use the law (or defy it) to define their own sexual and family lives, as well as the way some women were classified as deviant or criminal by the law, courts, and helping professions. I draw on North American sources to frame my discussion, but have intensively used primary sources from Ontario; my conclusions are thus shaped by this regional context but should still have some broader resonance with women's experiences in other Canadian jurisdictions. Many North American histories of moral regulation have focused on the Progressive period of reform, especially with reference to prostitution,[6] while criminologists tend to concentrate on the contemporary era. I have attempted to join these two together, examining the interwar, war, and postwar period, ending at the beginning of the 1960s when shifts in social theory and politics resulted in significant changes in law and criminology. Although this is not a study of incarceration, I have used penal records, as the histories of crime and punishment are intertwined, often implicating their mutual explanations for criminality. Finally, while conceding that the legal regulation of male and of female sexuality is intimately connected, my focus, due to feminist proclivities, is on the gender-specific supervision of girls and women, who I would argue—contra Foucault's aversion to the word—experienced a more *repressive* version of regulation.

Only a small percentage of the female population came before the courts, and women less often than men, yet the suppositions of the law, as well as women's reactions to their legal ordeals, reveal a broad gamut of social relations based on class, gender, and race. Indeed, the legal treatment accorded a small number of women reveals a much broader web of regulation shaping the proper definitions of sexuality, the family, and gender roles for *all* women. Examining the changing contexts framing women's conflicts with the law, and the strategies women employed to deal with these conflicts, also speaks directly to differences between women and to the importance of class and race in women's criminalization. The links between colonialism and criminalization are especially important because this period saw the alarming increase of the incarceration of Native women in training schools and reformatories, a 'tragedy of recent vintage'[7] that has become more pronounced in recent years. Finally, women's confrontations with the law also shed light on whether, and how, legal reforms facilitated or hindered women's ability to confront oppression, thus addressing issues of public power and the state, as well as private lives and subjectivity.

In the ongoing social and legal struggles to define women's sexuality and family life, there were recurring tensions between domination and defiance, official legalities and practised illegalities.[8] How these tensions worked themselves out is one question addressed in this book. How did the law, in contributing to moral regulation, reinforce but sometimes contest authority? How did the law construct an ideology of proper versus deviant womanhood but also become the focus for conflicts over these polarized definitions? My emphasis, however, rests decidedly on the side of regulation rather than resistance, in part because of the law's successes in inducing consent, but also because the historical sources I have used, including the records of reformatories and training schools, courts, Crown attorneys, professionals, and reform groups, were constructed primarily by those in positions of authority (see Note on Sources, p. 205).

The records of women before the court, or of those who were incarcerated, are especially problematic, highly mediated sources. Women's voices come to us through the enigmatic, sometimes contradictory narratives they and their regulators have left for us; these records are often biased by the recorder's views and incomplete, and may encompass justifications, fabrications, or supplications on the part of an expert, a state official, or the defendant herself.[9] While recognizing these limitations and silences, I believe that alternative stories and subjugated knowledges are perceptible in these records. However mediated, the responses of women, their families, and their communities to crime and punishment suggest that, if 'the face of the law was domination, it was not complete.'[10]

Theoretical Impasses and Advances

Since the 1960s an explosion of feminist research in history, law, and criminology has sensitized us to the inequalities that women as defendants and as victims face in the courtroom, and to how the very definitions of crime are shaped within discourses mirroring unequal power relations of class, race, and gender.[11] Ranging in method from quantitative to deconstructive analyses, this new research agenda marked a decisive break with the past. At the end of the historical period covered in this book—the 1950s—criminology had very little to say about women's experiences, or as Colin Sumner puts it, 'nothing much of value'.[12] Those who did address women and crime often assumed that females were subject to more effective informal controls in the family (an idea resurrected more recently in a new guise);[13] that their crime was more hidden and devious; and especially that their transgressions emerged from arrested or thwarted individual psychological development.[14] While biological explanations of women's lawlessness (still lingering in the interwar period) had faded by the post-World War II period, 'psychogenic'[15] or psychological theories were in full flower.

Staking out different territory, feminist, Marxist, and social control perspectives of the 1960s and 1970s stressed structural and social— rather than familial and pathological—interpretations of crime and criminality. The former may have been implied earlier in some labelling, cultural, or anomie theories of criminology, but new consideration was given to the way the law mediated class relations, conveyed and embodied domination, and reproduced gender hierarchies. Attempting to root the law and crime firmly in economic and social relations, new frameworks and questions centred on how the law constituted, explained, and reproduced forms of domination and, importantly, how this might be changed.[16]

Some emerging Marxist analyses, influenced by a New Left anti-statism and suspicion of policing, initially veered towards the one-dimensional and instrumental, suggesting that crime and policing were used by the bourgeoisie and the state to create a disciplined working class.[17] More often, Marxist analyses rejected the concept that law was simply the 'epiphenomena of the economic system';[18] they attempted to map out the law as a set of social relations and practices that reflected objective social, economic, and political circumstances but was also constructed in the realm of language, culture, and consciousness.[19] The ideological construction and mystification of the law and justice, the creation of 'willing subjects' to the law in democratic capitalist societies, and the way in which the working class might themselves use the law to claim legal redress were all explored by Marxist historians, often under the influence of Gramsci's writings.[20] Similar tools were applied in anti-colonial explorations of the law as a tool of conquest, a 'reflection' of racist tenets 'universalized' in Western legal discourse as 'natural' and just.[21]

Feminists also explored the reflection and reproduction of ideology and social power in the law, though often with reference to the patriarchal or masculinist assumptions underlying it, especially with relation to sexuality and the family. Women's law-breaking, feminists argued, was shaped and interpreted within a different political, economic, and ideological context from men's. Courtroom mercy, for instance, was measured out according to one's adherence to appropriate gender roles, and for women this necessitated an embrace of 'femininity, domesticity and pathology'.[22] While forensic psychiatry depicted women as less rational and balanced than men, often at the mercy of internal emotions,[23] feminist criminologists countered that criminalized women were responding understandably and logically to the difficult social, economic, and familial inequalities shaping their lives.[24] Indeed, the belief in a locatable social reality was a cardinal assumption in much early feminist writing on crime, with the corollary that class was an important structural category of analysis—titles such as *Women, Crime and Poverty* spoke to this assumption.

Some historical work was also influenced by conceptions of social control, a sociological concept defined in so many different ways over the century that, as Pat Carlen noted, it could become 'vacuous'.[25] By the 1970s the concept was often employed as a means of explaining the regulation and control, by informal or formal means, of groups such as the dispossessed or working classes by those with more economic, professional, and social power, as well as by the state. Early anti-delinquency efforts, for example, were linked to middle-class reformers' desire to control the unruly aspects of working-class life as much as to philanthropic concern.[26] In the hands of Nicole Hann Rafter, social control was used to expose the ideology of domesticity and purity underlying early penal reform for women, but also to suggest how criminalized women responded to the social agenda imposed on them by women from different racial and class backgrounds.[27] Similarly, the attempts to control French-Canadian women who 'broke the rules' of legal and social conformity were contrasted by Quebec historian Andrée Lévesque to women's attempts to flout the Church and state, making their own rules.[28]

By the late 1980s the whole terminology of social control was under intense critique. Marxist-inspired studies of the law were faulted both for ignoring gender and for slighting the subtle forms of non-legal and non-state regulation that shape everyday life. Social control theories in general were considered too all-encompassing, deterministic, and top-down in their approach, too much like Marxist instrumentalism in their actual use.[29] Social control became a synonym for mechanistic models that failed to differentiate the shifting historical uses of social/legal regulation, ignored human struggle, contest, and resistance to the law, and assumed a one-way street from formal (state) to informal (familial) control.[30]

Feminist versions of social control, which argued that women's experiences were structured by a patriarchal legal and welfare system, contended other critics, veered towards essentialism and ignored contradiction, negotiation, struggle, and complexity in the making of the law and social policy.[31] In early juvenile courts, for example, the judges and social workers were never the sole authorities shaping the fate of working-class girls and women. Women's interests were fractured by age, class, and race as well as gender, and the efforts of reformers were sometimes embraced by working-class families, or alternatively misappropriated by the state, with unintended, contradictory effects.[32]

The charge that social control theories were used like a 'hammer' is not without justification.[33] Nonetheless, though now scorned as passé in comparison to post-structuralist insights, such theories did spark novel efforts to ask how 'conformity was induced, even assented to, among the less powerful.'[34] They encouraged useful revisions of uncritical histories of reformers, reformatories, and asylums, as well as critiques of the supposedly neutral, benevolent welfare state; indeed, they brought the state 'back in' to challenge pluralistic, consensual views of law and social change. As Adrian Howe notes, the 'politicality'[35] of these works in revisionist criminology and social history was significant for the time. Spurning liberal and administrative approaches, and often critical of punishment in its many guises, this writing attempted to pinpoint the oppressive consequences of social control, implicitly positing an alternative vision of justice and equality.

Although social control terminology is now seldom employed in historical explorations of crime, Marxist or materialist critiques of law and society have not been totally abandoned. Economic determination, state power, and ideology remain important themes, or at least questions, in some historical analyses. Works detailing the creation of a 'moral culture' in the context of bourgeois economic relations, or the class distinctions inherent in the law's operation,[36] articulate concerns that remain compatible with theories of legal pluralism. While many materialists have been influenced by Foucault's emphasis on the dispersed operation of power, they maintain a critical interest in the linkages between 'little powers' and 'big powers, assuming that the "local effects of power are made possible or facilitated" by the condensation of power and its proximity to the coercive capacity of the state.'[37]

Also influenced by Foucault, some feminist scholars turned their attention to how legal discourses define immorality and how 'expert' knowledge normalizes and pathologizes, producing disciplinary powers that cross the boundaries of state and civil society. By the late 1980s, postmodern analyses also questioned the value of grand, overarching theories exploring the structures of class or patriarchal oppression inherent in the law.[38] One work on the history of female delinquency, for example, maintains that feminist indictments of girls' 'sexualization' by a patriarchal criminal justice system were reductionist and 'essentialist'; rather, one should explore the 'multi-plicity of discourses, norms and practices invoked to regulate' girls.[39]

Following on this trajectory, earlier feminist and Marxist analyses of the 'anti-social' family, as a site of oppression shaped by capitalist, heterosexist, and patriarchal social relations sustained in law by ideological consecration of a 'public/private' split, were rejected for their a priori doctrinaire assumptions. Challenging such feminist theories, Nikolas Rose presents the family as a 'complex grid of power relations' reflecting 'new forms of political rationality . . . and transformations in subjective realities', none of which were 'orchestrated by groups imposing the interest of one class or gender upon another.'[40] Though on the surface a more elastic, non-partisan perspective, his analysis is nonetheless also implicitly political in its very antithesis to notions of structure and oppression.[41]

Rose's antipathy to Marxist-feminist formulations reflects the immense influence of Foucault on contemporary social theory. No one writing on either criminality or sexuality today can avoid Foucault's power—myself included. This study has benefited from his appraisal of the law as an expression of power and politics, from his writing on biopower, the body, and sexuality, and from the impetus in Foucauldian theory to extend our gaze beyond the state, dissecting power as a multi-dimensional, complex process and analysing the disciplinary practices, discourses, and self-governance associated with expert knowledges. His trilogy of 'power/knowledge/body' has tested and enriched feminist theory, though even the converted sardonically concede that the 'Foucauldian industry' of replications and dissections of 'the grand master of penality' now approaches a 'religion'.[42]

By the 1980s, Foucauldian influence was articulated through the concept of moral regulation, that is, the 'discursive and political practices' whereby some behaviours, ideals, and values were marginalized and proscribed while others were legitimized and naturalized.[43] In understanding the regulation of sex especially, Foucauldian insights on the 'power/knowledge nexus' have been valuable, illuminating how medical, social science, and legal discourses defined normality and abnormality, setting out boundaries within which 'populations and bodies' were encouraged to act.[44] Medical and social work experts, as this study shows, produced 'classifications and typologies' of girls' delinquency, 'constituted individuals as cases'[45] to be investigated, and explored their actions as overt signs of covert feelings that could best be detected by their investigation and analysis. Foucault thus refocused attention on the operation of power at its micro level through the family, school, church, philanthropy, professions, sciences, and community—forms of regulation not apparently 'reducible to capitalism' or the state.[46] Challenging and even inverting Marxist theories (though often oversimplifying them), Foucault saw power as productive, not repressive, moving 'from bottom to top as well as top to bottom in socio-economic hierarchies of society',[47] dispersed, localized, 'never in anyone's hands'.[48]

By taking up questions relating to how bodies are constituted by and become invested with power relations, Foucault also posed a question already on the agenda for feminists.[49] Portraying sexuality as a social and historical construction, a 'dispersed system of morals, techniques of power, discourses and procedures designed to mould sexual practices to certain strategic ends', he inspired insightful feminist critiques of the female body as a 'strategic site of power'.[50] Women's bodies, Foucault also emphasized, though culturally constructed, may become 'saturated with sex' and thus 'the objects of discipline',[51] an observation that applies strikingly to the legal handling of prostitutes and 'promiscuous' women described in this book. Moreover, the dominant understanding of normal sexuality, circulating through the law and its apparatus, pervaded wider social groups, directing all women's self-governance. As Carolyn Strange and Margaret Little argue in their studies of moral regulation, the benevolent institutions and welfare policies established for young working women and single mothers were designed to chastise and isolate women heedlessly embracing extramarital sex. If only a minority of women were apprehended by the law or cut off welfare, their fate was not lost on the wider community of women.[52]

Finally, and crucially for this study, Foucault's influence has led to proliferating claims that, in the modern period, the law has increasingly been 'absorbed' by the norm.[53] The sovereign power of the law—direct, centralized, held and expressed through the state and its formal codes—was now permeated by non-legal forms of expertise and knowledge such as the medical and social sciences. In the case of delinquency, for example, emphasis was placed not on legal infractions as much as on the child's moral or psychological deviance and the need to reconstruct her conscience. 'The Juvenile Court', wrote Jacques Donzelot in a famous Foucauldian history of the modern family, 'does not really pronounce judgement on crimes; it examines individuals.'[54] Donzelot's work showed how familial regulation emanated not only from the state but from self-justifying centres of professional power or expertise. These experts created an important space in between the state and the individual, which he termed 'the social', a concept employed by subsequent historians of criminality, though with more critical attention to contest and conflict within this sphere.[55]

The time period covered by this study was supposedly characterized by the increasing regulation of daily life by the authority of such experts, including the 'long arms' of psychology, psychiatry, and social work, and some Foucauldian writing suggests that the law literally came to function *as* the norm. 'The operation of discipline', Foucault himself wrote, 'is not ensured by right but by technique, not by the law but by normalization.'[56] Yet the contention that the law has been displaced or 'invaded' by the norm[57] may be overstated, a linear interpretation of history that ignores the persisting plurality of forms of law. This results, as Alan Hunt contends, in the wrongful 'expulsion of law' from modernity.[58] Indeed, even some scholars sympathetic to Foucault are wary of this argument, reminding us that 'juridical power' remains 'formidable'[59] in our time; others, seeking to avoid a polarized depiction of sovereign law versus disciplinary power, have explored how 'social law was welded to the power of the norm.'[60] Rather than presuming the ascendency of discipline over the law, of the norm over sovereignty, I have found it more useful to ask how the law and the professions interacted and combined to regulate women. How, and why, did they produce a system that institutionalized relatively more girls than boys, failed to aid battered wives, and masked the sexual abuse of children? Moreover, were there changing stresses and fissures in this interaction? Why did certain disciplinary discourses come to dominate the legal agenda?

Emanating from his repudiation of the idea of a centralized state and the power of juridical law was Foucault's emerging emphasis on governmentality, that is, the regulatory strategies and techniques operating from and within many discourses, institutions, and practices that shape and guide the conduct of groups and individuals: the 'conduct of conduct', to use Colin Gordon's abbreviation.[61] This idea of 'government at a distance' allows us to see regulation not simply as coercive or objectifying, but as a process involving the 'cultivation of subjectivity', for as active agents, individuals come to make choices embracing regulatory aims, techniques, and strategies.[62] In the Family Court, for instance, women were not simply pressured to take back abusive husbands; they embraced the experts' version of the intact family and the forgiving wife as the best family form for themselves and their children.

Of course, the context that shaped their choices (which were hardly free)[63] is an issue evaded by theorists disinterested in historical determination or causation. Whether self-governance is itself a radically new idea has also been questioned.[64] Our preoccupation with governmentality may reflect the current transition from a 'welfarist' to a neo-liberal society, resonating also with the political moment of 'anti-modernity, anti-authoritarianism and a distrust of an increasingly regulatory society'.[65] Governmentality theorists argue persuasively that we are presently witnessing a heightened 'de-governmentalization of the state', as individuals are persuaded by a diverse array of interests and techniques to become privatized, self-regulating 'experts of themselves'.[66] However, this theory has been criticized by Marxists for its totalizing tendencies, implicit functionalism, and uncritical acceptance of neo-liberalism.[67] Most important for historians, caution needs to be exercised against the embrace of an 'iron rule' of intensifying de-governmentalization of the state over time. The period covered in this study was still characterized by substantial state control over—and by broadening definitions of 'delinquent' and 'deviant'—women but this pattern, like the current impetus towards governmentality, was never an inevitable, inexorable process.

Foucault's power over contemporary social theory has also been challenged on other grounds. Claims that power is diffuse, decentralized, and dispersed, suggest some feminists, mask the recognition that certain 'headquarters' of power do exist, with these interests reflecting and reproducing structural, social oppressions based on class, gender, and race.[68] Focusing on the operation but never the origins of power, on the 'techniques, but never the distributive consequences of rule', has the effect of obscuring discussion of capital accumulation and implies the *raison d'être* of regulation is simply more regulation—offering a grim picture of inescapable domination.[69] Indeed, some Foucauldian literature offers a more profoundly depressing view of 'top inward' regulation/governance than social control paradigms ever did.[70]

For those critical of this anti-foundationalist project, political pessimism, a brake on Utopian thinking, and the paralysis of skepticism are the outcomes of some Foucauldian analyses. One recurring critique of more relativist versions of post-structuralism is their rejection of any normative commitments or 'truth' claims on which to base appeals for justice and freedom—since those concepts themselves are 'invented' and discredited Enlightenment concepts.[71] Even Carol Smart concedes that such a postmodernist deconstruction of sexuality and the law sits uncomfortably with a politics of feminist action around violence, for the former so completely destabilizes the values and claims upon which feminist critiques of violence have been based.[72] Furthermore, even though Foucault pointed to subjugated, alternative discourses that challenge domination, resistance remains inadequately understood or theorized because it persists as a mere reflex reaction, never the product of conscious reflective agency or an awareness of differential access to power.[73] Finally, the calls of post-modern feminists to 'decentre the law', thus avoiding 'general theories' of women's oppression,[74] are a troubling prescription for feminists who see the connections between empirical research and the construction of metatheory as a valuable feminist project. This is especially so for those committed to a materialist analysis of exploitation and a deconstructive *critique* of the state, who believe the law 'and its application are [still] about the centralization of power',[75] often administered to the detriment of marginalized women.

The concept of social censure, developed by Colin Sumner and others, was one alternative means of analysing legal regulation, merging insights from Foucault with a commitment to a 'socialist criminology'.[76] Censuring processes of demarcating the good/bad, holy/demonic, they argue, are intrinsic in all knowledges, and these processes order social relations with political and moral judgements that simultaneously enforce power relations structured upon 'hegemonic masculinity' as well as race and class power.[77] 'Censures, as categories of denunciation', are 'lodged within historically specific moral debates and practical conflicts' that are ideological in nature, and are connected to the dynamics of class as well as gender and race relations.[78] Though drawing heavily on notions of normalization and the power/knowledge alliance, this approach emphasizes that the designation of particular behaviour as 'criminal, wicked, dangerous' is a contested realm of economic, political, and ideological constitution.

Regulation and Resistance

The semantics of naming regulation may be less important than understanding its operation, contradictions, and *raison d'être*. Without imposing a Foucauldian template on women's lives, it is important to explore the specific, local, mundane, lived encounters of women with the law to discover how power, domination, and resistance operated through and against the law. These confrontations must then be situated within a broader historical and theoretical framework: to understand women's criminality it is important to survey the material and social circumstances of women's lives, as well as expert discourses on the family and sexual morality, exploring their mutual imbrication.

In this regard, a materialist and feminist framework[79] allows us to draw on insights about discourse, power, and subjectivity while still allowing for a measure of structural determination; historical materialism makes intelligible how material life shapes the possibilities of discourse and social practice, how the materiality of discourse mediates social practices.[80] However important the discourse of sexualization was for delinquent girls, for example, we must ask why those sentenced to correctional institutions were overwhelmingly poor, working-class, and Native girls. Many women in this study came before the lower courts and were given the 'cheap' or 'low' justice reserved for the working classes, which offered them little in the way of majesty, mercy, or equality.[81] Their misdemeanours and difficulties were often construed by the courts as problems of 'therapy or morality',[82] but this discursive construction was inevitably conditioned by social relations based on class, race, and the sexual double standard.

Moreover, suggestions that we analyse forms of regulation expressed through the law need not lead to an avoidance or downgrading of the state. Rather, the pressure points between women, families, expert discourses, legal institutions, and the state can be examined with an eye to locating patterns and concentrations of power, to identifying how women used the law as a resource for redress while also suffering under its most punitive supervision. In the last resort, the law was an important means of conveying the authority of the state through arrests, fines, imprisonment, or even the refusal to act in women's interest. However important experts and families were to the process of familial and sexual regulation, juridical power offered the final, most coercive answer to women's immorality: incarceration. In some instances, such as with the creation and operation of state-run training schools, the state not only kept a close watch on disciplinary regulation in this period, but actually extended its political ambitions and administrative rule.

We should also be cautious of fully embracing Foucault's overly decentred power, totally subjected subjectivity, and completely governmentalized souls. Feminists and materialists need to engage with Foucault without embracing a universalizing reading of his oeuvre, remaining wary of a preconceived assumption of an ever-increasing, irrational urge to disciplinary power that avoids the central questions of who the agents and benefactors of power are, how social, racial, and economic relations of privilege reproduce that power, and whether resistance to the *unequal* access to power can be mobilized. Questions of privileged interests and strategies of control are critical to the history of women's criminalization, for we need to know which social groups or institutions promoted, used, and endorsed legal regulation, why, and how consent to this rule, including self-governance, was accomplished.

Moreover, interpreting normalization only as a 'libertarian negative'[83] misconstrues women's complex relationship to legal institutions, as well as our own ethical, interpretive responsibilities. Depending on how (and in whose interests) power was exercised, normalization might refer to the sexual restraint of so-called promiscuous women; it might also refer to the application of laws prohibiting incestuous assaults on children. To assume that we must limit ourselves to endlessly tracking the operation of power and normalization, while never distinguishing, ethically, between certain regimes of power, is not acceptable.

Uncovering or at least suggesting 'how it really was' for women in conflict with the law also remains one goal of this study. Some feminists perceive similar, contemporary questions to be potential minefields of essentialism and naïveté, a reflection of the completely compromised enterprise of positivist criminology.[84] Though this goal may be considered impossible (or perhaps unimportant)[85] in the current theoretical moment, I draw instead on older theoretical traditions of socialist humanism, feminist engagement, and even the traditional historical tenets of causation, explication, and empirical inquiry.[86] Indeed, some dissenting criminologists also continue to claim the possibilities of a 'transgressive' feminist scholarship that embraces political, humanist motives.[87]

I would concede that locating women's experience and understandings and assessing their resistance to the law remain deeply problematic, perhaps especially so for historians using closed rather than open-ended sources, which were usually created by the regulators, not criminalized women themselves. This may be even more difficult for those of us like myself whose privileged lives in the present mark our distance from criminalized women of the past. However, historians have long interrogated their sources critically and skeptically, 'working with their limitations',[88] reading them against the grain. Some also advocate attempting to write across boundaries of difference, avoiding a rigid insider/outsider stance on historical reconstruction.[89] Similarly, I believe women's responses and resistance may have been indirect, involving the smallest queries, verbal protests, or acts of non-compliance, but they can be uncovered and assessed. A focus on the coercive side of regulation need not lead to the presumption that all responses to authority-makers are merely knee-jerk reactions to the points of power, never 'active' or transformative in nature.[90]

As a process producing values, beliefs, and symbols and encompassing lived practices, the law worked as ideology, and its claim to truth and fairness offered it immense ideological power, often the invisible, naturalizing hegemony identified by Gramsci. Crime could thus be construed as immorality, in the process transforming other structures of being—poverty, violence, alienation—into narrowly legal issues and obscuring their social nature. Deeply 'embedded both materially and symbolically in the legal process',[91] power was often expressed through regulation, enforcement, or coercion, but it might also manifest itself through contentions and skirmishes over the law's meaning and application. As those contests unfolded, however, they bore the unmistakable markings of hierarchies of race, class, and gender.

The social relations of race and racism encoded in the law were inevitably intertwined with the ongoing project of the Canadian state to colonize and assimilate First Nations peoples. Even if 'race' as a legal category was not articulated in Canadian statutes, racist ideology and relations resonated through the operation of the law.[92] By the 1930s, nineteenth-century biological theories of race were in question, but racism in society and law was simply rearticulated in new forms with reference to culture and environment.[93] Moreover, these notions of racial difference were intertwined with gender and sexuality; though the Female Refuges Act described in Chapter 4 never mentioned race, its actual workings punished white women involved with men of colour and assumed the immoral and promiscuous criminality of First Nations women.[94] Creating and sustaining 'ideal' families through law and bureaucratic policy had long been an enduring ingredient of the state's nation-building project.[95] As a result, the regulation of white working-class and Native women's sexuality sometimes overlapped in intent and strategy, with monogamous marriages, patriarchal and nuclear families, female purity, and domesticity advanced as projects of legal and social 'reform'. But regulation—and by consequence resistance too—also differed in significant ways, as both the image of Native peoples' moral codes and the legal regime they faced were quite distinct.[96]

In an analysis of colonial and race relations embedded in the law, the linkage between law and ideology remains significant. Though it has embraced a postmodern skepticism with the natural classification of race, critical race theory often presupposes a legitimizing, mystifying, and falsifying role of the law in maintaining racial categories and racism. Granting the historical instability and social construction of 'race' does not negate the very real effects of racism. Often clothed in the legitimating language of necessity as well as justice, the law both confirmed popular beliefs concerning racial difference and defined racist boundaries, with whiteness invariably naturalized as superior, non-whiteness as different, inferior.[97] As a means of producing social knowledge, the law played a crucial role in encouraging legal actors and the wider community to perceive, and accept, the world through the racial categories and judgements it sanctified.[98] Moreover, as some critical race theorists have suggested, the law was based not just on consent but also on coercion, with the latter operating more decisively for the non-white and the dispossessed, in part due to 'their material oppression'.[99] The persistence of racism, Kimberlé Crenshaw argues, is produced both by coercion and by ideological consent, but for blacks, whose daily experiences continually contradict the dominant ideology of race equality and 'fairness', coercion is more central. 'Ideology', as she notes succinctly, 'convinces one group that coercion of the other is acceptable.'[100]

Her hypothesis aptly captures the legal regulation of First Nations women described in this study, who were subject, beyond the normal legal regulation of the courts, to an extra layer of state-orchestrated surveillance through the Indian Act. The Indian Act, like other forms of legal regulation explored here, must be interrogated both ethically and politically. More than the infinitesimal operation of power, more than an effect of racialized discourse, more than a normalizing strategy, the Act was grounded in the material and social foundations of colonialism and provided rationales, systems, means, and agents of oppression for generations of Native women. We should not, therefore, abandon as misguided and Utopian the search for other forms of justice for First Nations peoples or for women, even if the current constructions of justice leave much to be desired.

While embracing the 'invigorating skepticism' and deconstructive method of post-structuralism, then, this study remains committed to theoretical traditions of materialism and feminism, to the assumption that historical research can contribute to the construction of theories that analyse and critique exploitation and subordination. To cut ourselves off from these theoretical anchors means the perilous abandonment of a critique of the *systems* of social and gender inequality so clearly entrenched in the criminal justice system. The need to develop an 'emancipatory critical knowledge'[101] concerning women and the law is essential if we are to prevent ourselves from slipping into infinite deconstructions of criminality. The project, instead, is to direct our thoughts to the transformation of those oppressive social relations that sustain criminality.

2

Incest, the Sexual Abuse of Children, and the Power of Familiasm

Evidence that sexual relations have been defined, regulated, and punished in markedly different ways over time is starkly apparent with the example of incest in twentieth-century Canada. Placed officially in the Canadian Criminal Code in 1890, incest was explained and analysed within changing paradigms of legal, medical, and social discourse that are strikingly different today than they were a century earlier. Indeed, we might employ different terminology today, putting more emphasis on those kinds of incest that fall under the broader framework of the 'sexual abuse of children'.

This chapter explores the evolution of these changing understandings of incest, particularly relating to parents and children, and how they worked themselves out in legal contests in Ontario from the inception of the new Criminal Code of 1890 to World War II. The precise legal definition of incest remained almost completely unchanged until minor revisions in 1954 altered the definitions for its prosecution. Moreover, by the 1940s court records are difficult to locate or use.[1]

The evolution of incest in law, between its definition in 1890 and the post-World War II period, indicates how changing notions of sexuality, reproduction, and the family intersected to shape the dominant understandings of incest held by the legal, medical, and social work experts who exercised the power to define, discipline, and punish this crime. While the social and legal *construction* of incest assumes most visibility here, some indication of victims' resistance to sexual abuse also emerges from incest trials and from the case files of incarcerated females claiming incest in their background. Even if medical experts concentrated their ire on the eugenic and reproductive evils of incest, some complainants spoke of the domination and fear shaping their own experiences of abuse. Even if acceptance of familial privacy or rationalizations of 'individual pathology' curtailed legal prosecution, victims might later complain of the deep injuries incest had caused them. While an understanding of official definitions and rulings may outweigh our ability to understand actual human experience, this contrast between official discourses and personal narratives nonetheless provides a chilling and sobering recognition that human suffering may not be easily understood or compensated for by the processes of the law.

Incest in Feminist and Foucauldian Perspective

One of the most significant paradigm shifts in perceptions of incest occurred over the last two decades as feminist critiques of sexual violence in general and of power relations within the family in particular reoriented our conception of parent/child incest to stress the fundamental abuse of power involved in child sexual abuse. This was also linked to the shift in social theory from an emphasis on individual deviance to the larger social processes creating violence and to concerns with how and why definitions of criminality are constructed.

Also breaking with the past, feminist analyses gave new weight to survivors' stories as a more authentic source of evidence about incest; using these narratives, feminist analyses then challenged enduring myths about abuse, such as the conception that children enticed adults into sexual relations or that children experienced little psychic harm from incest.[2] Feminists influenced by Foucault warn that 'confessional' survivor accounts may be constructed and assimilated within the dominant discourses that deny and pathologize sexual abuse victims, but they still claim such accounts have 'transgressive and disruptive' political potential.[3] A major focus of feminist critique has been psychoanalytic theory. Although feminists debate what Freud himself said about incest, most agree that later Freudians dismissed incest as fantasy, denying its occurrence and thereby reflecting the 'androcentric, patriarchal milieus' in which they lived.[4] By the 1950s, argues Diana Russell, Freudians' dismissal of incest 'fantasies', along with Kinsey's new denials of the seriousness of incest, were well entrenched in psychiatric and social work practice, resulting in widespread suppression of survivors' stories.[5]

As a result of new feminist perspectives after the 1970s, the dominant explanations for incest (though there was not one monolithic feminist approach) no longer portray incest as a perverse and rare practice, but rather describe it as an outgrowth of masculinist, patriarchal, or violent social and sexual relations within the family and society. If women are perceived to be sexual possessions, if masculine sexuality is conceived of as a 'right' to sexual access to women, if older male/adolescent female sexuality is romanticized and celebrated in our culture, and if girls are socialized to be submissive and subordinate, feminists argue, then it is not illogical that incest will occur, particularly between male relatives and female children, though these power relations may also exhibit themselves in sibling or same-sex incest as well. 'Abusive actions are not sharply distinguished from accepted notions of masculine [and patriarchal] behaviour' that condone the objectification of the female body, romanticize a sexually predatory male, portray children as 'possessions', and endorse girls' self-effacing obedience to paternal authority.[6]

In their mutual emphasis on the social construction of sexuality through discourse and interest in the exercise of power relations at the heart of sexuality, feminist and Foucauldian interpretations of incest overlap. As Vikki Bell argues in *Interrogating Incest*, Foucault astutely locates modern discussions of incest at the crossroads between kinship/familial prohibitions and the proliferating expert measurement, discussion, and categorization of sexuality. Feminists have drawn on Foucauldian perspectives to question the labelling of the adult abuser as an essentialized, rare 'pathological' type and to explore the powerful gaze of surveillance that often renders victims defenceless, their subjectivity reordered and disoriented.[7] Using Foucault, Bell herself exposes the techniques of surveillance, examination, and hierarchical observation that create the very means of disciplinary power, exerted within the microcosm of the family, used by abusers to exert control over the abused.[8]

Yet, feminists and Foucault also part company in their approaches to incest. The former explore the decidedly structural social conditions that permit the sexual abuse, arguing that Judeo-Christian precepts and gender ideologies, the economic dependency of women, even the 'feudal-like' nature of family organization create a climate in which incest can take place.[9] While Foucault rejected notions of an authentic truth about sexuality, feminists are also more likely to see survivors' accounts in this vein, also accepting, in contrast to Foucault, the a priori existence of power based on patriarchal familial and social structures. The issue of unequal power, one feminist charges, mysteriously evaporates in Foucault's analysis of adult/child sex, which he believed should be completely unregulated.[10] Other writers are disturbed by his neglect of the crucial role violence plays in enforcing power between individuals; indeed, violence itself is 'masked' by the way in which the 'the technologies of power' are neutralized in his writing. The 'human experience of assault' tends to be obscured by Foucauldian theory, it is argued, for 'Foucault was enough of an advocate of power that he could not identify or speak in the voice of the victim. . . . *their* local knowledges are not incorporated into his understanding of power.'[11]

Even a sympathetic Foucauldian like Bell acknowledges that the 'juridical' power of a sovereign, head of family, or patriarch is not extinct but very much alive and central to the operation of incest. Some libertarian feminists sympathize with Foucault's critique of society's moral hierarchy of sexual practices and his rejection of legal and medical restraints controlling sexual activities. But this uncritical and unfettered celebration of the liberatory 'innocence of sexual sin'[12] and all forms of pleasure also makes his opposition to any legal curbs on adult/child sex and his calls for the decriminalization of rape very troubling to other feminists.[13] While agreeing on the need to uncover the production of sexuality through power/knowledge, they want to take this one step further, asking how knowledges about sexuality then create unequal access to power, domination, and violence of one person or group of people *over* others.[14]

These debates offer useful insights for historical explorations of the regulation of incest through the law. While the official legal statutes in the Criminal Code yielded an elementary text for the courts to draw on, this document was interpreted in the context of changing social, medical, and political discourses concerning sexuality, the family, and gender relations. Nor were these the only relations of power at stake. Incest was also perceived to be a cultural, geographical, and above all class problem, with the consequence that the prosecution of incest was shaped—if not distorted—by this discursive rendering of it.

While recognizing that perceptions of incest, even disavowals of it, were moulded by political, legal, and social ideologies and by the material reality of class and gender power structures, we should avoid the tendency to stress the multiple constructions and 'malleability of the idea of child abuse',[15] denying any obligation to understand its very real, debilitating effects. As Linda Gordon noted in a famous exchange with Joan Scott, historians studying family violence cannot ignore the physical reality of 'actual fists battering women's and children's bodies', even as we try to grasp the 'competing understandings' of these assaults by victims, perpetrators, and legal authorities.[16] Whatever their limitations, court and penal records offer some insight into victims' attempts to escape, resist, or come to terms with sexual abuse, thus unmasking the exploitation of power and violence located at its very core.

Incest in Law and Appeal

The law specifically prohibiting incest was first introduced into the Canadian Criminal Code in 1890, extending the laws existing in some provincial jurisdictions to create a consolidated, federal definition of the crime.[17] Introduced within a package of laws on sexual immorality, the incest provision offered severe punishment for 'sexual intercourse' and 'cohabitation' between parents and grandparents and children, brothers, and sisters who were 'aware of their consanguinity', though the Code noted that the female would not be punished if she had intercourse under 'restraint, fear or duress'.[18]

Other relations could be prosecuted under the criminal prohibitions against rape or having carnal knowledge of a girl under 16; indeed, these were the laws used to deal with incest in Ontario before 1890. Step and foster parents might be dealt with quite separately under Criminal Code sanctions prohibiting the 'seduction' of or sexual intercourse with these young women.[19] Presumably, the later 1908 Juvenile Delinquent Act might have been invoked for sexual assaults against children, as it contained clauses prohibiting parents from encouraging immorality in their children. The latter, however, was not routinely employed for this purpose, perhaps, as Tamara Myers argues, because the courts did not see incest as a direct cause of delinquent behaviour.[20]

The 1890 definition of incest reflected legal and social thinking of the late nineteenth century. As Vikki Bell has argued in the British context, lawmakers at this time feared inbreeding and emphasized the eugenic, health, and reproductive dangers of incest, though they also argued that incest was a violation of children and was immoral and sinful. All these points of view were articulated by Canadian parliamentarians in 1890, but most telling was that they were far more concerned with 'designing women' who might exploit the proposed prohibitions against seduction[21] than they were with the incest provisions, even though the Minister of Justice claimed that incest was 'not an uncommon' occurrence. In his presentation of the bill, the minister offered an example of incest in which a father cohabited with his own child 'and produced twelve offspring by her', an illustration undoubtedly meant to incite alarm about the reproductive consequences of continued legal inaction.[22]

His fellow legislators seemed to concur that incest was a 'gross offence',[23] and the only contentious issue was the concern that the whipping provision in the bill not be applied to women who were convicted. A small number of MPs also warned of the dangers of criminalizing the victim, as women were liable to punishment under the law. Echoing emerging feminist and temperance critiques of violent familial abuse by male patriarchs, they recoiled at the thought of fathers forcing themselves on their young daughters. 'These outrages', one MP noted, 'are generally upon very young girls who are absolutely under the power of their fathers.' Such 'helpless parties', he warned, 'should not be liable to the same prosecution.'[24] Indeed, the Liberal leader Edward Blake astutely warned that the 'liability of the child to imprisonment' might simply set up 'obstacles to securing the necessary evidence' to convict the father.[25] Their concerns, however, were allayed by limiting whipping to men and by reassurances that judges would use discretion in their 'provision of punishment'[26] to any female.

This 1890 definition of incest remained largely unchanged for decades. Familial sexual abuse, as a more broadly defined term encompassing all family members, both biological and step, and all kinds of sexual touching and relations, was not fully integrated into legal and social thinking at this time.[27] In 1934 the only amendment added half-brothers and half-sisters to the list of those who could be prosecuted. Over the next four decades, case law across Canada both reinforced the emphasis on the reproductive concerns at the heart of the initial bill and reaffirmed stringent parameters for conviction. Judges appeared reluctant to favour arguments and appeals that in any way infringed on the defendant's right to due process, thus ignoring the context of power and inequality already framing his relationship to the complainant.

Cohabitation, it was decided, had to be accompanied by intercourse, and occupation of the same bed was inadequate proof of incest; rather, the Crown must show *'corpus delicti'*.[28] Though an attempt to have 'emission of seed'[29] a *sine qua non* for a conviction failed on appeal, the fact that lawyers often used this argument attests to the anxieties about reproduction behind incest charges. One appeal even tried to argue that only if children resulted could incest be proven. Other appeals concentrated on the question of whether there was legal proof of either marriage or blood relations—other than the 'mere' testimony of the victims or others who knew the parents.[30] If ignorance of consanguinity could be proven, charges could be dismissed. Using a familiar defence in wife-battering trials, one appeal argued that the father was 'drunk' and therefore did not know he was having sex with his own daughter—though this was too much for the judge, who announced that 'if he was not too drunk to have sexual relations then he was not too drunk to know Hetty was his daughter.'[31]

The law was also contentious when it tackled issues of consent, complicity, and corroboration of evidence. Although it was established that minors need not produce corroborating evidence, in practice this did become an issue in some jury trials, and it became *de rigueur* for women 16 and over.[32] The technicality of age, not an understanding of the daughter's situation in the household—perhaps living alone with a father, relying on him for financial support—was thus the important measuring stick. Clearly, courts had trouble believing non-consensual incest occurred when women were older or when they were sisters to the defendant. If a brother is guilty, as one lawyer attempted to argue, the sister, if over 16, must *by definition* be guilty too; there must be dual convictions or none at all.[33] While power relations between siblings were generally slighted, a youthful victim of paternal incest could spark outrage from the court. When a Toronto man attempted incest with his seven-year-old and was convicted on the testimony of her and a four-year-old girl, the court acknowledged that the crime had technically not transpired but used another statute to imprison him for seven years.[34]

Prosecuting attorneys also had to be careful how they used corroborating evidence and witness accounts of previous or subsequent instances of incest; the jury might be 'warned against'[35] these being key to the case. Moreover, a girl's role as 'accomplice' could be confirmed by her failure to report the crime 'at the first opportunity'.[36] In one appeal, for example, a 15-year-old claimed her father came to her bed at night and threatened her, saying that 'if she called out, her brothers would wake up and they would all go to jail.' Six days later she told her stepmother about the incest and two days after that, her sister. Yet, this time lag was used to launch an appeal against his conviction; at that appeal, the defendant's lawyer also claimed her 'seventy year old' father was unlikely to commit such a crime due to his age.[37]

National statistics, available after 1922, suggest that use of Criminal Code section 176 on incest (after 1927, section 204) was uncommon (see Tables 1 and 2). In Ontario, for example, there were usually fewer than 30 charges a year from 1922 to 1960, although other Family Court records reveal instances of incest, buried in other charges and problems, that were never officially dealt with in court.[38] One study of sexual violence offences from 1885 to 1929 indicates that 14 per cent

Table 1
Incest: Charges and Convictions, Canada and Ontario, 1922–1939

| Year | Canada | | Ontario | | | | Rate of |
	Charged	Convicted	Charged	Convicted	Men	Women	Conviction (Ont.)
1922	47	36	26	19	14	5	73%
1923	39	7	19	15	15	0	79%
1924	37	25	14	13	12	1	93%
1925	49	31	25	13	12	1	52%
1926	36	22	14	7	5	2	50%
1927	45	35	19	16	15	1	84%
1928	47	32	27	19	15	4	70%
1929	40	24	14	9	8	1	64%
1930	71	48	27	17	16	1	63%
1931		43	30	22	19	3	73%
1932	69	57	21	16	14	2	76%
1933	46	31	23	15	15	0	65%
1934	55	42	25	22	21	1	88%
1935	74	59	23	14	11	3	61%
1936	90	75	33	22	19	3	67%
1937	56	43	28	16	14	2	57%
1938	81	68	21	14	13	1	67%
1939	80	62	31	20	19	1	64%

SOURCE: Statistics Canada, *Annual Report of Statistics of Criminal and Other Offences.*

Table 2

Incest: Ontario Commitments and Sentences, Selected Years, 1936–1960

Year	Commitments			Sentences			Per Cent Sentenced	
	Male	Female	Total	Male	Female	Total	Male	Female
1936	20	3	23	13	2	15	65%	67%
1937	26	1	27	17	1	18	65%	100%
1938	19	1	20	11	1	12	57%	100%
1939–40	26	1	27	15	1	16	57%	100%
1944–45	17	0	17	6	0	6	35%	0%
1950–51	10	2	12	7	2	9	70%	100%
1954–55	19	0	19	14	0	14	73%	0%
1959–60	30	1	31	18	1	19	60%	100%

NOTE: Provincial numbers showing commitments (rather than charges) may be greater than the federal numbers showing charges, as not all charges proceeded to a commitment to trial. The case could be dropped by the prosecutor or after a preliminary hearing.

SOURCE: Ontario Sessional Papers, *Report of Prisons and Reformatories for Ontario.*

of the Ontario cases involved family members, but rape or carnal knowledge charges were more frequent than charges of incest.[39] Moreover, between 1890 and 1929, only 25 incest charges were 'serious' or contentious enough to come before the Ontario Criminal Assizes, the higher court of criminal reckoning. Of these, four were deemed 'no bills' and therefore did not proceed to trial, 14 secured not guilty verdicts, and two secured reduced or different charges. A mere five resulted in guilty verdicts.[40] These conviction rates are lower than those for all the courts combined, both nationally and provincially, highlighting the usefulness of these higher criminal court records for revealing the obstacles prosecutors faced in securing convictions.

Ontario Criminal Assize Cases, 1890–1929

The reasons for the paucity of formal criminal charges for incest emerged from the nature of the crime, its effect on the victims and other family members, and its perception by society.[41] Victims felt shame and humiliation, and sometimes projected guilt onto themselves. They were reluctant to expose their experience to public view and were often pressured by the perpetrators with rewards and/or threats, including physical violence. Girls, who comprised the majority of victims,[42] were always caught in an inescapable contradiction: to fulfil their daughterly and feminine roles, they should be passive, accept paternal authority, and remain within the family, all of which precluded an escape from sexual relations they were also told made them immoral and sinful. Moreover, other family members, including mothers, might reject victims' stories, urging them not to precipitate family disintegration and shame with public charges. As in the present, economic, social, and psychological factors created a 'conscious and unconscious need *not to see* that could blind mothers to paternal incest'.[43] It is not surprising that some girls confided their stories first to neighbours, for they feared the implosion that would follow a confession within the family circle. Many girls ultimately used other strategies to escape sexual abuse, such as running away, leaving home to work, or marrying and establishing their own households. In her research on Quebec incest cases, Marie-Aimée Cliche found the average age of abused girls to be 11–15; after 16, she surmises, they could more effectively rebel against the unwanted advances of male relatives.[44] Her conclusions, along with Dorothy Chunn's research on British Columbia, suggest that regional variations in the application of the incest law were often outweighed by shared patterns and problems across the country.[45]

If a jury was involved, they were reluctant to convict without incontrovertible evidence, such as a confession, given the 'heinous'[46] shame of the crime and the severity of punishment. Like other criminal cases involving violence against women, the complainant had to fulfil the role of the 'ideal victim' if the court and jury were to take her charge seriously. Subsequent sexual relations out of wedlock, a lack of shame and guilt on her part, and a delay in coming forward with the accusations, or the father's respectability, were all seen as indications of her complicity or a false accusation.

All of these problems surfaced in the cases tried across the province in the county criminal assizes between 1890 and 1929. Incest often occurred over a long period of time, and a woman's failure to go to the authorities after the first instance cast suspicion on her claims. Women who were not minors, it was believed, had the ability to act completely independently; their material dependence on the family or even continued threats of violence from a father were not considered relevant to the context of their 'acquiescence' to sexual relations. Thus, even in a case where a 33-year-old woman was presented by the prosecution as 'rather simple', and therefore easily pressured, the jury did not believe her claims that unwanted sexual relations occurred with her father. She lived alone with her widowed father, who allowed her only two dresses, told her to 'stay in [behind a] locked door', and isolated her from the outside world, but her age and delay in reporting undoubtedly worked against her, and her father was acquitted.[47]

Two women who subsequently married were not believed, even in one case when a sibling verified that an assault occurred after her sister's marriage.[48] One 20-year-old woman testified that her father repeatedly raped her and threatened to 'kill' her if she told. Despite the fact that her new husband encouraged her to lay the charge, despite testimony from a sister and a neighbour about his assaults, her year-long delay in reporting the last incident due to pressure from her mother not to tell anyone, along with her age and marital status, cast doubt on her story. The fact that mothers sometimes doubted their daughters' claims, or repudiated them, fearing their husbands' violence visited upon them, social shame, family disintegration, the loss of other children to the Children's Aid Society (CAS), or their own impoverishment with the jailing of a breadwinner, created a wall of denial that some victims could not overcome.

Moreover, even when siblings or a mother supported the girl's story, the court might reject it. When a respectable locomotive engineer was tried in 1923 in St Catharines, the judge urged the jury to 'give him the benefit of the doubt', thus pressuring them to accept the 'veracity of the father's story, as opposed to the girl's'.[49] This was the second trial for the man, as the first jury could not reach a verdict, despite the fact that the mother herself laid the complaint and neighbours offered supporting accounts of the father 'with his hands up [the daughter's] clothes'. The father's letter to the mother, pleading with her not to allow the daughter on the stand, declared 'drink was my downfall' and asked for 'forgiveness' and the opportunity to 'change', certainly implying his guilt. However, the jury clearly sympathized with him rather than the daughter who claimed the father threatened to kill her if she told on him; perhaps they bought the defence argument that these 'are respectable working-class people', thus incapable of such crimes.[50] With incest perceived to be a vice of the underclass, a useful defence strategy was to distinguish one's respectable client from such immoral people.

Witnesses could also be discredited due to other family conflicts. In one case, two younger sisters who shared their bed with a 17-year-old sister corroborated her story that their father 'laid on top of her' in the bed, yet the father was still found not guilty. Presumably the sisters' youth made their testimony suspect; moreover, the mother, who laid the complaint, was accused of trying to get rid of a difficult, non-supporting husband.[51]

A similar defence strategy was employed in a Hastings County trial in which the husband was charged with incest against his nine-year-old daughter. It was claimed that the wife was trying to 'put him away' because he did 'not use her right'.[52] He was subsequently found guilty of the lesser charge of assault. In these scenarios, mothers were placed in a difficult double bind: if they supported their daughters' stories, they might also be blamed for failing to safeguard the morality of the home and to protect their daughters adequately.[53]

A girl's presumed intelligence level and her moral character (as well as her family's standing in the community) conditioned how her case was treated. In one case where a stepfather was tried for carnal knowledge, for instance, the girl's subsequent sexual relations were probed by the defence as a means of discrediting her. Ruby testified that her stepfather, who married her mother when she was three, began having sexual relations with her when she was nine, later encouraging her brother to do the same. He came to her 'crib' to fetch her when she almost 10, she claimed, and her mother also put her in her stepfather's bed sometimes, though she begged her not to. The abuse ceased when, as a 15-year-old, she left home to work for another family. Her stepfather had originally taken her 'to a man he

knew in town, and he used her wrongly when his wife was away.'
This relationship, however, became the focus of great scrutiny, and
the older man's romantic postcards to her were introduced as evidence by the defence. Since the second man was comparatively 'nice'
to her, even taking her on a trip, Ruby did not complain about his sexual advances. Moreover, the medical exam ordered by the court was
inconclusive. Her subsequent 'immorality' thus discredited her
stature as a true victim, a common problem in many incest trials.[54]

Some juries also clearly worried that children, perhaps under pressure, would fabricate stories. Favouring an adult's over a child's story,
many courts wanted some corroboration from other witnesses
(despite what the law said), a difficult requirement for a crime often
committed in secrecy. Incest might also leave no visible traces of
physical violence, and juries were thus unconvinced that sex was
forced upon the girl. Even if the man admitted having intercourse
with the daughter, the Crown might accept a reduced plea of assault,
which could be dealt with more expeditiously.[55] The difficulty of
proving that intercourse had occurred sometimes meant doctors were
called in to examine the girl to see if the hymen was broken. If they
claimed it was not, then incest was doubted; but if it was broken, they
might find other explanations, casting doubt on the girl's story, as
with the doctor who commented that this might simply be 'due
to masturbation'.[56]

Those on trial usually had lawyers, but the accusers were less vig-
ilantly protected by counsel in what must have been traumatic courtroom encounters, particularly if they had been physically threatened
by the abuser. A 14-year-old, with only a teenage sister (who was also
accusing the father) to stand by her, suddenly refused to speak against
her father once on the witness stand and, consequently, was given a
contempt charge.[57] In another case, which seemed to confirm the
fears of Edward Blake that victims would be criminalized, 14-year-
old Josephine was charged with incest, along with her father, but,
confused about times and places, she admitted she made a 'false
statement'. The father was acquitted, despite her brother's testimony
supporting her claims. Two years later he was charged with incest
again, after Josephine claimed his paternity for the child she bore in
the school outhouse and disposed of there. The father's lawyer, however, secured the jury's sympathy by reminding them of her previous
admission of 'false statements'. Josephine pleaded guilty to manslaughter and was sent to the reformatory for two years.[58]

The contentious cases represented in the Criminal Assizes were
more likely to result in acquittals, but some did not. Guilty pleas

were entered or returned when the accused admitted to the crime, when corroboration and the incontrovertible 'youthful innocence' of the victim seemed irrefutable, or perhaps when a pregnancy helped to confirm the girl's story.[59] In a famous case described by Karen Dubinsky, repeated pregnancies of three daughters and double infanticide committed by the mother were the catalysts exposing long-standing sexual assaults by a father on his daughters. The father was convicted of incest, the mother of infanticide, and her death sentence was only commuted after a concerted campaign for her release by women's groups—perhaps indicating their underlying sympathy for females caught in the maelstrom of violent and patri-archal families.[60]

The Lindsay Case and the Grand Jury Report

In 1915, the suspicious death of a 14-year-old girl, Lilly Lindsay, alerted the authorities in Peterborough County to the possibility of incest. The extensive records surrounding the Lindsay incest case, as well as its legacy, a grand jury report on sexual abuse and violence against children in this region, provide us with important insight into the legal and social construction of incest and the difficulties in securing convictions for it in the period during and after World War I.

The death of Lilly Lindsay, the daughter of Sandford and Phoebe, resulted in a coroner's inquest. The post-mortem on Lilly confirmed the fears of the local doctor called in by the parents to see the dying girl. Lilly died of a botched abortion, probably performed with an instrument that punctured the uterine wall and resulted in blood poi-soning. The coroner's jury concluded foul play and recommended further investigation.[61]

The provincial authorities immediately dispatched special Ontario Provincial Police (OPP) Constable Boyd to the area. His meetings with neighbours yielded enough evidence not only for an incest trial, but also for charges of murder and causing the death of an unborn child to be laid against both husband and wife. Neighbours testified at the inquest that the girl looked pregnant and admitted to being in trouble. Doctors had recently been visited by the mother asking for something to make her periods 'regular', and Lilly told neighbours that her mother was feeding her pennyroyal pills. Even more damn-ing, one female neighbour told Boyd that Phoebe had admitted Sand-ford 'ran his hands up [Lilly's] clothes', while an eyewitness recounted seeing Sandford on top of his daughter, her clothes dishev-elled, his pants down, while she was picking berries. Most tragic were accounts of Lilly's last hours in terrible pain, so much so that she could be heard from the road near their subsistence farm, 'crying and moaning'. The doctor who removed the afterbirth and administered an anaesthetic to the dying girl testified that, as she fell unconscious, she cried, 'Papa, take your hands away.'[62]

The parents countered that Lilly was impregnated by a former hired hand who visited one night earlier in the year and that she had simply miscarried. Contradicting themselves and their doctors, they were far from credible witnesses. In the face of damning evidence, they altered their names and fled with their remaining three children to the north of the province. Tracked down by the OPP, they were brought back to Peterborough to await their postponed trial, their children removed by the CAS.[63] When they came before the grand jury in February, 'true bills' (indicating enough evidence to proceed) were returned on every charge and Sandford was subsequently convicted of incest by a jury.

However, the presiding judge, William Mulock, ordered a new trial for Sandford after hearing three appeal arguments from his lawyer: first, the Crown did not prove 'emission of seed'; second, there was no legal proof of marriage between Phoebe and Sandford; third, the prosecution had unfairly pointed out to the jury that the prisoner's wife never testified. The first two grounds were common to other appeals, but the final claim that the jury had been prejudiced by the Crown's comment on Phoebe's failure to testify apparently secured a new trial, for this defence 'slip' supposedly contravened the Canada Evidence Act and case law concerning spousal testimony.[64] Once again, the rights of the accused were closely guarded above all else by the courts. In the next criminal assizes, with Supreme Court Justice Falconbridge presiding, the parents were acquitted due to 'insufficient evidence'[65] on all counts.

The judge's benchbooks do not reveal why the second verdict was an acquittal;[66] and newspapers were 'prohibited any detailed publication',[67] presumably because the Lindsays' lawyer claimed public feeling was preventing a fair trial for his clients. However, there were clearly weaknesses in the case, similar to stumbling blocks to convictions in other incest trials. First, the convincing testimony of an honourable victim was nullified by Lilly's death. Complainants were also doubted if any dispersion was cast on their sexual morality; since Lilly's parents asserted she had sex with the hired hand, this cast a shadow of doubt on her character, which, ironically, was already suspect because of her family's marginal social and moral status in the community.

Courts also looked for supporting evidence from other witnesses. In this instance they encountered the mutually reinforcing disavowals of wrongdoing by Sandford and Phoebe, for Lilly's mother *did* testify in the second trial. Finally, the most damning testimony had come from an older woman who had seen Sandford with Lilly in the berry patch and who later claimed to have heard Lilly confess that 'it was her father [who impregnated her], that he bothered her quite a bit.'[68] But this witness was not supported by others who had been with her in the berry patch. OPP Constable Boyd complained that neighbours would tell him 'all' in their homes, but did not want to appear in court: 'I was unable to get definite evidence from these parties. . . . They stated they knew things but would not tell unless they had to.'[69]

His frustrations reflected a recurring problem. Neighbours and relatives were reluctant to intervene in the privacy of the family unless the case was extremely egregious, violent, and brutal.[70] As Dorothy Chunn has argued persuasively in her study of incest cases in BC, attempts to punish incest with new Criminal Code interventions in the family drew on a rationale that such matters were now of public concern. Yet, ironically, a persisting ideological investment in the 'privacy' of the patriarchal family made it difficult to secure convictions: 'competing notions of family as private and crime as public made it difficult for legal authorities to deal with intra-familial crime. The way out was to construct incest as an aberrant act . . . by an abnormal, pathological father.'[71]

A plea for public, legal intervention in the family was precisely what George Hatton, the Peterborough Crown attorney, asked for in 1916 when he wrote to the provincial Attorney General requesting an investigation into the conditions precipitating child abuse in the rural areas of the county. Hatton drew on economic and eugenic arguments, pointing to the long-term social consequences if incest was not dealt with: 'the degenerates and the prostitution which always follow, the lowering of the standard of our people, permeating through generations'. His appeal had a humanitarian edge as well, perhaps even a critique of masculine power: 'when we take into consideration the suffering of these poor children, their health and lives ruined, the immorality of the crime with all its hideousness. . . . It is generally conceded now that a man's home is not his to the total exclusion of the State. . . . The State inspects cattle byres, back yards and outhouses . . . yet the homes of these defenceless children, subjected to the brutal lust of their fathers and brothers are completely neglected.'[72] His request was answered by the initial Lindsay trial judge who commissioned a grand jury in 1916 to report on conditions in the rural back country—soon labelled the 'Badlands'—where the Lindsays had lived.

Why this apparently unusual interest in the crime of incest during World War I? Although incest per se was never openly declared as a major concern by the strong pre-World War I child-saving movement, its overall concern with the mistreatment of children by parents undoubtedly created a hospitable context for such an investigation. Both philanthropic and state efforts (which were closely intertwined) had extended the reach of regulation over child-rearing, especially within poor and working-class families. Hatton's request seemed in keeping with these efforts.[73]

The grand jury report also emerged concurrent with wartime concerns about the loss of healthy white manhood on European battlefields and at a moment of perceived rural crisis in the province. Depopulation and the loss of good land and farmers, it was believed, would lead to social and moral decline.[74] Eugenic ideologies had also been in the public eye for some time, promoted by a social purity movement and health reformers who now warned that 'degenerate stocks are tending to increase' while the 'physically and mentally fit are carrying on the war.' An Ontario Royal Commission on the Feeble Minded took up this cause at the end of the war, advocating sterilization of the mentally unfit as one means of curbing prostitution, sexual immorality, and crime.[75]

Only two days before the Lindsays' final acquittal, this grand jury report was tabled and sent to the Attorney General.[76] Although it was supposed to offer recommendations to eradicate cases of violence against children, the report's underlying assumptions explain why it eventually shrouded, rather than unmasked, the sexual abuse of children. Many of these assumptions, in fact, persisted in medical, court, and penal thinking about incest for the next three decades.

On one hand, the grand jury report tried to avoid tarring the whole rural population of the county with the same brush, claiming violence here was generally 'abnormal'. The jurors listened to testimony from local experts and community leaders[77]—reeves, members of the provincial legislature, doctors, well-to-do farmers, as well as the CAS superintendent—some of whom were quick to defend their rural constituents as the 'honest poor',[78] rough though respectable, of 'good' and loyal British stock and therefore incapable of immorality. One politician argued that the very same conditions—a 'small percentage . . . living in squalid conditions'—were to be found in any 'urban slum' across the province, thus replicating the equation of lower-class culture with immorality.[79]

Assuming precedence, however, were the voices of those who agreed there was a problem of immorality, caused by poverty, over-crowding, isolation, and lack of moral training. The report combined prevailing images of urban and rural incest; the former was often attributed to overcrowding, the latter to isolation and backwardness. Both, it appeared, existed in the Badlands.[80] Poverty and illiteracy, a local doctor told the grand jury, were the sources of incest: 'I have come across cases where families . . . on account of poverty . . . live and eat and sleep in one room, thus familiarizing boys and girls with circumstances that should only take place in seclusion, and stimulat-ing their passions to like deeds.'[81] To these community leaders, abuse resulted from sexual passions run wild in an economically and thus morally impoverished environment. Crown Attorney Hatton's solu-tion for such conditions had already been offered: 'Separate bed-rooms, especially for female children . . . with proper locks on them, must be insisted on. If the people are too poor to make these improvements, the Government should take charge and lend them the money.'[82]

Three major recommendations were made by the grand jury. First, efforts should be made to improve and consolidate schools. With more and better schooling, values that 'make for a decent moral life [could be] inculcated'—a recommendation that implicitly saw the children as part of the problem rather than as victims of violence. Second, better roads would alleviate isolation (also aiding transporta-tion to schools), and third, a police patrol, like the RCMP, should be used to 'search out and expose every cause of low life and low living conditions, and with some power to act' against them.[83] Police could scrutinize squatters, supposedly the 'worst cases' of those drifting in from the outside, who were quickly resigned to a 'slackness in life'.[84] Finally, the government should consider relocating some families to more productive lands.

The Badlands report thus repeated prevailing concerns about 'inbreeding', equating incest with its pernicious eugenic/reproductive outcomes rather than focusing on the abuse of patriarchal power within families. It wove together an assumption of environmental causation, portraying a harsh land and troubled existence that created violence, with metaphors of individual blame and immorality. Sexual abuse, on the one hand, was socially created and alterable, but it was also portrayed as individual, almost innate, emerging from the des-picable depths of individual immorality—a contradictory view that persisted in the minds of psychiatric and social work experts in the interwar period. Ultimately, responsibility remained in the private sphere of dysfunctional families: parents were unable to overcome their 'wretched conditions' and succumbed to 'lust' for their children.[85] Of course, if the lack of sexual control was really the problem, locked bedrooms would be of little use. Nor had the Criminal Assize cases revealed communal sleeping to be the problem, for fathers attacked daughters in their separate bedrooms, as well as in barns, fields, cellars, kitchens, and their mothers' rooms.

The grand jury report thus ideologically managed sexual violence by creating it in the image of the lower class.[86] The construction of the 'imaginary geography'[87] of the Badlands was part of this process: sexual abuse was considered the purview of the poor and backward, contained in a geographical region, which then took on explanatory force as *itself* creating the problem. Such ideological constructions took place within the context of profound inequalities in social power. Sexual crime was projected as a characteristic of the 'other': the poor, ignorant, inbred, and backward, and it need only be policed among the lower orders in defined geographical regions or spaces, a notion that operated to 'veil and mystify the instrumentality of power' operating within the family and larger community.[88] While such characterizations of incest drew predominantly on class differences, they also resembled the racialized images of poor whites or 'white trash' present in the United States.[89] This same period saw the influential American Eugenic Records Office producing studies of poor, rural whites, claiming scientific proof they were 'genetic defectives . . . criminals, imbeciles and paupers',[90] the same kind of predictions of eugenic disorder characterizing the 1919 Ontario Royal Commission on the Feeble Minded.[91]

Thus, the grand jury recommendations would be unlikely to produce more legal prosecutions for incest, let alone convictions. By stressing reproductive and eugenic fears, the report reinforced a limited definition of abuse as sexual intercourse that threatened to produce children of blood relations. The report never questioned the courts' persistent doubts of youthful testimony or their demand for an honourable victim. Nor did it address the emphasis on female obedience and passivity, men's omnipotent familial power, or mothers' fears of violence and destitution, all of which kept cases hidden to begin with. Indeed, as I have argued elsewhere, the grand jury report was resurrected and used in a number of subsequent trials concerning familial violence and child neglect throughout the twenties, *none* of which involved sexual abuse. It became a facile and sensationalized explanation for all forms of violence, which, ironically, often located the problem with mothers, not fathers.[92]

Persisting Themes in the Legal and
Medical Treatment of Incest

The grand jury report was a prophetic indication of persisting themes in subsequent Ontario incest trials and the expert medical discussion about the causes of incest during the 1930s and 1940s. Courts continued to focus on the blood relation of the father to the complainant, often searching out birth certificates to establish paternity,[93] rather than concentrating on the social relations of power within the family. Equating incest only with intercourse, the courts relied on gynecological exams of girls, which might obscure as much as they revealed. Moreover, the prosecution might settle for a lesser charge if incest was difficult to prove.

Appeals to higher Canadian courts concerning the incest law became less frequent, and defence lawyers often resurrected conventional arguments. Lawyers pressed for the corroboration of girls' testimony, though the higher courts firmly defended the view that girls could not be 'accomplices' if they were under the age of consent.[94] A girl's 'moral character', including subsequent illicit relations with boys, might be also be raised by the defence to cast doubt on her story. Some even tried the long-rejected argument that 'emission of seed' and 'proof in the form of children' were necessary to conviction.[95]

The crime itself was also portrayed as so aberrant that more than one court appearance by a defendant resulted in a doctor's assessment to see if the man could be declared legally insane. After finding one father guilty, the judge rationalized that the case was so 'disgusting . . . it would indicate the man was suffering from some mental trouble as a result of his service overseas.'[96] Playing to similar ideas, men told the courts they were not responsible for their actions, as they were 'out of control'—much like the arguments used in some sexual assault cases. One 46-year-old tool-and-die maker, for instance, described the setting of his sexual relations with his daughter in detail. Yet, in his police statement, he also excused his actions as uncontrollable and irrational: 'something came over my mind . . . I can't explain it', he claimed about his first assault of his 13-year-old daughter. 'A devilish feeling came over me', he added about another assault, projecting the blame into a realm of inevitable evil. Echoing the biases of the medical literature, he described incest using a language of passivity with reference to his daughter, clearly to imply consent: 'I asked her if she would do it . . . and she took off her clothes and lay on the couch.'[97] Moreover, he offered reassurance that he usually avoided full penetration or practised 'withdrawal' as if to allay concerns about reproduction. His police statement could well have been written by a lawyer who knew all the standard legal buttons to push.

As in the earlier period, brother/sister incest was viewed skeptically, even if the sister was younger. In a rare instance, a Toronto Juvenile Court judge used his discretion under the Juvenile Delinquent Act to transfer a case to adult court, feeling the boy, who was over 14, fully understood the crime against his sister. After hearing the boy's claim that it was an accident of communal sleeping arrangements and that 'he did not even know what made me do it', the criminal court judge directed a verdict of not guilty.[98]

Some girls' claims about their brothers' forceful advances were simply disbelieved, or girls were presumed to be equally guilty despite age and strength differences. A young woman who gave birth to her brother's child at 13 testified that her 15-year-old brother 'came into her room and held her down' but that she was too frightened to scream or tell her parents. The judge admitted that she didn't even understand the term 'immorality', nor had she known what intercourse was, though ultimately this was attributed to her slow mental capacity. Her brother was charged but given a suspended sentence and returned to the family, leaving his sister no option after her sentence in the Ontario Training School for Girls (OTSG) at Galt, Ontario, except to forsake her family to which she had strong ties or return and live with him.[99] Because the prescription for recovery offered by medical experts was often for girls simply to forget incest, the emotional trauma they faced upon return home was little understood by social workers or doctors.

In this later period, girls also remained especially vulnerable to incest when they were young, isolated, and relied solely on their fathers for support, or when they endured especially authoritarian fathers. One widowed man and new immigrant, for example, brought his daughter, who may not have spoken English, to a rooming house and occupied the same bed, claiming she was his wife.[100] In another instance a daughter, who was the eldest in the family, helped to care for younger siblings and her widowed father, and became easy prey for his threats of isolation and violence; police intervention may have come only when she was badly beaten by him.[101]

Although some men professed shame, or blamed alcohol, others could not relinquish their sense of entitlement to complete control, including sexual access, to their daughters. One father, even though he had been convicted of her indecent assault, demanded to see his daughter who had been sent to the OTSG. Writing to the federal

Department of Justice, he railed that, as a 'Scotsman, a veteran, a Christian, a Salvation Army' member, he had a right to visit. His claim to respectability did not impress provincial officials, who denied his request. Tragically but predictably, the training school did not help his daughter, who was described as 'worse than before she was committed'.[102]

Training school records offer compelling evidence that incest was often hidden from legal and social view. It was not uncommon for judges to send victims of sexual abuse to training schools, even if the social workers and judges felt the girl was 'more sinned against than sinning'.[103] Because she was perceived to be morally polluted and potentially promiscuous, the solution was to isolate her from her family and society in order to reinscribe *her* moral conscience. One judge blithely disregarded a girl's court-appointed lawyer, who protested her sentence to the training school, pointing to the fact that *she* was the victim and should not be mixed with 'incorrigibles'.[104]

In another court judgement a young girl, 'Eileen', who was apparently pregnant by her father, was sent to the training school because of her 'immorality'. She had witnessed her mother's murder by a boarder when she was only seven, then went to live with her father in a lumber camp, where she had to share his bed. Pregnant at 13, she was sent to the OTSG to receive an 'education and moral training'. In a bland euphemism, her pregnancy was described as the result of her 'unhappy home', presumably because paternal incest could not be legally proven.[105]

Some girls did not even talk about incest until they were examined by OTSG psychiatrists; a veil of shame and anger had shielded relatives from prosecution. Others made references to their ill treatment by male relatives in ways that suggested they were victims of abuse, but they could not bring themselves to talk to the psychiatrist about it. Doctors, psychologists, and social workers involved in the juvenile justice system, as well as local CASs, believed girls should be removed from violent, sexually abusive adults, but this solution was sometimes experienced by the girls as *their* punishment. Also, experts working for the courts and penal system had trouble believing girls' stories unless the family fitted the incest stereotype, and they interpreted girls' confused retreats back to these families as evidence that incest had not happened or had not been serious. Some girls' stories were simply dismissed as fabrications, and even if they were believed, their moral complicity, at some level, was assumed.[106] Moreover, doctors' physical descriptions of incest victims betrayed the lingering potency of eugenic theories: they are described as 'big stupid' girls, or 'a [girl] with an 'unhappy . . . hangdog expression that almost makes her look defective.'[107]

A case that surfaced during World War II indicated how the Badlands image of incest had clung tenaciously in legal and medical minds. A 15-year-old, 'Priscilla', was sent to the Training School by a judge because she was 'sex obsessed', having intercourse with boys and men, and she had contracted a venereal disease. Years before, the girl had claimed she was sexually used by her (widowed) father and older brothers, from the age of six, but she was not believed until the school later became alarmed at her sexual awareness and 'amorality'. Nonetheless, her father's initial denials were accepted by the local police. Later, however, the father was sent to the penitentiary for incest after it was clear the girl's story was true.

The interpretative gloss on Priscilla's life proffered by local CAS officials sounded all too familiar. 'The home conditions are appalling', they wrote. These were 'subsistence farmers in the backwoods of [northern] Ontario, parents below normal intelligence, only one child normal, one in Orillia [the hospital for the mentally retarded].' The doctor who examined Priscilla at the Hospital for Sick Children in Toronto referred to her as a 'moral delinquent' and concluded that the 'environment she was brought up in was so bad it is impossible to say yet whether this is secondary to the environment, or if due to some *inherent defect*.'[108] In and out of foster homes and the OTSG, isolated, desperately wanting some kind of family, hostile, unhappy, violent and abusive to others, Priscilla was ultimately deemed unreachable by the institution. Asked to look into the future, her last words to the OTGS board, at age 17, may sum up her damaged psyche: 'it doesn't matter.'[109]

Combined with criminal court files, training school records also demonstrate how girls, and sometimes their allies within families, attempted to resist incest. Older sisters sometimes actively intervened to protect younger sisters. One 16-year-old in the late nineteenth century, already working and living away from home, returned to aid her 14-year-old sister who, like her, had been sexually assaulted by their father. From her testimony it seemed clear she had previously tried to shield her sister from her own fate when they shared a bed. 'My father', the younger girl testified, 'tried to do the same thing [have intercourse] to Katie when she and I were sleeping together. Before that . . . Katie would put me to the front of the bed.'[110]

Mothers might also aid their daughters' attempts to secure justice through the courts, and the courage needed to brave a courtroom with incest charges should not be underestimated. By the 1930s, these cases were often closed to the public, but in the late nineteenth and early twentieth centuries, public trials and newspaper coverage resulted in intense community scrutiny. Still, daughters and their familial allies testified against fathers or brothers and even registered their vocal objections to acquittals. When one 'respectable' man was acquitted in St Catharines, after strong pressure from the judge, a mother and daughter shouted out 'liar' as the father spoke in court.[111]

Simply telling someone else took fortitude and bravery, for family members might easily reject the story and thus, also, the daughter telling it. One mother conceded on the witness stand that she initially rejected her daughter's account of her father attacking her 'in the hay loft, in the barn and in the house' when the mother was away and only the younger siblings were at home. 'She told me five or six times' before [she] believed her, she admitted, finally accepting the daughter's story when it was substantiated by her brother, and also because she knew 'her daughter was not a bad girl.'[112] Other daughters, such as one hearing-disabled girl, were never believed, especially if they became problematic runaways afterwards.[113]

Indeed, most responses to incest never involved the courts. Often, agencies such as the CAS would warn the family or remove the daughter, placing her with a relative, in a foster home, or even in a training school. In many cases, girls responded by running away and using sex as a means of barter or a form of rebellion—a topic discussed again in the chapter on juvenile delinquency. Some, as we have seen, also escaped into marriage, though if they lived close to abusing fathers this did not necessarily stop the attacks. These instances of resistance to incest do not, admittedly, provide us with transparent, absolute understandings of its effects on its victims. Psychiatrists working with survivors in the OTSG could not even agree on possible treatment; some advocated repression of the past, others claimed the girls needed 'intensive psychotherapy', which the school could not provide.[114] Nor could they understand why some survivors could live through the pain and others seemed defeated by it. In two cases of very young victims, both noted above, one young woman managed, outwardly, to become an OTSG 'success' story, securing an education and a job and assuming her own family responsibilities. The other young victim, Priscilla, travelled in and out of foster homes for nine years. Even though she admitted that some foster parents offered her affection, she could not deal with her anger, resentment, and hatred of herself and others. The experts eventually designated her hopeless, with some blame attached to her 'weak' personality. Instead, they might have concluded that for some young women the ability to lead a 'normal' life had simply been crushed by the violence and domination at the heart of sexual abuse.[115]

The Triumph of Blaming the Mother

The damaged psyches of such young women would find little comprehension in the medical and psychiatric writing of the time. In the interwar period, and indeed into the 1950s, expert interpretations of incest stressed its abnormality and location in very peripheral social groups. Moreover, the legal preoccupation with accomplices was closely intertwined with medical suspicions of girls' complicity.

While few medical and social work journals broached the subject until the 1960s—a crucial silence—those that did, often focused on incest taboos in non-Western cultures[116] or on its eugenic outcomes. One famous psychiatrist writing in the 1930s, for example, examined the three offspring of a brother and sister, looking for mental defect, and expressed some surprise that two children were 'normal' in behaviour and scholastic ability.[117] Often basing their conclusions on one or a few cases, psychologists and psychiatrists also portrayed incest as the product of marginal, 'sexually lax' communities in 'slum areas'[118] and of families typified by 'poverty, alcoholism and poor education'.[119]

By the 1940s, eugenic themes were increasingly replaced by psychoanalytic ones. Generalizing on the basis of five women who supposedly 'sought out substitutes in promiscuous sex' to replace earlier incestuous relations with their fathers, one study concluded that the emotional impact of incest on those in adolescence was more severe than for younger children. The former understood the incest taboo, they reasoned, while the latter often 'unconsciously desire the sexual activity and become a more or less willing partner.'[120] Indeed, the language in medical writing often betrayed a view that girls were complicit, referring to their 'indulgence', 'compliance', or 'attachment' to their fathers. We should not 'cloak all children in innocence', concluded one learned study, since some play a 'cooperative and initiating' role in sexual relations with adults.[121]

The Freudian thread of influence was starkly evident in one case study, published in the *Psychoanalytic Review*, which was then utilized by later experts as well. The doctor writing up the case first mused over whether he was dealing with anything other than incest 'fantasies'. After conceding the incest had happened, and even that it had severe emotional consequences for the woman he studied, he went on to offer his final conclusion concerning her 'neurotic' behaviour: it was explained by the fact that her 'early acquaintance with male anatomy led her to strongly envy the possession of a penis.'[122]

By the 1950s some Freudian interpretations had the benefit of including social fathers, such as step and foster fathers, as well as biological fathers in their analysis of sexual abuse. But incest was still located within the purview of the poor and, increasingly, the blame was placed squarely on inadequate mothers. In their first interviews, the mothers of incest victims appeared 'careless in dress, infantile, extremely dependent and intellectually dull',[123] wrote one team of experts. Moreover, scarred by 'controlling' maternal figures in their own families, these women often emotionally and sexually 'deserted' their husbands, then implicitly offered up their daughters as sexual surrogates for the father. Thus emotionally 'abandoned' by their mothers, girls 'in their loneliness and fear accepted the father's sexual advances as an expression of affection', though they would later compensate with 'repetitive [sexual] compulsion' towards other men.[124]

Such Freudian interpretations 'gave [experts] the opportunity to explain away incest'[125] rather than face its traumatic effects, a problem worsened, as Diana Russell argues, by the deliberate disregard, or rather, acceptance of adult/child incest by Kinsey researchers in the 1950s.[126] Well into the 1960s, criminologists writing on sexually delinquent girls repeated the idea that incest might be a fabricated response of girls to difficult relationships with mothers and fathers, or they reverted to the notion that it was an uncommon, aberrant, deviant behaviour of the 'lower classes'. A strong current of 'mother-blaming', with mothers portrayed as 'colluders, as helpless dependents, or as victims', permeated the expert literature until it was challenged by feminist analysis 20 years ago.[127]

It is hard to escape the conclusion that, as women's child-rearing roles were accorded more significance and were heavily scrutinized by professional experts after World War I, women were made responsible for preventing violence against children. A recent historical overview of sexual abuse in the United States has suggested that a number of interrelated factors produced a virtual silence on sexual abuse from the 1920s to the 1960s: the decline of feminism, blurred definitions of categories of violence and neglect, conflicting social work strategies for prevention and protection, the impact of psychoanalytic theory, and a focus on the difficult economic conditions in the 1930s.[128] These same factors shaped the Canadian silences about sexual abuse, as well as its representation as uncommon, emerging from poor, dysfunctional, possibly feeble-minded families.

In the years after World War I, the child-saving work of the Children's Aid Societies and Juvenile Courts focused on the ill treatment and desertion of children, as well as the immorality of parents (such as their adultery and drinking). Although violence against children was a concern for the CAS and the courts, family preservation often remained a central goal. In the interwar period, for instance, the Peterborough Children's Aid Society declared it aspired 'not to break up homes but make them better',[129] while simultaneously voicing its belief that only *mothers'* efforts would counter immorality against children.[130]

The logical end of these social and legal processes was vividly displayed in the parliamentary discussions concerning changes to the incest law (new section 142 of the Criminal Code) in 1954. Once again, the issue of corroboration reared its head. During an overhaul of the Criminal Code, parliamentarians discussed whether there should be consistency with regard to judicial warnings about the need for corroboration of rape, carnal knowledge, and incest charges.

Discussing the existing incest law, MP and lawyer Patrick Nowlan immediately invoked his personal experiences as evidence. He recently defended a case, he claimed, in which the girl was forced by her mother to testify against the father and thus send him to the penitentiary, as the mother wanted to 'take on' a new boyfriend. Defending his masculine lawyerly reputation, Nowlan added, 'I didn't have much trouble breaking [the girl] down on the witness stand.' He also claimed that he had recently seen three such incidents, noting that false accusations might be more prevalent in intra-family charges, though admittedly, this happened with a rather 'poor type' of family.[131] John Diefenbaker, known for his defence of civil liberties, agreed judges should be required to issue warnings to juries about convictions for incest where there was no corroboration. We need to 'protect the accused who is innocent from being convicted by those who by *design* invent a story. . . . I do not believe parliament intends to take away that element of protection against the kind of unfounded charges frequently to be found in families when wives decide that they wish to disassociate themselves from their husbands.'[132]

The matter was complicated further by their discussion of incest between adults, which, one MP reminded his fellows, 'implies consent upon the part of both parties . . . with the lady giving evidence, the accomplice.'[133] It was ultimately agreed that an incest conviction, like these other crimes, required 'corroboration in a material particular of evidence implicating the accused' as well as the testimony of 'one witness'.[134] This tightened protection for the accused, making it even more difficult to secure convictions. These deliberations were a stark contrast to those undertaken by MPs in 1890. There was no voice, like that of Edward Blake, speaking of the abuse of power involved in incest or worrying that girls would be wrongly convicted. Instead, the rights of the accused and a deep suspicion of women's abuse of their power to falsely accuse men predominates. Indeed, the 'designing' women that MPs feared would exploit seduction charges in 1890 were replaced in 1954 by the 'designing' mothers who would pressure their daughters into making false accusations of incest. In the context of a weakened feminist movement little concerned with violence, with the triumph of Freudian thought shrouding incest, and with persisting class biases that denied violence existed across the social spectrum, the turn of events in the 1950s was entirely comprehensible. For incest victims, however, it was entirely tragic.

Conclusion

The irony of the incest law was that the late nineteenth-century discussions surrounding its creation incorporated a modicum of insight into the abuse of paternal power involved in familial sexual abuse, a view subsequently lost in the legal treatment and medical discussion of incest by the mid-twentieth century. Of course, we should not idealize the early legislative and legal attempts to deal with incest. The incest laws were also shaped initially by narrow reproductive and eugenic concerns, and conviction was always circumscribed by an intense concern for the rights of the accused, with little understanding of the situation of victims. For those girls and women who did attempt to use legal means to secure justice, the criminal justice system provided more barriers than encouragement. The court cases examined here, from the late nineteenth century to World War II, indicate that judges and juries were reluctant to convict without clear confessions, some corroboration, or the untouchable testimony of an ideal victim.

Incest trials, of course, were not undertaken in a vacuum; the legal process was intertwined with the dominant social, medical, and political ideologies of the time, as well as by the material realities of gender and class power structures. Social and economic conditions profoundly shaped the options of those who were abused and their ability to escape, resist, or confront abuse.[135] The possibility of pursuing incest through the courts was also restrained by a strong investment in familial privacy, an acceptance of paternal power, and disbelief that abuse occurred outside of very poor, immoral, and depraved families. The ideology of familial privacy always coexisted uneasily with intermittent calls, like the one articulated by Crown Attorney Hatton, for public protection of disadvantaged children through the legal regulation of sex.

The medicalization of sexual offences and the increasing influence of psychoanalytic categories on legal processes, especially during the interwar period and after, meant that male perpetrators were seen as 'pathological'[136] individuals, and the very 'ordinariness' of sexual abuse was overlooked, just as the Badlands report displaced incest onto a small, abnormal rural population. Moreover, medical discourse increasingly justified and accentuated the legal preoccupation with women's 'complicity', as mothers and daughters, not fathers, were held accountable for the abuse or perhaps were accused of fabricating it. Until a full-fledged critique of this medical model, of the sexual double standard, of familial privacy, and of the material, social, and emotional imbalances of power within male-dominated families emerged, efforts would be made to patch over, if not suppress, the fissures of sexual abuse within the family.

Given the strength of these forces, the resistance of girls to incest, their public testimony against abusers, and their clear articulation of resentment, anger, and hurt seems all the more remarkable. Abuse often reinscribed their subjectivity, and no moral makeover offered by a training school would alter that. For many girls, incest was a nightmare that lasted with them, working itself out in different forms of unhappiness, despair, or violence. More recent attempts to unravel these very real effects of abuse on survivors differ profoundly from earlier medical and social analyses of incest; they also owe less to Foucault than to feminist analyses of power, knowledge, and sexuality.

Incest presents feminist theorists of law and society with contradictory and troubling questions. The use of the law to monitor and police sexual relationships raises questions about how scholars, under the influence of Foucault, have interpreted such state intervention and moral regulation. Often, a subtle interpretive thread poses regulation as intrusive, repressive, anti-libertarian and ineffective. Foucault's skepticism that either the law or scientific theories of sexuality have successfully uncovered injustices, defended the needs of the victims, or offered up sexual 'freedom'[137] may have some legitimacy. However, his disavowal of the moral and ethical condemnations of certain kinds of sex sits less comfortably with some feminist analyses. If feminists accept the authenticity of incest survivors' accounts, if they accept the existence of a priori power relations shaping incest, then regulation may appear attractive in some areas of sexual life—such as adult/child sex—if not in others. The argument can be made that, historically, attempts to protect girls from sexual abuse using the long arm of the law were dismal failures. But does this always have to be true?

3

Rhetoric of Shame, Reality of Leniency: Wife Assault and the Law

In January 1950 a Peterborough man appeared in Magistrate's Court charged with wife assault. The magistrate reprimanded the husband severely, as his wife was badly beaten, her 'face almost unrecognizable' after the vicious assault.[1] Making his abhorrence of the man's actions clear, the magistrate sentenced him to a jail term and a whipping. While the magistrate's cure for the man's violence—prescribing more violence—would be seen today as counterproductive, his condemnation of violence against women would not. But was his denunciation of wife-battering distinctive to the 1950s? Twenty years earlier, in the very same courtroom another local magistrate had similarly castigated a husband who had assaulted his wife for abandoning his paternal role as protector and prescribed a jail sentence, pronouncing, 'I don't believe in condoning wife beating and you may count yourself fortunate for receiving as light a sentence as you did.'[2]

Were these two pronouncements, over 20 years apart, apparently similar? Were the courts in the past sympathetic to the plight of battered women? While family violence was by no means limited to wife assault, this was one of the repeated, seemingly intractable forms of brutality that the courts tried to deal with. This chapter examines women's attempts to use the law to end or escape their partners' violence and the responses of the legal system to wife assault. Women's options included the laying of formal charges, under section 292 of the Criminal Code, which prohibited men from 'assaulting and beating' their 'wives and other females',[3] but there were also more informal solutions, such as probation, mediation, and counselling. Legal strategies for dealing with violence were linked in turn to the broader material and ideological context of the time: social and expert attitudes towards wife-beating,[4] the views of police and legal authorities towards their clients, the prevailing familial and gender ideals, and the economic and social choices women faced as alternatives to marriage. They were also influenced by the predominant, though sometimes contested, definitions of masculinity and by the attempts of husbands to confront, manipulate, or evade the law.

Drawing on legal records, such as Family Court, criminal court, and Crown attorney files, as well as published accounts of violence, I examine women from both rural and urban Ontario in three counties from 1920 to 1960, with the purpose of locating similarities and contrasts over time and place in the treatment of wife abuse. While the Toronto Family Court was established in 1929 specifically to deal with problems like violence, non-support, and juvenile delinquency, Welland and Peterborough counties contained small cities and surrounding rural areas, which used Magistrate's Courts until Family Courts were established in the later 1940s. Welland was distinguished by a more varied ethnic mix than the very Anglo-Celtic Peterborough County, but both were small manufacturing cities surrounded by farms and villages. Smaller cities like these lacked many social services; moreover, kinship ties and community reputation were often well known to local legal authorities. As a consequence, patterns of paternalism persisted in such small cities in the operation of the criminal justice system. In contrast, the Toronto (York County) court dealt with a larger, more ethnically diverse population, and its work was supported by probation officers, a psychiatric clinic, and links to many other social service and welfare agencies.[5]

Although there were differences in attitudes towards spousal violence, as well as in women's strategies for dealing with it, shaped by these different geographical and social contexts, there are also striking similarities among the three jurisdictions. Moreover, despite some changes over this 40-year period, particularly because the founding of new Family Courts augmented the means of dealing with wife assault, there were stubborn consistencies over time. Whatever the laudable intentions of the Family Courts, they could not and did not significantly transform the lives of women trying to find peace and security through the court system. These depressing continuities across time and place arose because, more than the letter of the law or the kind of court involved, the broader ideological understanding of gendered violence and the social and material options women faced were the deciding factors in their efforts to escape domestic abuse.

The law was a resource that women drew on, hoping that its regulatory potential would offer them respite or freedom from abuse. It was also profoundly limiting, for its operation implicitly legitimized the ideas and conditions sustaining unequal power relations between men and women. Unlike nineteenth-century law, which displayed its investment in patriarchy quite openly, these new post-suffrage legal regimes (now often incorporating professional female social workers) apparently promoted more autonomy and rights for women. Because the law replicated gender inequality at a far more subtle level, a feminist critique of it was difficult, if not unlikely, in this period.

Feminist Views of Wife Assault

It is a tragic truism that the place women should feel safe—their homes—is actually the place where they are most vulnerable to violence, which is often perpetrated by the very people women are taught to trust and love.[6] Yet, until the last 20 years, expositions on history and law rarely discussed violence against women, sustaining a 'myth of marital bliss'[7] in which the asymmetrical power relations of the family were hidden from history. Some writers have suggested that wife abuse is a recent phenomenon, or at least that it is increasing, stimulated in part by women's new attempts at independence.[8] Historical research, however, has begun to expose extensive evidence of wife-battering in late nineteenth- and early twentieth-century Canada, though given the limitations of historical sources, quantifying the increases and decreases in violence over time has been extremely difficult. It is evident from these emerging studies that such violence was encouraged by power struggles within the patriarchal family and was linked to patterns of masculine control and hostility towards women. Violence was also resisted by some women, but with marginal success; from the police, courts, and social services women received minimal protection.[9]

The feminist movement has challenged both conscious and unconscious attempts to sweep wife-battering under the patriarchal rug. In the late nineteenth century feminist suffragists and temperance advocates made the first attempts to critique wife abuse, though their analyses were partial, ethnocentric, and class-biased. They often assumed working-class and immigrant men were the culprits and that drink was the primary cause of, rather than the excuse for, battering.[10] In the two decades after World War I the issue was occasionally discussed within the realm of social welfare provision for deserted wives and broken families or in relation to calls for Family Courts, but more often it was obscured both in the popular press and in such social work journals as *Canadian Welfare*. In popular culture, a masculine

humour that reflected a demeaning view of women and marriage—
sometimes even mocking marital violence—predominated in the
interwar period,[11] and as Linda Gordon notes for the US, economic
concerns about family disintegration occasioned by unemployment
and the Great Depression resulted in the 'de-emphasis' on male violence within the family during the 1930s.[12] Nor did the issue become
a significant social issue in the 1940s or 1950s, when liberal and radical feminist organizing was relatively weak and when the domination of Freudian and functionalist models in social work and
psychiatry, both influential forces in the newly established Family
Courts, set their therapeutic sights on protecting family unity.

The suggestion that violence against women was discounted in
Canada until a renewed feminist movement of the 1970s exposed it
thus bears some truth.[13] Violence became a more central political
issue when second-wave feminists developed a critique of women's
oppression within the family and when they were willing to consider
alternatives to the traditional nuclear, heterosexual family. At the
same time, feminists are not of one voice on the issue. Radical feminist thinking, which dominated early discussions of domestic violence,[14] often searched for a 'universal model of patriarchy'[15] to
explain the connections between sexuality, violence, and male dominance and the way men's physical threat and control of women conditions both women's oppression and men's social power. In contrast,
materialist feminist theorizing, by concentrating on other dimensions
of women's oppression, such as class exploitation and the relationship between patriarchy and capitalism, initially ceded much of the
explication of violence to radical feminism.[16] While maintaining the
importance of historical change and variation in gender relations,
socialist feminists have nonetheless tried to come to terms with the
alarming persistence of violence against women. Rather than stressing the inherent tendency of all men to dominate, they suggest that
violence is shaped by 'material deprivation as well as women's
dependence and powerlessness, and men's assumptions of their right
to control women'.[17] As Lynne Segal argues, if domestic violence
appears to prevail among the poor and working class, this partly
reflects more intrusive policing and surveillance of groups. It is fal-
lacy to think that middle-class men do not use violence (for their status has protected them from public censure and they may use other
means of control over women and children), yet the cultural equation
of masculinity and control over women may well take on different
forms according to class and material situation.[18] Segal suggests,
though this is controversial, that since society equates masculinity

with control over others, men who are themselves socially and economically subordinated may be more likely to resort to familial violence as a means of asserting masculine power.

Linda Gordon's study of domestic violence in the US offers the most convincing historical, materialist-feminist account of violence to date. Stressing how violence is itself redefined as a political issue over time, and placing violence firmly in the context of familial contests for power, Gordon grounds wife-battering not in timeless masculinity but in the structural and social relations of women's economic, social, and psychological subordination and men's privileges within the family. Contemporary explorations of the changing 'genealogy' of domestic violence discourse echo Gordon's warning that anti-violence campaigns may not be necessarily feminist or transformative for women; indeed, in the US they have recently been absorbed into a conservative 'crime control' agenda of the state.[19]

Gordon's study pays close attention to the social and cultural meanings attached to domestic violence without surrendering a notion of its cruel reality. As with incest, the issue of domestic violence poses contradictory, difficult questions for a Foucauldian analysis of legal and moral regulation. Despite some initial, superficial efforts by researchers to integrate Foucault into their analysis of wife assault,[20] his work has not been embraced uncritically by feminists. While the increasing legal and social governance of the modern family has been criticized by Foucauldian followers like Donzelot,[21] an intrusive regulation of domestic violence was actually welcomed by many women who tried to use state and philanthropic agencies to remove themselves from oppressive families. Donzelot's analysis, as feminists have pointed out, implies a lament for paternal authority lost, a reminder that Foucauldian perspectives do not necessarily encourage critiques of masculine dominance.

As Dean and Juliet McCannell argue, masculine violence may be obscured by Foucauldian analyses portraying power as 'neutral, diffuse and freely available',[22] and that cannot 'see' the exercise of power through the victim's eyes. Foucault's theoretical claim that power can be distinguished from the exercise of 'force' also veils the manner in which power fundamentally structures and limits women's freedom as victims of violence, neglecting the subtle, psychological, and ideological, as well as coercive, measures creating women's vulnerability. Nor should we discount the brutal, corporal nature of such coercion. Far from simply reflecting Foucault's designation of modern disciplinary power as 'invisible, anonymous and lighter (if more comprehensive)', domestic violence is personal, physical, and sporadic: it imparts direct terror of punishment, just as Foucault claims 'pre-modern' power did in the past.[23]

It is true that the concept of governmentality aptly describes how women and men were encouraged by medical and social experts to monitor and transform their inner character to alter domestic violence. The increased use of medical and social work counselling by the courts offered couples a scheme of Foucauldian 'normalization' that was itself disciplinary, often pathologizing the battered as much as the batterer. Such expert monitoring tended to reproduce women's 'docile bodies' and prevailing gender and familial power relations. The crucial question for contemporary feminists, as Andrea Westlund points out, is whether all modern legal and social institutions are doomed to reproduce Foucauldian disciplinary power in new, perfidious forms, or whether there are openings for resistance and alternative expert discourses that can truly offer women some freedom from violence.[24]

Although feminist writing of the last 20 years has laid bare the oppressions underlying family life and exposed the depressing normality of wife-battering in our culture, we should not forget that women in the past still recognized its malevolence and resisted its practice. The court system, legal reformers, and social workers were also well aware of wife-beating, even if they recommended solutions—like the whipping mentioned above—considered ineffective today. Ironically, as this chapter shows, women's sense of entitlement to a violence-free family life may exist and even increase in periods of meagre political agitation on the issue and when they are receiving little ideological encouragement from the court system.

Informal Mediation in Magistrates and Family Courts

In the interwar period, women in rural and urban areas alike endured domestic violence in silence, with a smaller number attempting to use the law to secure peace and security. Few women laid formal charges that made their way into the courtroom.[25] Police and lawyers claimed that many women were reluctant to air their tales of violence in public, and however embarrassing it was to reveal one's domestic life to the court in a large city, it must have been doubly uncomfortable for women living in small towns and rural areas where one's family history was already well known. In recognition of this public shame, the *Peterborough Examiner* announced in the 1920s that it would no longer broadcast the names of those involved in domestic disputes in Magistrate's Court, though the paper sometimes reneged on its policy, especially for cases affording the opportunity to reiterate class and ethnic stereotypes.[26]

The press thus selectively reported on assault trials, and some court columns bore resemblance to melodramatic nineteenth-century newspaper accounts or to earlier temperance morality lessons. In one report, for instance, a wife went to the local tavern where her husband whiled away his time to persuade him to return home. He hit her so severely that her black eye was still visible in court. The wife's honest pursuit of her family's well-being, the callous husband's misuse of money, and his cowardly violence were all conveyed to the newspaper's audience through repetition of the magistrate's lecture of shame. Sentencing, of course, could still be lenient; offering the man a suspended sentence, the magistrate pointed out that the man 'may lose his job if he is sent to jail.'[27] This newspaper report, like other sources pertaining to wife assault, points to the inherent class bias in much historical evidence, which recorded the more public policing and conflicts of working-class families but not the conflicts in more affluent families.

Many cases of wife-beating also never made it as far as the courtroom. Women were reluctant to lay charges, for reasons discussed below. Second, when cases were brought to the police, they were often informally mediated to avoid a court appearance. In Peterborough County, for instance, the Salvation Army police matron was involved in this process, counselling battered wives. Given her religious beliefs, one assumes that her advice leaned towards reconciliation rather than separation and litigation. More important to this process were the magistrate and the chief of police, who engaged in efforts to secure payments for deserted wives or to repair the family after violence occurred. The Peterborough chief bragged about this tradition of informal justice, claiming few marital cases 'are ever fought to the bitter end'; rather, he and the magistrate used their influence to secure 'reconciliations' and 'placate the parties' and, with the deliberate aid of the local lawyers involved, 'preserve the marital relationship'.[28] In fact, when a sensational case of suspected violence against a child surfaced in 1927, the stepmother of the boy admitted that she had previously tried to separate from her husband, whom she claimed was violent, but that the magistrate had persuaded her to return to her husband.[29]

This ongoing practice of informal mediation by the chief of police, rather than public airing of disputes in court, may have been one rationale for delaying the establishment of a Family Court in this small city. Another was the lack of money and social services to deal with family problems. Until the early 1940s some local Children's Aid Societies resisted the emerging emphasis on professionalization in social work, and city aldermen muttered about spending *any* money on services such as the CAS. In Peterborough, the Children's Aid Society was the only agency even tangentially involved in family violence, and it constantly reminded citizens that it was *only* meant to deal with neglected or abused children, not adults. There were simply no agencies helping battered women at this time. The Mother's Allowance program was largely restricted to widows; the YWCA concentrated on recreation, resocialization, and recruiting young women for domestic work, and the churches' philanthropic efforts did not encompass battered wives.

Indeed, the social authority of the church, as a moral voice and self-appointed commentator on family life, should not be forgotten as part of the context for women's responses to violence. Although these decades were characterized by increasing secularization,[30] churches retained some social influence, likely more so for the middle classes than for working-class families, whose absence from the pews church leaders had lamented for some time. The Catholic Church's retributive promise of excommunication of divorcees sent a strong message to anyone contemplating leaving a family.[31] Mothers were also urged to embrace the ways of saintly self-sacrifice; one priest, for instance, reminded Catholic women in his sermon that 'duty [to the family] was the way to heaven . . . Roman Catholic women must be the stuff of which martyrs are made.'[32] Two decades later, a woman who went to her priest detailing an unbearable life with an alcoholic husband was sternly told that 'she made her bed'.[33] While not all Protestant churches were so resolutely opposed to divorce, their religious messages nonetheless idealized the *permanent* bonds of marriage as well as the imperative of family unity; women's wedding vows were to 'obey', not question, their husbands' authority. As late as 1954, a minister's 'Frank Talk to Brides and Grooms', published in *Chatelaine*, urged women not to make too much of a 'little pushing around' that might leave a visible 'bruise'.[34] While there is no doubt that some women found refuge in their faith, and did not simply obey the missives of patriarchal priests, the general message of Protestant and Catholic churches did not encourage the honest exposure of family violence. The middle-class 'maternal feminist' alliance with Protestant clergy, which supposedly lingered on as a positive force after World War I, thus had a negative side: idealization of women's 'selflessness'[35] in the family might obscure the dark side of family life for many women.

The extensive use of informal mediation fostered within this broader context affords one explanation for the very low number of official arrests for wife assault in the interwar period,[36] though statistics on wife abuse drawn from sources such as county jail registers and police complaint files are clearly deficient. A comparison of these sources with newspaper accounts in one city alone indicates that the number of men appearing before the legal authorities for wife assault was greater than those officially cited for arraignment.[37] Moreover, Family Court records reveal that assault cases could be bundled with and subsumed under other charges, such as alcohol offences, creating an unfit, 'immoral' home for a child, or contributing to delinquency.[38]

In Magistrate's Courts, not guilty pleas dominated for wife assault (in contrast to other cases) and withdrawal of the charge by mutual consent was frequent. From 1921 to 1949, for instance, 35 per cent of the cases in Peterborough County were withdrawn, 22 per cent were dismissed, 26 per cent received a light suspended sentence, and only 18 per cent were jailed or fined, with the remaining few found not guilty. Withdrawals seemed especially likely when the case was delayed by a number of remands; these were used to create a cooling-off period in which informal mediation might occur. A common practice for wife-battering convictions was the use of a peace bond: the man put up collateral and signed a bond agreeing 'to report once a month to the police, support his wife and children, and stay away from liquor.'[39] Although the number of common assault charges in the county was not much greater than the number of wife assault charges, the former were far more likely to receive convictions.[40]

Informal mediation, however, was also the intent of Family Courts, which were established in response to a lobby of social and legal reformers who believed socialized justice was the best way to deal with desertion, non-support, violence, and juvenile delinquency. The Toronto Family Court[41] advertised its faith in 'investigation, diagnosis and probation'—the essence of socialized justice—as a means of upholding the family. Indeed, one Family Court judge argued that Canadians should have the right not only to fair 'legal trials' but also to these 'social trials' based on 'social investigation and clinical evidence' submitted to the court.[42]

Non-support, as Toronto Judge Hawley Mott admitted, was the Family Court's first priority,[43] but violence also fell within the court's purview. Acting on complaints from family members, probation officers met with the couple involved and sometimes questioned neighbours or other relatives to ascertain the nature of the problem. Mediation, counselling, and informal settlements arranged by social work and medical experts were the means used to avoid formal trials. 'We felt it dangerous to take a family quarrel to court on oath,' explained Mott, 'for such testimony broadens a chasm between husband and wife.'[44] If the latter did occur, private hearings with a judge and probation officer were encouraged. Avoiding publicity was lauded as a major achievement of Family Courts, not only because this saved family members from 'shame' but also because publicity hindered reconciliation. 'Many men never forgive their wives when brought to court', remarked Judge Hosking in the pages of *Child and Family Welfare*. Comparing marital failures to army deserters(!), Hosking also worried that press coverage of family breakdown would seriously undermine the public's faith in family life, thus subverting the goal of the court to 'preserve the family as a unit'.[45]

The Family Court encouraged working-class families with few resources to use its complaint and mediation services, and as a result the Toronto court dealt with family disagreements ranging from adultery and sexual incompatibility to violence.[46] Informal mediation was also a form of 'cheap justice' for people who lacked the cash for carfare to the court, let alone to hire an attorney—though the involvement of lawyers had become more common by the 1950s and 1960s. Many couples (quite correctly) understood the probation officer to be the front-line purveyor of justice, and they carefully shaped and pleaded their own cases to him as if he were the judge. One husband, who claimed he kept a log, told the probation officer that his wife was 'never home looking after the house' as she should. But his wife's efforts to gain the upper hand of sympathy were more convincing—she maintained she had suffered 21 years of 'degradation, hell and humiliation' from a husband who drank, swore, threw things at her and hit her daughter: 'I've done my utmost to make the best of a cruel situation, being of a quiet nature, but my life is a living hell.'[47]

In a large city like Toronto, and dealing with both poor and reluctant clients, the probation officer often had to rely on letter-writing as a means of intervention. This was sometimes a follow-up-strategy after a meeting with a couple, but given the reluctance of accused men even to speak to the officer, it was also a means of dealing with the impenitent. The court letterhead and stern tone were supposed to alter the man's behaviour. Guilt, it was hoped, might also help: 'your wife is complaining you are drinking to excess', wrote one officer after a complaint of drunkenness and physical abuse. '[I]f this is true, it would be a pleasure for your home, especially in this festive season [Christmas] if you would discontinue drinking and make your home a happy one . . . as your wife is in a nervous state.'[48]

By the 1940s, after political and legal battles had conclusively secured the place of Family Courts as domestic relations tribunals 'for the unfortunate classes',[49] they spread across the province. Like the existing Toronto court, they provided private, technocratic, and non-legal justice, using court-employed probation officers (increasingly social workers) supplemented by links to other social agencies and mental health clinics. By the end of World War II, 23 counties had Family Courts, though in many cases (including Peterborough) the local magistrate simply doubled as a Family Court judge. Thus, there were strong connections to earlier Magistrate's Courts: both dealt with a largely working-class and poor clientele, and both used methods of informal mediation.[50] The clients were the same, even if the professionals dispensing advice and justice had changed.[51]

The Peterborough Family Court was set up in 1946 as a result of lobbying by the Children's Aid Society, whose concerns about juvenile delinquency often dominated the court's agenda. Nonetheless, because of its broad legal jurisdiction, it also claimed the ability to 'solve domestic disturbances and ruptured family relations'.[52] Similarly, the Welland Family Court emerged from attempts by the local county council in 1944 to enact the federal Juvenile Delinquent Act for the county. In searching for its first probation officer, the Welland council was less concerned with a degree in social work and more anxious that the new officer have a history with the local community. They selected a married, middle-aged man with children who had 'experience with boys' work . . . and among persons of foreign birth'.[53] The former undoubtedly spoke to their image of the probation officer as a paternal arbitrator, the latter to their belief that non-Anglo families were more likely to be in court.

In the newly established Welland Family Court the probation officer tried to reconcile husbands and wives by having the husband and/or wife agree to go to the mental health clinic and by having an alcoholic husband put on the interdicted list, join Alcoholics Anonymous (AA), or sign a no-drinking bond. His own counselling of the couple was also crucial. He might exert moral pressure on men, reading them a 'riot act' of legal responsibility and punishment: 'I explained the law to Mr. E. and he was surprised. This will now be a deterrent to his pugilistic methods.'[54] Finally, if mediation failed and the case went to court, the probation officer had prepared case files, with rather partial views of who was guilty and innocent, which were given to the judge to help him make a decision.

Small-town intelligence remained an integral part of investigations in rural areas and smaller cities and towns. The Welland probation officer knew just where to find his male clients, searching them out and chatting with them in local streets and restaurants. In direct contrast, he usually saw women in their homes. He also visited neighbours, employers, or other community leaders to ask their opinion on the case. In one instance, he found out where the accused man was working and went to speak to his foreman, who lamented the fact that these 'nice kids' were having 'troubles at home'. He then spoke to two local lawyers. As his case notes reveal: 'later talked to lawyer G, and he knew the couple. thought there was no reason they should separate. talked to lawyer H, he felt the same.'[55] His own assessments were sometimes based on the local lore of who came from the right and wrong side of the tracks. 'Knew him when he was a boy and they were fine people . . . [but] they have been around with a group of people which I would not suggest being the best type and am not surprised he is having family problems',[56] he concluded in one case. Appearance was also an indicator of reputation, even guilt: 'she [the wife complaining] was a big fat woman and does not look as if a man could harm her much . . . and She came in with Mrs M. and that is no recommendation for her.'[57]

Ethnic and class biases were sometimes integrated into his evaluations. Violence in more middle-class families was perceived to be unusual or infrequent, and help for a wronged woman was offered with few questions. Commenting on a woman who left her husband, whom she had met in the armed forces, because he was apparently 'cruel' to her, the probation officer asked for 'more help' for her and her five-year-old son: 'these are splendid people with a very fine record for integrity and good work in the community. Her father was Deputy Reeve.'[58] Occasionally, ethnic stereotypes also shaped his assessments. An Italian woman, he wrote, was conceivably exaggerating her complaint of assault as 'she is perhaps a naturally excitable woman.'[59] He was also quick to assume that a black woman's reputation for 'immorality' was true.[60] Some cultural backgrounds—not Anglo-Protestant ones, of course—were assumed to foster patriarchal and controlling men: 'He is a Central European type, and believes he can beat his wife as he pleases', noted one case file.[61] While similar assumptions crept into some Toronto files too, probation officers in Toronto primarily judged their clients using a barometer of social and economic factors denoting respectability: whether they were 'steady workers', had clean houses and children who were cared for, and did not drink to excess.[62] It is also likely that recent non-Anglo immigrants avoided using the Family Courts, seeking out agencies that offered counselling in their own language.[63]

Despite the distinctions between Magistrate's and Family Courts, small and large cities, professional and less professional probation officers, noticeable patterns relating to wife-battering had emerged by the 1940s. Investigation and mediation by non-legal experts was the first, preferred recourse of the courts, and hopes of family reconstitution, aided by social work and medical expertise, were highly placed. While women often sought out this informal justice, was this process really the most important factor inhibiting or encouraging their complaints?

Women's Complaints, Women's Strategies

Going to court to protest abuse was not an easy decision for most women. Financially, many women were dependent on their husbands and had few alternative means of supporting themselves and their children, and they often had no legal share in the family assets or home (if there even was one). In fact, the husband could return to the family home after a charge was laid. Socially, they might not have the support of friends and family to effect a legal separation, still considered a sign of marital failure or disgrace. In general, they faced a social and culture context that discounted marital violence and, to a great extent, still stressed women's sacrifice and duty in marriage. Given these obstacles, it is perhaps surprising how many courageous women did publicly protest their battering. In all three counties throughout this period, for instance, women were the authors of the vast majority of complaints, though other family members initiated some, and occasionally the police responded to especially loud or violent scenes by laying a charge on behalf of the Crown.

Often, women had already attempted other strategies to deal with violence before they went to court. They moved out temporarily and stayed with family, occasionally called on neighbours' help, withdrew their own sexual and domestic services from their husbands, or called in the police to scare their husbands while not pressing charges. Leaving the family home, however, might mean leaving children behind and was especially difficult for rural women, as men often controlled the means of transportation on the farm. Involving neighbours seemed to work only when an especially violent or public incident occurred; for example, when one husband beat his wife in the yard in front of neighbours, they took her and her baby in, then testified on her behalf in court.[64] But not all women could secure neighbourly aid. In one farming area, neighbours were so scared of the violent husband, particularly his threats of arson, that they did not help the wife.

Simply reporting the abuse to the police and courts was also a strategy. Like the women in Linda Gordon's study, these women were using the police and court system as a tool to secure assistance and protection. Many returned more than once, begging the probation officer to intervene to warn the husband, to ask for strategic advice, or sometimes actually to lay charges. Even if charges were laid, they were often withdrawn with women's permission. Women wanted to stop short of sending husbands to jail; a court appearance, they hoped, would jolt them into better behaviour. Opting for the private procedures of Family Courts, many hoped, would also help them to avoid public shame. 'I prefer the problem dealt with in the office as he had been all right since he received the last letter',[65] explained one wife to the probation officer. Another wife asked that a warning be issued, but 'I don't want things taken any further. I will meet him half way, after all it is just a matter of him controlling his temper. I am willing to help him with no further humiliation.'[66] In the most extreme cases, women anticipated (with some accuracy) that the beatings would escalate should they shame their partner with a court appearance: 'He beats me and tells me that he wants to murder me. He is full of spite since I went to you', wrote a desperate wife to her probation officer.[67]

Women living in rural areas felt particularly vulnerable to night-time attacks. A farmwife in Welland County wanted the court to prosecute her husband for the many verbal threats of violence he made at night, but because it was verbal, not physical, intimidation, which was harder to prove and less 'serious', her requests were dismissed.[68] Although farm women were often isolated from family and neighbourhood supports, about 50 per cent of the complaints in Peterborough County actually came from women outside the city.[69] Their case files point to lives of physical terror and violence far removed from any romanticized notion of bucolic rural life. Because farmers often had guns with which to threaten wives, the terror was quite intense: 'I just as soon kill you as the dog', shouted one husband to his wife, pointing out that he kept his gun ready, beside their bed.[70]

Recent immigrants might share similar experiences of isolation. A post-World War II Italian immigrant in Welland County was informed by her abusive partner that he had only married her to gain entry to the country and he intended to leave her. With no family here, she had to support herself immediately, even though she had suffered a miscarriage after one beating. Because she made $5.00 more a week than her husband, she was told by the Family Court she was ineligible for support payments. After she laid the charge, her husband agreed to reconcile; although the file was closed, we have no way of knowing if the abuse stopped.[71] Similarly, a Dutch immigrant admitted that she was too frightened to 'take legal action' against her husband because it might jeopardize her application for citizenship.[72] However, recent immigrants did not always succumb to blackmail. A Polish woman who lived with her husband on a tobacco farm ran away to Toronto to start a new life with her daughter after both were beaten and threatened by her husband. His lawyer argued that she should return home as she could not speak English and the husband could, but the judge disagreed, positioning his court as the superior defender of womanhood: 'no woman in Canada needs to stay with a husband who beats her.'[73]

Often, women pressed charges only when the beatings were habitual, when they could provide substantial visual or corroborative evidence, when they were desperately afraid of escalating violence, or when they were also frustrated by other domestic problems, such as lack of economic support for their families.[74] One Peterborough woman who took her husband to court in the 1930s told the court that the 'first time he hit her was seven years ago shortly after they were married'; the violence continued, with her husband finally 'throwing a butcher's knife' at her.[75] Twenty years later, a Toronto woman took action against her abusive husband only after he began to 'threaten to take her baby away'.[76] Women who were initially afraid or reluctant to lay charges sometimes came to an emotional breaking point that led them to court. For one woman it was her husband's assault on the day of her daughter's wedding. Another client claimed her husband 'had beaten her many times, but she was only afraid when he took a knife to her.'[77] Women might suffer in silence the ongoing tyranny of husbands for as long as 21 years before they finally involved the law. As 'Sandra' explained, her husband rotated his abuse, focusing on each member of the family: first he used sexual force and threats with her; then he harassed her teenage daughter, whom he 'screamed at, called her a whore, a pig'; finally, when the daughter left, her son was verbally abused and assaulted. In the end, her son's decision to leave home prompted her to go to the probation officer to press for a psychiatric exam for her husband. She was not even able to bring herself to lay assault charges.[78]

The results of violence were sometimes visible when the woman appeared in court. Though husbands threatened women with guns and farming tools, the vast majority of batterers used their fists or kicked their wives. In one case, the physical consequences of a man's hands were so appalling that the magistrate warned him to desist or 'you will soon find yourself charged with murder in this court.'[79]

Some court reporters' vivid descriptions of bruises, cuts, and scars, undoubtedly provided with the intent of shocking the newspaper's 'respectable' readership, suggested that only the 'lower classes' or those from the 'backwoods' engaged in such behaviour.[80] Nevertheless, the emphasis on women's visible injuries in court reporting may also indicate that many women only resorted to formal charges when they were absolutely desperate, battered repeatedly, or, importantly, when they had dramatic evidence that would convince the magistrate they were telling the truth.

Those women who had bruises and injuries or corroborative witnesses to back them up might secure the sympathy of the probation officer or the judge. When a war bride from Blackpool came to the Peterborough court in 1947 she stressed both the repeated nature of her husband's assaults and showed her bruises as well as her broken nose to the court.[81] Where injuries were substantial, where the woman was seen as totally helpless, as with the case of a disabled woman, the Family Court's sympathy was unwavering. 'He is a bully, belligerent and hostile', the Welland probation officer wrote of the latter case of a disabled woman, 'she has a bruised eye, back and legs, so she can't even wear her back brace.'[82] But minor injuries were often overlooked with a chilling acceptance. 'Only minor bruises which don't amount to much', noted a Toronto probation officer in the late 1930s. He did not dispute the attack, but excused it by pointing to the husband's 'despondency after an accident' as the cause of violence.[83]

Women's testimony indicated again and again that contests for power in the household, and attempts by men to assert and preserve their dominance, often precipitated violence. In his historical study of wife assault, David Peterson del Mar distinguishes between men's 'instrumental' violence, used as an immediate, direct, coercive tool, and their 'affective' violence, a more generalized expression of anger and anxiety directed at all women.[84] While both were found in these Ontario court cases, they sometimes overlapped or merged with one another. Family life was already structured economically and socially on the basis of a strict gender and age hierarchy. Violence often resulted when the authority of the male head of household was questioned or when men felt it needed to be reasserted. Women's claim to financial support, their control of possessions, their social lives, their sexual autonomy, and disputes over the treatment of children were the most common excuses for men's violence. Women often objected to their husbands' use of money (especially for alcohol), or to their husbands' use of *their* wages, and consequently faced violence. These cases thus bear some similarity to those described in contemporary studies. As Lisa Freedman points out, battering is often precipitated by husbands' criticisms of their wives' domestic work or their friendships, by financial battles or contests for control of children, or by the husbands' attempts to refract their humiliation and frustrations back onto their wives.[85]

Women were not passive in these contests for power. They often sought to assert their influence, criticize husbands, or defend other family members. For instance, in the twenties, Anne, a rural woman, intervened as her husband tried to send a child to the store to buy tobacco and wheat. Anne became angry with her husband as she objected to the purchase of tobacco when there was little food in the house. Her husband responded by striking her so hard she was dizzy. As the child later testified, his father told Anne that she couldn't tell him 'not to make whisky anymore' or what to buy, as 'he was running the place . . . [and] if it doesn't suit you, take the door.' Anne complained of 'splitting headaches' after the assault, but in court her husband's lawyer called in her barber to attest to the fact that he had not seen any marks on her head when he recently bobbed her hair! As in many cases, the husband's defence lawyer convinced the judge that the man was usually a decent provider and thus should be let off.[86]

Women occasionally fought back, too, with words, destruction to household items, or violence—though the latter certainly discredited their case in the eyes of the court.[87] Women threw household items, such as pots and pans, at violent husbands; they hurled rocks at departing husbands' cars. If a woman fought back physically, became involved in a public fight, or had other charges (for example, alcohol-related ones) levelled against her, the man's violence was perceived more leniently. In one case, for instance, a woman who claimed non-support and assault jumped on her husband's car as he departed. Her case was easily dismissed.[88]

In a very few cases truly desperate women responded by killing their husbands. In Peterborough County, for instance, the Criminal Court dealt with two murder cases during the 1940s in which the woman argued she was abused. In such cases women who appeared immediately physically victimized, who were defending the sanctity of their family, or who were literally hysterical were accorded more public and legal sympathy.[89] In 1947, for instance, Jean McAllister, a 'diminutive, attractive' war bride, who had been beaten and verbally berated by her husband, especially after a hysterectomy left her unable to have children, was tried for murder. Her defence counsel portrayed a woman isolated in a hostile environment, emotionally traumatized by her recent discovery of infertility; indeed, he argued that hysterectomies created massive depressions, confusion, and blackouts. McAllister's body became part of her pathology, but also a cause for pity. Her physical vulnerability, widespread public sympathy for isolated and unhappy war brides, and pity for her loss of 'womanhood', as well as clear evidence of repeated abuse, made her into an object of public sympathy.[90] Surrounded by other war brides, she heard her reduced sentence of three years, which was lenient, the judge said, because she was so 'provoked'.[91] Yet, only a few years before, an older woman, more obviously poor, who claimed to have suffered abuse, including threats with weapons for many years, was given 15 years for killing her husband. Described unsympathetically in the press as 'pathetic and haggard',[92] her attempt to explain her actions by pointing to the ongoing forceful 'lustful' sexual demands of her husband was treated derisively by the authorities, who were convinced that her actions were premeditated.[93] To secure the court's compassion, women had to appear mentally out of control, if not temporarily insane; rational self-defence was unlikely to secure mercy.

More often, of course, women's violence was a limited response to men's violence. One such case from a small town in Welland County reveals a number of continuing themes in the court files. The probation officer investigated an assault reported by the wife and, though he acknowledged that it happened, he orchestrated the couple's reconciliation. The real problem, he noted, was that 'they (had to) get married and he does not want responsibility . . . he does not like children and hasn't even asked her to stop them, if possible. If we could get him some counselling, we could help.' Within four months another assault occurred: 'he kicked her and pushed her down the stairs. She is expecting . . . she came back upstairs and clubbed him over the head with a dishpan. . . . He said he would kill her. She moved out. . . . the CAS agrees that she is the worst for filthy language, is arrogant and stubborn. He is not a bad fellow except when nagged by her.'[94] At that point, the case was closed. Her violent retaliation discredited her, and she now became the problem, a wife who would not stop getting pregnant, who used bad language and nagged. On occasion, both CAS workers and the probation officers were openly hostile to women perceived to be provoking violence. When one abused wife who clearly hated her husband fought back with violence, her case was not even taken up: 'she would drive anyone crazy with her prattle', the probation officer concluded.[95]

The wider material context of family life and women's economic vulnerability were crucial in shaping when violence erupted and how women dealt with it. When women relayed their fears of losing

children to orphanages and their struggles to provide the most basic
clothing and medicine for children—as one woman noted, her son
was almost deaf because his tonsils were so bad—their decision to
stay with violent partners becomes understandable. Often, they were
encouraged to do so by probation officers, who told them in the 1930s
that 'you cannot split the relief with your husband', or in later years
that you 'don't have the money to live apart.'[96] Not only did women
withdraw complaints because they were afraid to lose earning husbands to jail sentences,[97] but some women only complained about
violence when non-support also became an unbearable problem.
Their trip to the court was as much about getting financial support as
about protesting physical abuse they suffered. Occasionally, they indicated they might endure the violence, if only their husbands would
work or give them some money.

The connection between non-support and violence cannot be
underestimated; in many cases the two were intertwined, and women
used whatever legal strategy appeared best to escape battering and
still obtain support for their children. While many were not well
versed in the law, they were vaguely aware that a verified charge of
cruelty, after they had been forced out of the family home, could
secure them support payments. For these women, like the nineteenth-
century Halifax wives Judith Fingard describes, separation was
sought as a 'poor woman's form of divorce':[98] it was the only path
many could see out of violent marriages. Still, their financial security
was precarious. The judge often secured weekly payments only for
the children, not the wife, who frequently had to search for paid work
to keep the family solvent.

Social workers sometimes directly blamed family poverty for violent disputes. 'The real problem here is lack of money due to unemployment', wrote a probation officer in the thirties. '[S]he takes in
three boarders to eke out survival for the children, then the husband
accuses the wife of being too friendly with one.' The officer's solution
was for the husband to get work as a farmhand. Wives also blamed
violence on joblessness and poverty, and there was no doubt that
financial frustration and despair precipitated some men's violence,
most noticeably during the lean 1930s. The slightest reference to
financial problems could incite violent anger, as one wife found when
her punishment for giving her child a second glass of milk was 'a slap
across the head'.[99] But violence born of frustration did not totally disappear in more prosperous times; it reflected a persisting understanding by men that their frustrations could be visited violently upon
other family members. Moreover, though especially prevalent as a

'fatalistic' explanation for violence during the Depression, this explanation was used by social workers during World War II and the postwar period. Judges, however, did not always accept this argument once a case came to court.[100]

Many other disputes involved the wife's social outings or her control over the children. In one case, Lilly protested her husband's whipping of their child only to be assaulted herself; another woman was ordered home from the neighbours', where she was socializing, and was struck unconscious in front of her father-in-law.[101] Women's protests about their husbands' sexual demands, and their threats of violence if they did not comply, were also evident in these files.[102] I 'have so many children', said one mother of 10 children in the 1930s, because 'he threatens me'.[103] Accusations of marital rape or attempted rape were made to the probation officer, though charges were rarely laid. One woman with a black eye and bruises claimed her husband assaulted her after she refused to have sex with him, 'which I cannot have as I haemorrhage.'[104]

Women's complaints about violence were often accompanied by charges that husbands were setting a bad example for children by drinking to excess and swearing. It is possible these working-class women suspected that middle-class social workers and judges would sympathize with these accusations, but it is also clear that women resented men's drinking—for both financial and safety reasons—and they equated cursing with a lack of respect. Though historians have tended to see increased surveillance of working-class morals by emerging Family Courts in a negative light, as evidence of middle-class moralism, it is clear that some women brought complaints about language and demeanour to court as a means of asserting their dignity. One woman, for example, testified that 'she didn't want her children growing up hearing obscene language.' She had not simply internalized middle-class prudery, however, for she described, quite clearly, what feminists would later call emotional abuse. She recognized that her husband's constant swearing, ridiculing, and condemnations of her, and his encouraging the children also to denounce her as a 'damned whore' (one of his politer terms), undermined her sense of self-worth.[105]

Some women who were aware of the difficulties of convicting husbands on assault charges tried to use other laws to deal with the violence. In a case in the 1940s, Linda first charged her husband with assault, but found no change in behaviour after his 10 days in jail. She later called the police repeatedly, explaining that her husband spent his time at the Legion and came home drunk and abusive; she tried to get police to charge her husband under the vagrancy law as he was drunk and disorderly. Finally, she tried to have him certified mentally ill.[106] None of her strategies succeeded. Women looked to professional experts such as doctors to validate their accusations, but this was not always effective. When one woman's assault case was dismissed, she tried to have her husband designated insane. While one doctor agreed that the husband was unstable, he rejected incarceration, and his assessment revealed an unsettling acceptance of violence in the home: 'from the wife', he wrote, 'I learned of family quarrels and some bodily injury to herself, but she did not seem to be badly hurt.'[107]

Too terrorized to testify once their cases came to court, some women abandoned legal action quite quickly. Wives often told magistrates and judges they didn't want husbands sent to jail; they just wanted one more chance for the abuse to stop. When a rural Ku Klux Klan organizer was charged with wife-beating in the 1920s, his spouse agreed to effect a reconciliation: 'wives always want to give their husbands a second chance', commented Peterborough Magistrate O.A. Langley cynically.[108] His fatalistic attitude, seeing wife-beating as an inevitable part of working-class married life, was not unusual. Sitting in the same seat 20 years later, Magistrate Gee could be dismissive, too. His 'jocular' pronouncements indicate the influence of local judges and law enforcement officers in shaping attitudes towards domestic violence. What we need, Gee lightly remarked during an assault case, 'is a Wives' Protection Society'; on another occasion he told a man to give his wife a 'kiss and make up' after she was persuaded to withdraw assault charges.[109]

Moreover, some husbands were profusely and convincingly repentant, promising new behaviour, so that women wrestled with contradictory impulses: they feared leaving marriages as much as they feared staying. 'Loves him, but says he is an animal' and 'I cannot take this anymore, but I do not want to lay charges' were common, anguished assertions on the women's part.[110] At least 25 per cent of the Welland files in the 1950s had a subsequent complaint after women 'forgave' the violence. Those who returned often regretted their earlier decision. 'I have to get out of this house. I haven't a friend I can turn to . . . no money, but I may be able to find some housecleaning money or fruit picking. . . . I won't take any more of this beating, I know I made a mistake coming back last year, and now the CAS doesn't want to help me',[111] lamented one woman in a letter. Probation officers, CAS workers, and the local justice of the peace sometimes complained that women went back and forth to abusive husbands; yet, their pursuit of reform and reconciliation encouraged this very strategy.

Men's Responses

If they were reported to the police or court, how did abusers justify their own actions? Some men clearly believed they had an inherent right to their wives' sexual and domestic services and that they could secure these, on their terms, with physical coercion. Similarly, men articulated their prerogative to discipline their wives to obtain obedience. What is remarkable, from our perspective, is how adamant many men were, even in public, of their *right* to hit their wives.[112] 'She was hysterical', claimed one husband to justify his action, who then added that 'he will do so again when he feels inclined.'[113] Indeed, men sometimes asked for a jury trial, clearly believing their peers were more likely than a judge to accept their violence.[114] When a judge threatened one man with deportation in 1932, after police had testified that his repeated beatings left his wife too terrified even to call them, he faced the judge down and retorted: 'I'm not scared.'[115]

Most often, men cited uncontrollable external forces on their behaviour as excuses for violence, perhaps an indication that they and their attorneys thought they were more likely to be treated sympathetically if it was 'beyond their control'. Men blamed their unemployment, destitution, and especially alcohol for battering. The claim that unemployment had robbed men of their rightful role as providers, creating 'frustration', was especially apparent during the Depression, but the same excuse was also used later on. In the early 1940s, a man claimed his eight years on relief had left him unable to cope with stress: 'when you are together 24 hours a day, it gets on everybody's nerves', he told the magistrate.[116] In attempt to reverse the blame, men even resorted to the most trivial excuses, from a wife being 'irritating' or 'not turning the light off' to purchasing too many pairs of shoes.[117]

One rationale was used again and again by men: they were drunk. As many authors have pointed out, alcohol offers the licence to batter; it is not the simple cause of battering. Husbands 'overstep boundaries selectively' when drunk, committing violence that may be 'ostensibly but not really unacceptable' to society.[118] For both the husbands and court workers, however, alcohol became the most prevalent and simplest of explanations for violence. In mediation, men repeatedly professed their 'repentance', claiming 'it was drinking which caused all the trouble.'[119] Alcohol certainly was involved in many assault cases; men often linked their right to leave the domestic sphere and drink excessively with male friends to their right to control their wives, and both of these 'rights' were related to their masculine identity. For women, too, alcohol was an explanation they could cling to in seeking to understand their husbands' violence; as a result, they pushed, again and again, for their husbands' entry into AA. (And the most successful mediation cases were ones where AA was successful with the male partner.)

Family Court personnel did not make a connection between alcohol abuse and issues of power. Rather, drink transformed men into uncontrollable creatures; this rendition of masculinity was a Jekyll-and-Hyde portrayal of the good husband transformed into an unruly, animalistic man. 'He is out of his head when he drinks, when sober he is mild and good to her'[120] was a typical conclusion of social workers. Yet this same justification was used in one of the most horrific cases in the Welland court. The husband held down his pregnant wife so his friend could forcibly rape her, then he beat her up afterwards. While the probation officer found the case 'disgusting', he still held out some hope for reconciliation: 'I tried to have her see that she might go home . . . and the family might be held together . . . she did not know whether she could.' Despite the misgivings of the police that the case against the men was a weak one, the two men were jailed. Five months later the woman was so near destitution, on relief and with five children to support, that she tried to secure her husband's parole.[121]

Violence often took place in the bedroom or kitchen; in the latter case, men assaulted or raped wives after they came home from the bar at night. One unemployed husband demanded his wife (with four children, five and under) get out of bed at 2:30 in the morning to make him supper. She said she was 'too tired' so he pulled her out of bed by the hair and threw a table at her.[122] The kitchen, supposedly women's domain, was also a site of violence, precisely because husbands wanted to assert their total control of the household. The number of assaults precipitated by the wife's failure to put dinner before the patriarch when and how he demanded was striking. When 'Kathy' didn't put her husband's 'potatoes on the plate properly, he punched her, bruising her eye and nose.'[123] Criticisms of the way wives raised the children and charges that children didn't offer respect and obedience were also made by batterers to justify their attacks.

Men also felt they should control family monies, however meagre they were. While many authors have stressed the respected role of working-class homemakers in the managing of the family finances, these files tell a different story. Both magistrates and later Family Court officers assessed the husband's character by asking if he was a good provider. 'Hands over his pay', noted the probation officer approvingly of one husband, but then the officer was forced to admit that 'he beats her. . . . Last week hit her with a frying pan when his lunch was not warm enough.'[124] But the man's pay packet also became an instrument of power: 'Husband won't give her money. Hydro to be turned off . . . he expects her to work, and threatened her with a hammer', detailed one file. Another noted, 'Five kids under 15 and only gives $4.00 for groceries, drink and assault are problems. She is pregnant, so we agreed she would stay till baby is born.'[125]

Women's economic, social, and sexual freedom were all perceived as threats to some men. Occasionally, they objected to their wives working outside the home. One husband told the probation officer 'he wants a separation unless she stays home and looks after the house and kids';[126] another complained that his wife was getting dangerous 'ideas about independence from separated and divorced women at her factory', thus causing marital problems. Probation officers seldom advised women to quit jobs (in fact, by the 1960s working-class women were expected to earn wages to support insolvent families), unless it appeared the family was economically comfortable. One such wife came to the Welland probation officer complaining of an assault, and the husband readily conceded that he gave her a 'back-hander' but added, 'I don't abuse her all the time.' Noting that they 'both have their own car, wage and bed', the probation officer criticized the wife's transgression of gender roles: 'It looks as though you, Mrs. C, are working just to have your own car but it is also making you feel too independent and you are giving your husband a rough argument with that attitude.' He implied she should sleep with her husband, but her response that her husband 'had beaten her so much that he has driven all desire out of my mind and body' seemed to fall on unsympathetic ears.[127]

Women's sexual independence was particularly grating to men. Even women's past sexual lives could be threatening. As 'Ellen' found, her admission of a 'wild' life before marriage became the excuse for her husband's violence: 'he is very suspicious, jealous of me looking at other men. . . . He wants total obedience, doesn't want me to go to night school and take courses.'[128] Women who were out at night, especially if they were drinking with other friends, were often seen as overstepping their bounds. One husband explained his violence by telling the probation officer his wife 'taunted' him with tales of her sexual exploits with men 'across the river' (i.e., in a US bar).

In such cases, the offended male found a sympathetic mediator. 'You are going to dance halls with a man and have a child two years at home who needs your attention', lectured a Toronto court official in a warning letter to a wife during the 1930s. Despite bruises and claims the husband tried to choke her, the probation officer persisted with his advice to limit her social life to 'going to dance halls' only with her husband. Many years later, a similar lecture was endured by a wife who took her $6 worth of bingo winnings and went to China-town with a girlfriend, then came home 'late' with their landlord. Though admitting the husband had 'no right to strike' her, the proba-tion officer admonished her conduct, which 'was not proper for a wife with five children . . . if she won $6.00 she should of [*sic*] spent it on the children instead of going to Chinatown.'[129]

Many men blamed assaults on 'promiscuous' wives, though they clearly had different standards for their own behaviour. One man's sense of entitlement to sexual predominance was so strong that he assumed the court would accept his right to two partners. When his legal war bride appeared from England with their baby in arms, she found him living with another woman. He set his wife and baby up in nearby rooms and alternated his domestic residence week by week, but, angered by his wife's claim that 'things could not go on like this', he hit her. Affronted by the interference of the court, he announced that 'other husbands did this' and he did not consider slap-ping her an 'assault'.[130]

While his sense of domestic entitlement was rather extreme, the assumption that the husband's adultery was not as serious as the wife's clearly existed in the mind of both husbands and court author-ities, even if the latter were not as rigidly wedded to the double stan-dard as nineteenth-century officials had been. When linked to notions of provocation and men's uncontrollability, this could literally be a fatal combination for women. In Welland, for example, a man took an axe to his wife and their boarder because the two were having an affair. The husband confessed immediately, but after a long murder trial the judge advised the jury that murder was an unlikely verdict since the man was 'provoked' by finding his wife and the boarder in a 'compromising position'. When the jury ignored him, the murder verdict was successfully appealed in favour of a seven-year sentence for manslaughter.[131]

A woman's sexual relationship to the battering husband was ques-tioned in another manner. If a woman had sexual relations with her husband after the assault,[132] it was assumed that the assault was not serious or perhaps never happened. When probation officers attempted reconciliations, they often pressured women to resume having sex, to 'submit to your husband' in return for the spouse's promise to stop drinking and beating her: 'she says he drinks too much . . . she won't sleep with him. . . . Once in a while, he admits to pulling her out of the bed in the kids' room, to sleep with him . . . to sum [the case] up: he agrees to stop drinking, but she must be affable and sleep with him. He will let loose on money and she will only go to bingo once a week. She should keep his clothes clean and look after the house.'[133] Similar advice was given to many couples. Part of the 'bargain' women had to agree to, to gain protection from violence, involved providing domestic and sexual services to their husbands.

Finally, many husbands claimed their wives' insults were the cause of their violence. In domestic disputes, women often resorted to derision, particularly of the husband and his family; verbal indignities, the husband believed, deserved physical revenge. 'He admits to pushing her in the face', noted one official in the 1930s, but added that 'she has a sharp tongue and insults his sisters'.[134] Women were not above using ethnic slurs. When one wife complained about her husband's assault, he admitted to striking her but claimed she had insulted his father with 'racial slurs', calling him a 'wop'. I did 'slap her', he told the probation officer indignantly, and 'I am a Canadian'.[135] This was only one of a multitude of variations on the theme of provocation, which many men raised as their defence. Consideration of women's provocation of the attack resonated with the courts as well. That social workers also absorbed this ideology is clear from the curt response of a female probation officer to the question of 'abuse' on one man's form. 'Yes', she answered, 'when aggravated.'[136]

Men's justifications for their violence remain remarkably constant over this period, centring on their right to rule wives and families, their hostile responses to women's demands for autonomy, their fearful claims that women were undermining their authority. If anything, however, violence seemed to become more random and men's anger more acute in the post-World War II period—though this may reflect the richness of sources for this period as much as actual trends. However, there are some hints that men's general hostility to women and marriage and to women's social or sexual autonomy were more intensely intertwined with outbursts directed at the specific control of wives' daily work and actions.[137] If women were seeking, even marginally, more autonomy and control over their marriages after World War II, men were not ready to give any ground.

The Family Court Responds

Even if the agitation for Family Courts was primarily focused on delinquency and non-support issues, we need to ask if these courts encouraged women to press charges against violent husbands or modified the attitudes of legal authorities and the helping professions towards wife battering. Looking at all three Family Courts, particularly in the late 1940s and 1950s, we can better assess whether they operated as 'police courts in another guise', imposing middle-class norms on the working class and poor but with little actual relief for women's pressing familial problems.[138]

Although Family Courts were supposed to offer more productive solutions to family discord, their assessment of the causes of wife assault altered only slightly from that found in Magistrate's Courts. In fact, in the post-World War II period, men's violence was often obscured by the prevailing definitions of family dysfunction: social science and medical discourses themselves operated as disciplinary practices that focused on women's psychological flaws and 'normality' as much as on the abnormality of violence. Describing the causes of domestic violence, the newly appointed Peterborough Family Court Judge Philp offered a gender-neutral inventory that assumed equal culpability for marital discord: 'Lack of maturity in young couples marrying and raising a family, lack of the ability to recognize mistakes made and how to rectify them, lack of desire to forego [sic] the apparent pleasures of bickering, the lack of interest in the moral development of those composing the family circle and an overwhelming selfishness and devotion to pleasure coupled with the attempted escape of many by the use of liquor—each plays its part.'[139]

Similarly, the York Family Court had a standardized occurrence memo that measured the causes of family violence according to an a priori assumption of causality. 'Drink, immorality, Venereal Disease, ill temper and abuse, interference of wife/husband's relatives, lack of support' were the designated origins of violence and could apply to women and men. These assumptions were both encouraged by and reflected in social work journals of the period. In the forties and fifties *Canadian Welfare* contained anguished articles asking 'Whither the Family?' but they were more likely to decry divorce and marital breakdown, citing factors such as sexual jealousy and 'hasty marriages', than confront issues of violence.[140] Although social work references to broken or disrupted families may well have been codes that implicitly acknowledged violence, the issue was rarely confronted openly as a concern for casework. Discussion of 'marital failure' in the pages of Canada's premier social work journal focused more on the need for 'good home management' and responsible parenting, especially proper mothering, as the means to preserve the family.[141]

In both informal mediation and courtroom hearings, probation officers and judges usually embraced three general aims: first, they tried to see the assault within the overall picture of the dysfunctional family;

second, they aimed to preserve the family unit if at all possible while still ending the violence; third, if separation or a jail sentence was perceived to be the only answer, they tried to make the husband pay for the support of his family. Family Courts did offer increased avenues for mediation and probation, more referrals to mental health aid, and, after World War II, an increased emphasis on the psychological health of individuals and families. All these factors encouraged women to bring their marital problems to the courts, sometimes gaining at least verbal reassurance from probation officers, but they did not necessarily provide them with the peace they were seeking. And though many of the legal authorities were men, their gender alone did not account for their view of family violence. Their emphasis on reconciliation was shaped by the material realities facing their working-class clients, by a prevailing ideology of family preservation, and by an increasing reliance in social work thinking on simplified Freudian and functionalist models of the family. Paradoxically, these forces sometimes created an image of masculinity under attack, even though it was women who were being assaulted.

According to the Welland Family Court probation officer, for instance, men's tendency to strike out at wives reflected masculine insecurity over breadwinning issues: 'Mrs. P claims he slapped her more than once . . . but I believe that if he had the security of a steady job, she could live with him.'[142] 'What he needs to boost his manhood', he noted in another assault case, is 'a more secure income earned by himself.'[143] Indeed, probation officers often assumed that some female acquiescence to male authority was necessary to preserve men's sense of masculinity. In one case, both the wife and the probation officer agreed that the husband was still 'acting like a stern army officer' from his wartime days: 'he has to be the leader, the power in the home.' Although he is 'cruel and unbending', the officer concluded that 'she is fighting him at every move because she is hostile too. . . . I checked with the police. They said it is not all this man's fault, but rather the flighty, overbearing attitude of the wife, who is just like the rest of the K family.'[144]

Authority issues were directly connected to the assessment by the Family Court of women's provocation of the assault, supposedly by nagging, by swearing at their husbands, or by being unfaithful. Probation officers often tried to help the wife understand how her affronts to the husband's masculinity promoted the violence. Even the most cursory glance at the Family Court files would lead one to believe that nagging had suddenly become a major social category in the 1950s.[145] Comments such as 'she is a bit of a whiner', 'she is a nervous nagger', and 'a neighbour says he doesn't drink too much and she is a nagger'[146] appear repeatedly in assessments. This language of derision used by court officials, with women described, for example, as 'wild vixen' with 'vile tongues', is striking.[147] Certainly, some domestic disputes were complex, and we should not ignore women's use of hurtful insults, their own addiction problems, and sometimes their violence against their children. Nonetheless, physical assaults on women were consistently downplayed when they were accused of nagging. In one case a wife whose eardrum was broken by her assaulting husband agreed to mediation. The Family Court officer concluded: 'she is an addictive bingo gambler, and hits the kids. She is the poorest looking human being . . . face pockmarked, and looks like a gambler to me.' Mediation produced an agreement: 'the husband will sign a peace bond and the wife will limit her gambling. He is rough type, drinks a bit at night, but has a good heart', pontificated the officer. '[H]e will be OK if she does not *antagonize* him.'[148]

The dysfunctional family of the forties and fifties was also supposedly caused by outside family interference, infidelity and sex, and, as before, alcohol abuse. Mediating officers were particularly concerned about in-laws trying to take sides in disputes and sometimes criticized women or implied they were spoiled if they drew in their parents as allies. Although the Family Court saw a valid role for itself as a professional mediator, extended families, it was assumed, were amateurs, exacerbating marital problems.[149] The increased emphasis on nuclear family privacy in the post-World War II period—with only the experts allowed to intervene—hindered women's ability to draw on aid from neighbours and relatives, who previously provided a limited means of community control over batterers.

Lack of sexual fulfilment and adultery were also perceived to cause violence. The frequency with which sexual incompatibility is mentioned by women in their interviews indicates a yawning gap, *especially* in the post-World War II period, between the promise of sexual fulfilment in popular culture and the reality of unhappy marriages. The increasing emphasis in advice literature and popular culture on sexual and emotional fulfilment in marriage, overshadowing duty, obligation, and reciprocal work roles, engendered new tensions and dissatisfactions. Psychological counselling was almost always the answer of the court, but there was a frequent subtext: failed sexual relations might be the result of women's frigidity. This partly reflected the male gaze of some probation officers, but also prevailing Freudian images in psychology of the domineering or frigid woman. In one separation case, for instance, a woman said her husband had always been unhappy with their sex life and was involved with another woman. The officer urged her to 'go home and try to be more of a wife to him, to submit to him . . . wait and see if he does get in deeper with this other woman. It will do her good to reflect for awhile', he concluded, 'she is not so badly off as others.'[150]

Similarly, when assault cases turned into inquisitions about adultery (and counter-adultery) by the probation officer or judge, there was an assumption that a woman's adultery might excuse her husband's jealous violence. Although one husband 'admitted to beating and choking'[151] his wife, the judge adjourned the case in order to investigate claims that she was involved with another man. Charges of adultery could obscure the original assault charge. In a noticeable exception, the judge allowed a charge to stand against a man who assaulted his wife, supposedly because of her adultery earlier in the marriage: 'you may have been outraged at what your wife did but you have no right to treat her this way.' Presumably, his repeated violence and threats to kill her and the children, once with a loaded gun, precipitated the judge's stern response.[152]

Even if Family Court judges claimed to deplore wife assault, they sometimes went on to chastise women for causing it with their promiscuous behaviour. When a Peterborough woman was prosecuted for her 'idle and dissolute' life (she had VD and the Crown wanted to incarcerate her), she adamantly refused to return to her husband, claiming he beat her up. Although the husband *had* been convicted of assault, the judge, in this closed session, was relentless with her. 'He keeps you, doesn't he? Why don't you get a job?' he asked. 'Did you stay out at night and that caused the trouble? . . . You can't run around with other men and have your husband ignore this . . . you can tell about how bad he is to you, [but] what about how bad you are to him?'[153]

The emphasis of the Family Court personnel on reform and reconciliation reinforced women's understanding that formal charges should only be a last resort. In the Toronto court, for instance, one file starts in 1931 and stretches to 1957, with many incidents of assault; less than half of them led to court charges, and usually the husband was simply bound over to keep the peace.[154] Similarly, another woman who first asked for help in 1935 suffered through three incidents before a summons for threatening was given to her husband. Despite the involvement of the probation officer in the case, the husband continued to assault her, and when the children intervened, they, too, were physically abused. By 1944, after a judge finally declared him 'unfit to live with', she gained her freedom.[155] If women were

Table 3
Occurrences Processed and Offences Brought to Court,
Toronto Family Court, 1920–1940

Year	Occurrences	Offences Brought to Court	%
1920	955	284	30%
1922	1,753	619	35%
1924	1,243	807	65%
1926	1,636	696	43%
1928	1,637	1,004	61%
1929	3,371	1,397	41%
1930	4,127	1,837	44%
1932	4,021	1,013	25%
1934	3,962	851	21%
1936	4,780	839	18%
1938	6,538	842	13%
1940	6,900	1,015	15%

SOURCE: Toronto Family Court, *Annual Report*, 1920–40.

persistent in pressing their cases, their untrammelled determination stood out as exceptional. 'I don't care what I am called', wrote one Toronto woman who was 'habitually beaten' to the court. 'I will leave and work or . . . walk out, but the father is not fit to care for these children. . . . I will leave but not until I've sold my property. I realize that it is your duty to try and keep homes intact but you have not been persecuted day in and out for ten years.'[156]

Statistical evidence supports the emphasis on placation and probation in Family Courts. In the Toronto court the number of assault cases concealed a much larger number of assaults processed as 'occurrences' by the staff of probation officers. During the 1930s all occurrences in the Toronto Family Court outnumbered court cases by 3:2; by the 1940s, this was 6:1—and rising.[157] Moreover, assaults, almost all of which were perpetrated by men, were always a small percentage of occurrences: in 1930, they were 6 per cent, in 1940, 3 per cent (see Tables 3–4, Figure 1).[158] Table 5 indicates all of the offences that brought adults before the Toronto Family Court for formal hearings during the 1930–50 period, including assault and contributing to delinquency.

The socialized justice of the Family Courts may ultimately have been far more effective in collecting support payments than in controlling violence in the home. Dorothy Chunn argues that the Toronto

Table 4
Adult Occurrences Processed by Toronto Family Court, 1920–1940

Year	Contributing to Delinquency	Non-Support	Desertion/Neglect	Domestic Problems	Assault	Children	Total
1920	7	39	125	57	40	687	955
1922	244	272	93	74	2	1,068	1,753
1924	195	129	60	61	68	730	1,243
1926	143	100	39	48	108	1,198	1,636
1928	153	120	49	58	110	1,147	1,637
1929	224	851	128	449	220	1,499	3,371
1930	267	1,197	158	912	248	1,345	4,127
1932	185	766	179	1,119	242	1,530	4,021
1934	217	687	234	822	297	1,705	3,962
1936	343	881	208	805	303	2,240	4,780
1938	310	1,116	115	1,027	271	3,699	6,538
1940	209	1,468	63	1,001	216	3,943	6,900

SOURCE: Toronto Family Court, *Annual Report*, 1920–40.

Table 5
Formal Court Hearings of Adult Offences, Toronto Family Court, 1930–1950

Year	Contrib.: Drink Male	Female	Contrib.: Other Male	Female	Contrib.: Truancy Male	Female	Non-support Male	Female	Assault Male	Female	Other Male	Female	Total
1930	178	30	340	207	105	103	751	5	71	4	30	13	1,837
1932	66	9	135	28	56	65	577	9	39	3	13	13	1,013
1934	42	3	95	14	66	74	510	0	44	1	1	1	851
1936	62	9	107	13	78	56	456	1	54	1	0	0	839
1938	70	4	106	13	59	57	410	4	101	1	1	1	842
1940	65	4	86	2	17	0	728	0	84	0	0	0	1,015
1941	86	2	75	4	4	1	488	0	87	0	0	0	747
1942	79	8	71	8	14	3	562	2	93	5	0	0	845
1943	85	3	58	8	32	23	565	1	139	0	0	0	914
1944	96	7	52	3	123	98	577	0	143	2	0	0	1,101
1945	96	10	29	2	110	140	660	0	137	3	0	0	1,187
1946	106	14	37	11	62	109	714	1	116	4	0	0	1,174
1947	117	3	44	2	31	50	609	0	115	6	0	0	977
1948	84	3	31	16	16	31	579	0	98	6	0	0	864
1949	66	5	55	6	13	18	576	0	107	1	0	0	847
1950	69	6	73	11	12	22	579	0	87	0	0	0	859

Contrib.: Drink = contributing to delinquency through drink.
Contrib.: Other = contributing to delinquency through other means.
Contrib.: Truancy = contributing to delinquency through truancy.

SOURCE: Toronto Family Court, *Annual Report*, 1930–50.

Figure 1
Assaults vs Total Offences, 1930–1952

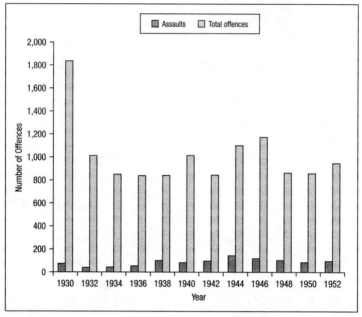

SOURCE: Toronto Family Court, *Annual Report*, 1930–53.

court did aid support collection,[159] and the number of women trying to use the Peterborough Family Court for support payments skyrocketed in the 1950s, though battering charges apparently did not.[160] This may have reflected women's increasing sense of entitlement to financial support or even the pressures on the women from local social service agencies that wanted fathers, not the state, to support deserted families. But because many support cases actually involved battering, women were also likely using the Deserted Wives and Children Maintenance Act as a strategy to leave violent marriages.

One or two incidents of violence were seldom seen as cause for separation, and judges often pontificated against 'easy' separations. In one complicated case, the Welland Family Court judge could not decide whether to believe the son (who said his mother was beaten) or the father. He urged reconciliation: 'It takes two to make trouble. You have been married 28 years. You could get along. It is a disgrace to separate now. . . . [If you do] a lot of hard earned money will go down the drain and it will be costly with custody of the children. It will hurt the children. You are well advised to get back together and make a home.'[161] By the 1950s, if the court did find the husband guilty of assault, if suspended sentences and peace bonds did not work, and if it deemed cruelty could be proven, it was increasingly adamant that the woman had a right to separate and that the man should pay support to his family—though the court had a lot of trouble collecting that support.

If the man was convicted in court the most likely outcome was a suspended sentence, probation, or a choice of a fine or jail. In the 1930s a standard $10 or 10 days was offered; by the 1950s an assault was worth up to $30 or 30 days. In a sample of cases from 1954 to 1961 in Welland County, jail sentences were involved in 9 per cent of cases, withdrawals accounted for 37 per cent, suspended sentences, 19 per cent, further counselling or referrals, 23 per cent, and dismissals or granting of separation orders, 12 per cent.[162] Judges were reluctant to send men to jail, arguing that the loss of the family breadwinner would only increase tensions in the home and possibly place women on the welfare rolls. Women's economic dependence was thus central, not marginal, to the issue of violence. The ideal of a male breadwinner, the reality that women's earning prospects were dim, and the poverty of some families all contributed to the legal system's continuing indulgence of wife assault. The few men who received jail terms for wife assault were often repeat offenders, had done extremely severe physical damage to the woman, or were convicted on other charges as well.[163]

Throughout this 40-year period, both earlier magistrates and later Family Court judges did not challenge the idea that the man was the rightful head of household. Rather, they advised men to exercise this authority with compassion instead of physical intimidation. 'Go home and take the leadership in the house, act as a man . . . . You have lost the reins of control [to the wife], you have made a mess of it', moralized a judge to one man in a separation case, adding that he should 'be her protector' rather than 'casting her off, so she will be fair prey for the lust' of other men in the community.[164] Judges often reminded violent husbands of their manly duty to protect their wives; if the man abandoned his duty, the law would take the woman under its wing for protection.[165]

This outlook must be seen in the wider context of legal and social views of all kinds of violence against women. Although wife assault was perceived through a different lens than sexual assault (who could imagine a magistrate asking a victim of sexual assault to kiss and make up with the man!) there were overlapping themes in the courts' assessment of violence. Both men charged with sexual assault and abusive husbands were chastised for abandoning their role as paternal guardians of women,[166] and like many wife-beaters, sexual assault defendants claimed that their physical actions were provoked or beyond their control. The testimony of medical experts was often necessary to corroborate or support a woman's case, and the victim's own marital, sexual, and family life was relevant to the court's sympathy and sentencing. The rape victim was grilled on her sexual past, while the wife was interrogated about her fidelity and the proper exercise of her domestic duties.[167] Women's cases were stronger if other witnesses testified to support their claims and if the violence appeared to be totally 'unprovoked' in the court's view. In short, the woman had to be an honourable victim—a good wife and mother, not promiscuous, adulterous, or violent. Women might lay claim to some protection from the courts, but this always fell short of an endorsement of their sexual autonomy and complete freedom from all violence. 'Benevolent concessions, not absolute rights'[168] remained the tenor of the law.

Conclusion

In the interwar period, women in rural and small-town Ontario tried a variety of strategies, not unlike those of their nineteenth-century grandmothers, to try to deal with their spousal violence. Calling on legal authorities was often a last resort of tremendous fear, a response to habitual violence, or an attempt to deal with family poverty combined with violence. Once in the courtroom, men justified their violence with a language of authority and obedience or by seeking to portray their violence as beyond their moral and physical control.

In response, the legal authorities offered a rhetoric of shame—repeated in the press as a reminder of the uncivilized, lower-class character of wife-beaters—but also a reality of leniency in sentencing. Women were persuaded to buy into the operation of this system precisely because they saw so few financial or social alternatives to their existing marriages. To rural women, alternatives seemed particularly remote, given their lack of transportation and their isolation from wage work, family, and sometimes even sympathetic neighbours. Patriarchal relations and women's economic dependence thus set the scene for violence, creating the opportunities and rationale for it to occur.

Within this social context, not all women were characterized as equal and honourable victims needing the protection of the law.

Assumptions concerning the essential character of masculinity and femininity and the duties of wifehood and the rights of husbands, as well as a double standard of sexuality, influenced the informal and formal operation of the law. Concerns that some women had provoked their attackers, or that they were immoral, were voiced by court officials, detracting from their right to protection.

Evidence also indicates that those cases making it to court were the tip of the iceberg, for long before Family Courts were set up across Ontario, the seeds of socialized justice had already been sown. The earlier practices of mediation, reconciliation, and informal justice exercised by the police and magistrate established a pattern of patching up families in which husbands had beaten wives. Once Family Courts were established, this informal justice did take on a new form; non-legal experts, trained in a grammar of medical and psychological analysis, tried to conciliate, counsel, and mend family discord so a court case could be avoided. The court no longer legitimated police conclusions: it now legitimated the diagnoses of professional social workers, probation officers, and doctors.

This new emphasis within the Family Courts on private investigation and counselling, as opposed to public trials, encouraged more women to voice their complaints. Certainly, in the 1940s and 1950s, the increasing numbers of women seeking separations and support to escape violent marriages, voicing their marital unhappiness to the probation officer, and attempting to use the Family Court apparatus to alter a husband's behaviour may point to the 'seeds of revolt' percolating beneath the surface of a claustrophobic culture of unhappy family togetherness. By the 1950s some small changes were clearly evident. Women articulated an increased sense of entitlement to peace and sought separation as a means of coping with violence, while the courts and related social services indicated a marginally increased toleration for women's social freedom and their need to work outside the home. However inadequate the Family Courts were in ending violence, women's quest for a talking cure with the probation officer suggests a new attempt to negotiate and/or resist unhappy, violent marriages. Women's increased use of the Family Courts also suggests a push for autonomy and independence, undoubtedly framed by increasing numbers of women (even married women) in the workforce, and a very slightly improved welfare and social service provision to single mothers.[169]

But was socialized justice more effective than the earlier patterns of informal justice in actually ending battering? Despite the good intentions of their sponsors, Family Courts did not substantially change the alternatives of many abused wives. It was not simply the existence of a Family Court but the ideological climate surrounding it, the nature of its socialized justice, and especially women's material and social alternatives—or lack of them—that shaped the outcome for women. In the intensely pro-family climate of post-World War II Canada, the emphasis was placed on preserving the family, and women were still urged to give their abusive partners a second chance. The psychology and psychiatry experts of the 1950s—who provided important backup to the new court process—were not really more critical of the power relations behind family violence than the earlier police investigators had been.[170] As Elizabeth Pleck points out for the US, the pervasive influence of Freudian interpretations, along with an emphasis on rigid gender roles and on family privacy and preservation, actually had a detrimental effect on the perception of family violence in this period, 'obscuring, hiding, even excusing it' with the image 'of the nagging wife'.[171] This does not mean we should idealize criminal justice solutions as opposed to socialized justice solutions to wife assault. Many contemporary studies offer the sobering reminder that increasing court appearances and convictions do not necessarily 'further feminist goals' and better the lives of women, and some maintain the 'criminal justice solution' merely reinforces race and class oppressions.[172]

Over this entire period, the crucial issues of power and control at the heart of wife-battering were eclipsed. The gendered ideology of protection ingrained within the legal system reproduced the notion that freedom from violence was not an inherent right of all women but, rather, was limited to decent, dutiful, and loyal wives. The protection offered by the letter of the law supposedly applied to all women; the practice of the law was quite different. That some women continued to press the law into their service, given such uncertainties, indicates courage and determination to seek out lives without violence. Although little public, feminist agitation over wife assault was heard until the 1970s, women had already been protesting wife assault for some time.

4

Prostitution and Promiscuity: Sexual Regulation and the Law

A fundamental tenet of feminist political critique throughout the twentieth century has been that the law regulated the sexual activity of men and women in profoundly different ways, with heterosexual women subject to stricter policing and harsher stigmatization for sexual activity outside of marriage. The double standard that castigated women for their rejection of chastity and fidelity, for childbirth outside of marriage, and for the sale of sex was the focus of suffragists' ire before World War I. The latter continues to be a focus for feminist critique today. While most suffragists agreed that limitation of sex to monogamous marriage for *both* men and women was the desired goal, current feminist discourse is more multi-vocal in its assessment of sexuality in general and of the sale of sex in particular. Some feminists argue prostitution is a form of alienated work, but also the inevitable outgrowth of patriarchal social relations; others analyse it as a form of wage labour and as a constructed social problem, criticizing the 'covert moralism' still underlying some feminist appraisals of prostitution.[1]

Unlike such contemporary advocates, feminists in the period from 1920 to 1960 rarely suggested the decriminalization of prostitution. Rather, most liberal feminists agreed with the tenets of the reigning legal discourse: first, women's unrestrained or pecuniary sexual activity outside of marriage was a social problem, and second, the law was an appropriate instrument to regulate sexual activity and familial roles for men and women. However, the criminalization of certain sexual behaviours was not simply a juridical matter. The deviant sexuality censured by the law was also constructed within a wider economic, social, and cultural context. Sexual regulation stretched across state and civil society, crossing the borders of the public and private, linked through formal and informal systems of power and authority—the nuclear family, religious precepts, expert medical knowledge, and the court system. Criminalization, in short, always went hand in hand with a broader process of Foucauldian normalization.

Normalization, as feminists have also been at pains to add, was not gender-neutral. The question Foucault leaves out, Sara Bartky maintains, is 'why female bodies become endowed with certain meanings and *not* others', for the construction of sexuality and one's 'embodiment' through discourse are gendered, and asymmetrically so, sustaining unequal and oppressive relations between men and women.[2] Moreover, the body so often interrogated by Foucauldian theory is not an isolated 'site of pain and pleasure';[3] it is connected to the pre-discursive, again reminding us to ask those messy materialist questions of social and economic context.

Foucault's *History of Sexuality* did refer to 'class sexualities', suggesting the need to ask how sexuality was experienced and regulated differently according to class. Rejecting the repressive hypothesis of sexuality—the idea that the middle class denied and avoided discussion of sex and embraced sexual repression as a means of controlling the working class—Foucault argued that the modern bourgeoisie embraced the examination of sex, creating a sexual identity first for itself. But this identity, he concedes, was meant to distinguish bourgeois sexuality from proletariat sexual 'degradation', and the bourgeois did attempt to 'deploy' their sexual standards among the working classes, even if their lack of success meant that distinct 'bourgeois' and 'class sexualities' persisted.[4]

An analysis of class and race, the pre-discursive context, and feminist questions concerning sexual inequality and subordination are thus necessary additives to a Foucauldian emphasis on the deconstruction of sexual truths. Histories of prostitution, for example, began by exploring the structural roots and social organization of prostitution, sympathetically portraying it as a 'choice among limited choices' for working-class women. More recent works, drawing on cultural theory, have explored the symbolic representation and expert discourse on prostitution. Both approaches are useful, and though the latter invites considerable doubt that the 'subaltern'[5] voice of the prostitute can be located, I would argue that her brief ripostes in penal and court records provide some clues to her social life and thinking.

With those questions in mind, this chapter will examine two concrete examples of the legal regulation of women: first, the policing of prostitution through bawdy-house laws and vagrancy provisions prohibiting streetwalking and soliciting, and second, the use of the Ontario Female Refuges Act to curb women's 'incorrigible and dissolute' behaviour, these usually being code words for promiscuity. While concerns about prostitution declined over this period, other methods of policing working-class women's promiscuous sexuality were strengthened. As Foucault argued, the notion that the so-called sexual 'repression, taboo, and prohibition' characterizing the Victorian period were surpassed by more modern 'liberating' proclamations of sexual expression obscures the way in which the regime of 'power/knowledge/pleasure' simply reinvented itself over time.[6] There was, on one hand, a continuum of sexual regulation, with persisting goals reflecting power relations of class, race, and gender, but on the other hand there were different definitions and rationales and shifting focuses of concern and methods of censuring women deemed sexually deviant.

Sexuality and Criminality:
From Feeble-Mindedness to Frigidity

Despite the supposed unsettling of gender roles during World War I and the image of the liberated flapper in the 1920s, the double standard of sexuality did not disappear in the interwar period. It remained deeply embedded in Canadian society and law for decades, not only in statutes dealing with prostitution but also in cultural constructions of gender roles, social welfare provision, and the regulation of wage work. Nor were feminists necessarily critical of the double standard; they consciously and unconsciously endorsed it. Social welfare reformers, for instance, insisted that only sexually 'moral' mothers should receive Mother's Allowances and middle-class birth-control advocates deplored sex outside of marriage.[7] Even socialist and Communist women, who challenged some sexual norms, could not completely shake off a moralistic abhorrence of the 'degradation' of prostitution.[8]

Discourses demarcating normal and abnormal sexuality did change from the interwar period to the post-World War II period, though medical and psychiatric doctrine was always prominent and, indeed, proliferated over time. These theories made their way into the criminal justice system through the training of court and penal professionals and into the public mind through public advocacy groups (such as the Canadian Council on Social Hygiene) and the popular press. Social workers, doctors, psychiatrists, and psychologists were increasingly integrated into Ontario's system of socialized justice,

and with psychological and intelligence tests backing up their diagnoses they made influential judgements about the sexual lives of
working-class women.

In the interwar period especially, feeble-mindedness was seen as a
cause of both promiscuity and prostitution, a view promoted by
Helen MacMurchy and C.K. Clarke, leading Canadian doctors with
eugenicist sympathies. Using dubious measures of intelligence, Dr
Clarke claimed that over 75 per cent of prostitutes were feeble-
minded, an idea reproduced in the 1919 Ontario Royal Commission
on the Treatment of Venereal Disease and Care of the Feebleminded.[9]
MacMurchy's statistical equation of mental defect and prostitution
was sometimes higher.[10] Clarke also quite consciously popularized
his research from the Toronto Psychiatric Clinic, which claimed that
the genesis of factory girls' sexual 'immorality' was 'low mental
capacity', not 'low wages'.[11] Not surprisingly, one of the constant
refrains of superintendents from both the Mercer Reformatory for
Females and the OTSG was that promiscuous feeble-minded women
were clogging up the penal system when they belonged in an institution for the mentally deficient. While the equation of feeble-mindedness and prostitution weakened after the thirties, it did not entirely
disappear; in 1945, a few medical experts were still calling for the
'incarceration' of the 'mentally defective sex offenders'.[12]

A second medical theme, which took on special significance during both world wars, was the coupling of venereal disease (VD) with
promiscuity and prostitution. Urgent concern about VD during World
War I resulted in new, coercive federal legislation used to detain
women suspected of having VD,[13] and in the aftermath of the war,
provinces followed suit with their own interventionist laws as well as
participation in national educational campaigns. Ontario's law, passed
in 1918, required all cases to be reported to the medical officer of
health, provided for free treatment (but fines for those who refused),
and compelled examinations of those in custody and possible forced
treatment through incarceration. After World War I, some doctors continued to advocate the forced confinement of 'pestilential' prostitutes,[14] while social hygiene activists used the perils of this disease in
their attempts to keep faltering anti-prostitution campaigns going.[15]

Although fears about VD were displaced during the Depression,
they resurfaced during World War II. A military and state campaign
against the 'patriotute' reflected fears that, as women left the home
sphere for untraditional jobs and lives, they would become 'proletari-
anized'[16] and thus promiscuous. Educational material tended to cast
women either as innocent victims, perhaps contacting the disease

unwittingly from husbands, or as predatory, sexually loose women and prostitutes spreading the disease with no moral compunctions.[17] Describing the campaign against prostitution in Vancouver during World War II, a military doctor first portrayed the prostitute as a pitiable and 'unfortunate' human being used by pimps and 'badgered' by legal prosecution 'into the depths of underworld subjection'. But in his eyes she could also morph into a promiscuous predator: we need to ensure that 'tired war-industry workers' going into beer parlours are not 'confronted brazenly by venereally-infected women at adjacent tables.'[18] Well into the 1950s, VD remained an important concern; controlling infected women with forced treatment or incarceration was rationalized as a public health necessity to protect current citizens and future progeny.

Other experts in criminology and social work also endorsed theories that reinforced rather than questioned a polarized view of the dissolute versus the normal woman. An influential study of female delinquency in the 1920s, W.I. Thomas's *The Unadjusted Girl*, did note the material logic behind working-class girls' embrace of prostitution, a theme taken up by social workers who worried that less-than-innocent girls were callously embracing a new consumerism and lax morality in the form of sex-for-sale.[19] Despite his materialist insight, Thomas, like other experts of this era, never questioned the basic equation of deviant female sexuality with criminality.

This was also true of a 1934 American study, *Five Hundred Delinquent Women*, still referred to positively in the 1940s by Canadian social workers. Although its authors, Sheldon and Eleanor Glueck, claimed an environmental approach, concluding that incarcerated women were the products of broken homes, foster care, inadequate parenting, and impoverished and unhealthy families, their definition of criminality was closely tied to sexual transgression, especially promiscuity and prostitution. Their recommendation of reform was to inculcate sexual self-control into working-class women who lacked moral training. Old-fashioned and superior moralism permeated their conclusions: with 'this swarm of defective, diseased, anti-social misfits', the Gluecks concluded, it is a 'miracle' the proportion we do rehabilitate.[20]

Suppositions about class and race informed most expert discourses on sexuality in the interwar period. It was assumed that those 'lingering near the bottom of the social ladder' were more promiscuous, contributing to the spread of venereal disease.[21] Furthermore, because houses of prostitution were located in poor areas of the city, working-class children were exposed to this 'corruption' and were thus likely to adopt similar 'sexual behaviour'.[22] J.J. Heagerty, chief of Venereal Disease Control for Canada, cited Canadian studies showing that prostitutes 'are recruited from girls who leave school before fourteen years of age', adding that they were 'women with the mentality of children'. They were similar, he claimed, to those of the 'primitive and semi-civilized races' from Siam or Haiti, whose culture was so completely promiscuous that it lacked any notion of 'morality'. It is well known, this doctor continued, that the 'smaller the amount of education . . . the more prostitution'. As a result, 'almost the entire population [of Russia] is infected with venereal disease.'[23] Both the ignorance of the poor and the amorality of the 'uncivilized' non-white races were thus equated with prostitution.

By the post-World War II period, psychoanalytic theories were increasingly used to analyse everything from unwed motherhood to prostitution; the latter was traced to both women's frigidity and their hypersexuality (as Barbara Hobson notes, 'psychoanalytic theory had it both ways').[24] Once separated in the mind of sexologists, lesbianism and prostitution now were linked as signs of women's sexual excess and their dangerous rejection of the familial ideal. As one discussion of a female training school inmate noted with horror: 'she has tried dope, lesbianism, prostitution—*everything*.'[25] Earlier, sex experts had come to the conclusion that the 'disease' of nymphomania originated not simply in the biological body, but in the damaged psyche, and was defined not only by 'too much sex, but too *aggressive* sex'. By the 1940s and 1950s, psychological theories of women's 'hypersexuality' had taken firm root in the mental health profession, which informed the wider public of the multifarious causes of nymphomania: 'a hunger for power, hostility, incestuous desires, latent homosexuality, narcissism, need for affection, rebellion, self hatred, a sexually repressed childhood, among others'.[26]

Psychoanalytic studies such as Harold Greenwald's influential *The Call Girl* stressed the affluent lifestyle of prostitutes but downplayed 'economic need' as the reason for their embrace of commercialized sex. Rather, 'emotional dispositions and early personality traits' were to blame, especially 'early feeling of deprivation because of rejection by the mother'.[27] He threw in some other causes, including broken families, low self-esteem, and early lessons in 'bartering' sex for affection or presents, though the latter was clearly his neutral formula for his patients' descriptions of familial sexual abuse.[28] Another author, a court social worker with day-to-day contact with street prostitutes, was far more attuned to these women's social and economic marginality, even suggesting decriminalization, but she also tended to see prostitutes as pitiable, unfortunate outsiders: 'these broken women who sell their bodies are their own worst enemies, not ours.'[29]

Yet, the psychoanalytic theme of blaming the mother was most enticing to many journalists. This theme suffused a *Chatelaine* exposé of the late 1940s, penned by Canadian journalist Gwenyth Barrington, who based her story on 'Barbara', a prostitute she interviewed in the Mercer Reformatory. Barbara's selfish, materialist mother had run off with another man when she was a mere child, leaving her to a hapless father's care. Lacking a role model, Barbara 'didn't give a damn about herself' and her low self-esteem led her directly to prostitution. Barrington's story made clear that the real criminal was the delinquent, selfish mother: 'When you've read this story you will know which one should be in jail.'[30]

The 1950s fascination with call girls—surely an assumption that prostitutes must be sharing in the post-war boom—and the turn towards psychoanalytic theory were also promoted by Canadian journalist Sidney Katz, who analysed 'the sleazy, grey world of the call girl'. Katz relayed theories that these women were often 'frigid' because they had been 'rejected' when young and did not grow up in a 'normal home learning what it is like to be a wife and mother'. Thus, they were confused about their sex roles, even engaging in 'homosexual activities'. Though Katz portrayed the call girls as outcasts from *Father Knows Best* domestic bliss, alienated and subordinated to pimps (and often small-town, naïve immigrants to the big city, as in earlier white slave narratives), he inadvertently revealed their views as well: many simply stumbled into or chose prostitution to make good money.[31]

Renditions of prostitution and promiscuity in the popular press often drew on the views of medical and psychological experts, but they were also undoubtedly influenced by other cultural and religious ideals. Indeed, the 'embeddedness' of Judeo-Christian precepts within the larger culture offered propitious conditions for the production of 'scientific' expert knowledge.[32] As Cynthia Commachio points out, during this period 'no organized religion tolerated sex outside of marriage, even if the gravity of that sin varied.'[33] The Catholic Church's abhorrence of premarital sex and prostitution was articulated not only through the pulpit but also in reform work with unwed mothers, which offered those who transgressed little in the way of forgiveness, more in the way of condemnation.[34] Even as more churches took up the cause of unwed mothers in the post-World War II period, offering them shelter and aid, they persisted in the view that girls who had fallen from grace needed reform and rehabilitation.

What of women's so-called normal sexuality in this period? The post-World War I era was popularly portrayed as a liberation from Victorian norms of repression as there was new emphasis on adolescents' normal sexual curiosity, and on women's heterosexual expression and satisfaction. Sexologists like Havelock Ellis, Marie Stopes, and later Kinsey were gaining credence, constructing in their wake, 'a myth of [past] Victorian sexual repression'.[35] Yet, the new image of sexual fulfilment created its own imperatives: it pathologized same-sex relationships, maintained the idea that women's sexuality was responsive and passive, and limited women's true sexual feelings to monogamous, committed, spiritual relationships. This definition of normal sexuality still spawned an opposite: the promiscuous and the prostitute were abnormal women, 'sexually indiscriminate . . . acting against their *true sexual nature*'.[36] The prostitute, it also warned, could potentially destroy normal family life.[37] As one anti-prostitution politician wrote, she was so entirely 'alien' from the normal women that she was unable even to survive in their geographical midst: 'most of all, [prostitutes] will shun residential areas where every housewife knows her neighbour and is the guardian of her family.'[38] In common with earlier eras and other countries, the prostitute in Canada represented more than the mere sale of sex: she might be transformed into an 'allegorical threat' to family and nation.[39]

Redefining the Legal and Social Problem of Prostitution

The rejection of ideas of Victorian purity did contribute to a declining interest in white slavery and prostitution in the interwar period.[40] Politicized women did not place prostitution on centre stage as suffragists had, nor did the issue assume such an obsessive place in the cultural and social imagination as it had in the previous era.[41] Prostitution was increasingly seen as a symptom of other ills, not a signifier in its own right. Moreover, the changing nature of urban leisure and the increased use of the telephone meant that prostitution could recede to new spaces, less visible than red-light districts. Many police forces, always skeptical about the eradication of all prostitution, turned instead to 'selective toleration, geographical segregation and fines'[42] to control it.

Ironically, prostitution was never itself illegal, though many activities associated with it were. The 1892 Criminal Code had created two primary means of criminalizing prostitutes.[43] First, both men and women could be prosecuted for keeping a common bawdy house (later, as inmates or frequenters of these houses), and the same was true for disorderly houses, though this offence included illegal gaming and drinking. The vagrancy statute also made it illegal for a woman to be a 'common prostitute or night walker' who is 'found in a public place and does not, when required, give a good account of herself.'[44] This streetwalking/vagrancy law equated females only with the category of prostitute, made prostitution a status offence, and generally made suspected women 'outlaws'[45] whom the authorities had wide latitude to harass or arrest.

Moral crusaders had also secured stricter amendments to the Criminal Code in 1913 and 1915, some of which drew more men into the disciplinary orbit of the law by making procuring easier to prosecute, adding offences such as living 'wholly or in part off the avails of prostitution' and concealing a woman in a bawdy house. The bawdy-house provisions were extended to include landlords and the new offence of being 'found in' a bawdy house was added to the Code. Along with the new laws monitoring VD, these provisions created a mighty legal arsenal—and thus social justification—for the prosecution of prostitution. John McLaren shows that national conviction rates for prostitution-related offences rose through the moral reform era, peaking in 1914–16, with numbers of arrests never approximated again for decades.[46]

Indeed, it would appear that this arsenal was not used to its fullest after World War I. Legal historians usually ignore prostitution law after 1920, claiming that recorded cases 'fell off in volume dramatically', reflecting a declining national concern about prostitution.[47] Prostitution laws challenged in the higher courts from 1920 to 1960 often focused on laws dealing with procuring and living off the avails of others, leading one sociologist to conclude hastily that 'greater attention was finally being paid to the males involved in prostitution', though he also admits that 'the courts were initially reluctant to convict males for ancillary prostitution offenses.'[48] A Montreal study also suggests that, by the post-World War II period, women were losing control over their work to pimps, a sign of increased male control over prostitution.[49]

It is true that some significant higher court judgements focused on men; indeed, legal decisions reinforced the understanding that *only* men could be procurers and pimps and only women were prostitutes.[50] Increasingly, the onus was on any man living with a prostitute to prove he was *not* living off her earnings;[51] he was guilty until proven innocent. Also, procuring was interpreted broadly and could be punished severely. One appeal, for instance, upheld a stiff prison term for a café owner for levying a 'value-added' tax on prostitutes using his rooms.[52]

Table 6
Prostitution Charges, Toronto, 1920–1955

| | Inmate of Bawdy House | | Keeper of Bawdy House | | Procuring | | Vagrancy* |
	Male	Female	Male	Female	Male	Female	Female
1920	40	28	12	15	2	1	184
1921	111	55	20	37	5	2	159
1922	200	101	48	64	1	1	137
1923	141	67	46	60	1	0	106
1924	215	110	64	88	2	0	117
1925	256	106	63	137	1	1	178
1926	140	76	40	80	1	0	129
1927	151	50	39	87	2	5	139
1928	108	36	29	53	0	0	102
1929	110	43	21	64	2	1	141
1930	100	42	28	54	2	2	193
1931	53	25	22	52	3	2	234
1932	93	24	16	74	0	1	155
1933	86	34	23	67	0	0	109
1934	56	25	15	47	5	0	96
1935	90	33	19	60	1	1	103
1936	107	35	28	71	0	0	116
1937	88	30	15	62	0	0	92

(continued)

Table 6 (continued)

| | Inmate of Bawdy House | | Keeper of Bawdy House | | Procuring | | Vagrancy* |
	Male	Female	Male	Female	Male	Female	Female
1938	60	28	14	28	0	0	158
1939	118	37	24	81	0	0	177
1940	190	55	39	133	2	0	183
1941	152	37	28	108	2	1	212
1942	48	12	8	36	4	1	186
1943	60	14	7	33	1	0	171
1944	27	10	4	32	0	0	192
1945	26	2	5	27	0	0	292
1946	43	15	10	32	0	0	233
1947	26	17	7	16	0	0	222
1948	11	8	2	9	8	0	216
1949	8	4	2	9	0	0	216
1950	20	7	4	10	0	0	136
1951	40	12	11	15	0	0	114
1952	22	7	6	5	0	0	122
1953	33	0	5	6	0	0	19
1954	45	64	16	3	0	0	173
1955	47	21	32	17	0	0	166

*Vagrancy included some prostitution arrests.

SOURCE: 'Crimes Committed in the City of Toronto', *Annual Report of the City of Toronto*, 1920–55.

Figure 2
Prostitution in Ontario: Male vs Female Commitments

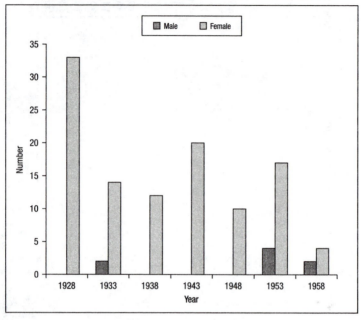

SOURCE: Ontario, *Sessional Papers*, selected years.

The courts might hand down severe sentences when they perceived young women were pressured or literally beaten into prostitution. In 1937 a Toronto Criminal Court judge clearly pitied a young woman of 16 who married her husband because she was pregnant, then was pressed by him to support their impoverished household with street prostitution. Because of her age and condition, his beatings of her, her claims that she tried to resist, and supportive testimony from her neighbours, the husband was given a two-year sentence by the judge, who declared 'there should be no leniency here.'[53]

Ontario-wide committals and sentencing numbers also reflected the new impetus to draw men into the moral parameters of the law, especially using the charge of being an inmate of a bawdy house. However, increasingly after the 1930s, women were still more likely to receive a sentence for keeping a bawdy house, and they were overwhelmingly those charged under the streetwalking/vagrancy clause. In Toronto, female arrests for 'keeping' outnumbered male

Figure 3
Prostitution in Ontario: Female Commitments vs Sentences

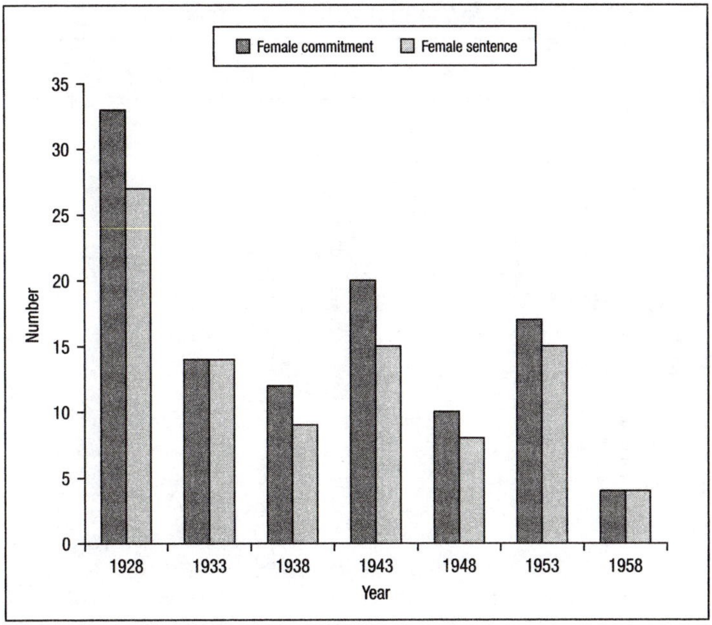

SOURCE: Ontario, *Sessional Papers*, selected years.

arrests, as indicated in Table 6.[54] Moreover, higher court decisions also made life miserable for women working as prostitutes. The definition of a bawdy house was stretched to include just about any place, including a woman's rented rooms, if they were used even twice in the exchange of sex for money, and mere 'reputation'[55] could be a factor in convicting her. Furthermore, the implementation of the vagrancy/streetwalking law could be arbitrary and draconian. Across the country, some courts interpreted it very broadly, allowing easy convictions, though some interpreted the law more narrowly so that all three elements of the vagrancy clause had to be satisfied.[56] It is revealing that Ontario conviction rates for the latter 'female-dominated' prostitution offence remained considerably higher than for the 'co-ed' bawdy-house charges. Figures 2–7, based on Ontario-wide statistics, indicate both the extent of prostitution-related charges and the differential treatment of females and males for sex-trade crimes. Figure 2 shows the female dominance under prostitution

Figure 4
Bawdy-House Inmates/Frequenters:
Female Commitments vs Sentences

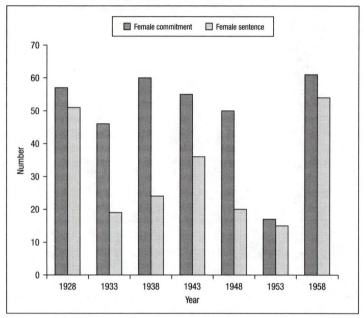

SOURCE: Ontario, *Sessional Papers*, selected years.

(as opposed to bawdy-house) charges; Figures 3–5 indicate the higher rate of conviction (commitments to sentences) for prostitution, as opposed to convictions for being an inmate or keeper of a bawdy house. Figures 6 and 7 compare male and female commitments. Note the high number of men pursued as inmates in the 1920s but a falling off afterwards. With a few exceptions, women came to dominate slightly in charges for keeping a bawdy house. From 1930 to 1959, female charges dominated in 19 of the 29 years. These are highly dubious measures of actual prostitution, of course. They tell us more about policing, though possibly also about increased male participation in or control of a female job ghetto. Finally, given the increased reach of the law over men, it is significant that social discourses on prostitution remained so decidedly fixed on women as the 'problem', whether they were constructed as evil predators or naïve victims.

Figure 5
Bawdy-House Keepers: Female Commitments vs Sentences

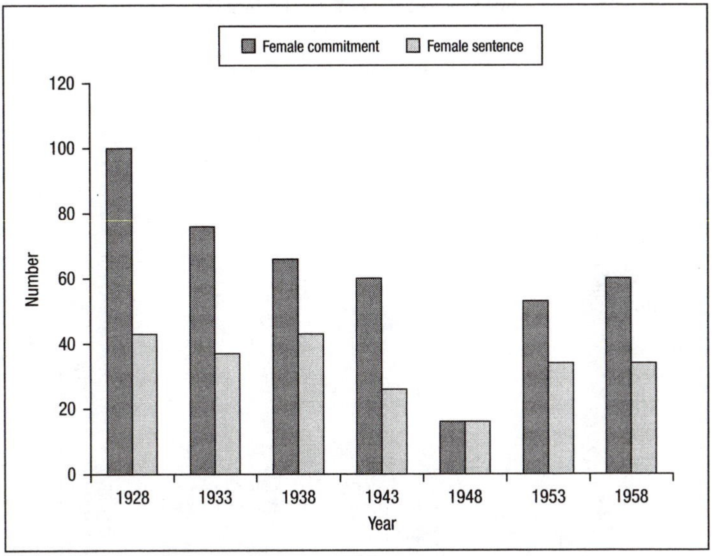

SOURCE: Ontario, *Sessional Papers*, selected years.

It is also important to remember that the disinterest in prostitution after World War I was neither immediate or complete. The interwar period, especially the twenties, witnessed a last gasp of reform efforts, especially because prostitution was connected to anxieties concerning feeble-mindedness and the drug trade. Responding to a public panic about increasing drug use in the early 1920s, legislators introduced new anti-drug laws, aimed at and then disproportionately enforced against Asian and black men.[57] Pressure for legislation was aided by 'narratives of narcoticism' published by notables such as Judge Emily Murphy, in which a recurrent theme is the 'innocent girl addict' whose fate is inevitably a degraded life in prostitution.[58] Charlotte Whitton, a prominent social worker and secretary of the Canadian Welfare Council, pressured the Canadian government to abide by League of Nations resolutions on white slavery, expressing dismay that the RCMP were lax in locating prostitutes imported to Canada, while the virtuous US authorities were 'rounding up and prosecuting large numbers of prostitutes'.[59] She argued before the League of Nations that 'promiscuous voluntary' prostitution was now

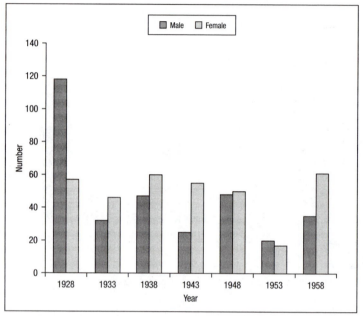

Figure 6
Bawdy-House Inmates/Frequenters:
Male vs Female Commitments

SOURCE: Ontario, *Sessional Papers*, selected years.

the real problem. The combination of a 'demand for sex' by men, 'the existence of amoral attitudes' among women and girls searching for material comforts, and 'public indifference' to the problem led to prostitution, not 'poor working conditions or poor home life'.[60] Whitton's views signified a new, pessimistic emphasis on character defect rather than environmental causes of prostitution—one reason why feminist reform efforts were in decline.

New female magistrates (their appointments often the result of maternal feminist lobbying) also maintained a strong, and punitive, interest in prostitution. Margaret Patterson, who presided over the Toronto Women's Court, created a binary picture of 'good versus bad girl' in a 1935 *Chatelaine* article describing her work. Patterson juxtaposed the 'unfortunate, underprivileged' girl, lacking maternal guidance, who might foolishly fall into trouble with a 'pernicious' minority of promiscuous women who were inherently 'anti-social',

Figure 7
Bawdy-House Keepers: Male vs Female Commitments

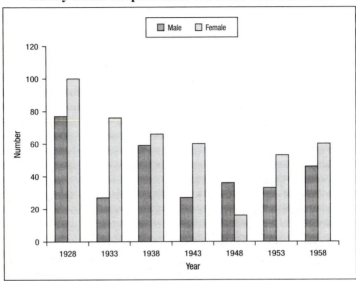

SOURCE: Ontario, *Sessional Papers*, selected years.

irretrievably 'bad . . . wicked, unprincipled, immoral and corrupting'. Some of these women, Patterson charged, actually enjoyed wrecking marriages and families, 'deliberately encouraging the attention of men whom they know to be married'.[61]

Patterson's analysis bore strong similarities to the ambiguous pre-war image of the prostitute as both victim and victimizer. So, too, did a 1937 *Chatelaine* article, which claimed that some young, naïve women were enticed into prostitution by cunning procurers. The depiction of poor, unsuspecting country girls lured into compromising situations by men, as well as the suggestion that 'foreigners' were procuring, bore depressing similarities to white slave narratives. In a similar vein, the *Chatelaine* author suggested that middle-class 'club' women should extend their maternal goodwill to these fallen women, some of whom were of 'inferior mentality', while others came from 'poor families living in overcrowded hovels' and were easily dazzled with 'tales of beautiful clothes' and luxurious surroundings.

While these themes were familiar, others were not. The author also linked prostitution directly to the Depression, blaming unemployment, 'low wages and dreary living conditions' for prostitution.[62] The Depression was thus the problem; prostitution was the symptom. Second, the significance of the article was its isolation in the mainstream press. By the 1930s, Canadian magazines rarely discussed the problem of prostitution. Instead, the Depression and the threat of unemployed angry men, encouraged by socialist and communist parties (which also represented alternative and immoral sexual activity), were the focus of popular and political concern.

As Margaret Hobbs shows, middle-class women's groups, such as the National Council of Women and the YWCA, repeatedly fretted that low relief levels or downward pressure on wages, especially of domestics, would lead 'even the normal' woman to prostitution.[63] Similarly, socialists and trade unions warned that unemployed girls, ground down by capitalism, might 'abandon the social moral code' and resort to prostitution.[64] This refrain had a wider, popular resonance. One of R.B. Bennett's many correspondents on the issue of the economy admonished the Prime Minister on the problems of unemployed women: 'Are you going to stand aside and see prostitutes made of our Canadian women?'[65]

Despite this public hand-wringing, the National Council of Women admitted that 'there is little being done in Canada towards the rehabilitation of prostitutes.'[66] When police, provincial authorities, and private reform groups were surveyed about rehabilitation for prostitutes by Charlotte Whitton in 1935, it became clear that few organizations were interested. The Toronto police knew of no social services, and added that 'low wages' and a lack of employment prevented rehabilitation.[67] The Salvation Army did attend the Toronto Women's Court and regularly visited the Mercer Reformatory, but their efforts were suffused with moralism, and prostitutes may not have embraced the Army's view that they were 'lacking in discipline . . . never having learned to exercise self-control'. The Salvation Army believed the prostitute had to renounce her 'evil associates' and 'adopt good moral standards and a change of heart', not surprisingly, through the 'saving power of Jesus Christ'.[68] A similar conviction was espoused by the Good Shepherd Catholic Refuge for Women, which also offered domestic training and moral 'regeneration' through the power of 'Faith'.[69] Although some women used the Salvation Army's hostel as a halfway house, none of the cases I examined in the Mercer indicated an openness to their religious proselytizing. The Army itself admitted that few prostitutes took advantage of their aid in securing domestic jobs as they 'considered [themselves] above service'.[70]

The decline of the reform impulse was also seen in women sentenced to the Mercer Reformatory. Some convicted prostitutes were always sent to local jails, used as 'holding tanks' to 'keep [unreformable] women with shorter sentences off the streets.'[71] But in the aftermath of Progressive-era social purity campaigns, by the 1920s many Ontario magistrates were giving younger women longer, variable, and indeterminate sentences in the Mercer, believing this sentencing strategy offered the best chance of altering their character. By the 1940s a very different pattern of sentencing and incarceration emerged. Sentences were shorter, fines were used more often, and women were very slightly older.[72] The 1950s provided a more striking contrast, with sentences of less than two months, fewer women under 21, more Toronto women, and more women paying fines. Women were being processed, held, and let go, with little or no attempt at reform.

During World War II, concerns about other sexual offences also momentarily displaced prostitution. The Venereal Diseases Act, amended in 1942, was used extensively from 1943 to 1945; in fact, more women were incarcerated in the Mercer for breaches of that Act than for bawdy-house and streetwalking infractions combined.[73] In Toronto, VD arrests, already increasing just before the war, peaked in 1941, a consequence of a concerted police campaign in collaboration with local medical authorities. Although the public rationale for such vigilance was the control of disease, the VD law was also directed against the moral blight of the so-called 'casual' prostitute, who offered sex far too indiscriminately, or cheaply, for the authorities' taste.[74] The increased use of the VD law indicates how the means and rationale for sexual regulation altered over these years, though a censure of non-marital, heterosexual sexual activity remained a constant.

Indeed, the precise use of prostitution laws remains difficult to measure since policing was a local responsibility and varied from one community to another, and because streetwalking arrests are hidden within overall vagrancy numbers. Nationally, arrests for bawdy-house offences peaked in 1914–15 and remained significant, though fluctuating over the 1920s and 1930s, but such arrests had declined decidedly by the 1940s and 1950s.[75] The same decrease in the formal policing of prostitution was apparent in Toronto, Ontario's primary city of sin. Despite the claim by the Toronto chief of police in the early 1920s that 'bawdy houses received increased attention', this was not sustained into the 1930s, when the Morality Department no longer listed prostitution as a major problem. The police boasted that a decline in bawdy-house charges during the forties was due to their 'vigilance',[76] but the chief, arguing like a good materialist, also admitted that a buoyant war economy and 'good salaries for women'[77] played a role. The early 1950s witnessed increased concern with street prostitution; however, given the increase in the urban population, the arrest numbers were not large. Moreover, if total arrest numbers are any sign of policing concerns, prostitution did not assume a significant proportion of Toronto officers' time, which was spent on auto infractions, theft, domestic disputes, assaults, and so on.

Even in Peterborough, the police chief noted in 1930 that the city was now 'practically free of houses of ill-fame'.[78] Perhaps this had something to do with unorthodox police methods. Rose, a convicted 33-year-old female bawdy-house keeper, claimed in the twenties that the police chief had tricked her into confessing, then reneged on a deal to offer her freedom, presumably in return for her silence about a prominent citizen's 'visit' to her house.[79] Writing to a younger woman arrested with her, she pleaded:

> I can get our good name back, by giving evidence into the . . . case. We can put the chief out of his job also some of those policemen, for . . . we got whisky to drink in the Police station, also more than that took place, and we were all fools. We did not tell how the Chief said if we told nothing he would get us out on parole. . . . We sure have . . . to get our own back at them.[80]

Rose did not, it appears, get her revenge. And by the post-World War II period there were few prosecutions for prostitution offences in this small city, perhaps indicating that prostitutes were more interested in the promise of a more supportive work culture in larger urban centres such as Toronto, or that here, too, a measure of police tolerance prevailed.

Mercer Prostitutes and Their Keepers

That no reform group singled out prostitution as its *cause célèbre* in this period is also evident in new attitudes towards rehabilitation and incarceration. In the nineteenth century, Christian and feminist women had set up refuges such as Toronto's Magdalene Asylum to take in fallen women. By the early twentieth century, however, the Asylum, now the Belmont Refuge, shifted part of its charitable work towards the indigent elderly, though it continued to admit young women deemed dissolute or incorrigible by the courts. By the late 1930s, Belmont abandoned this work, its female incorrigibles transferred to the Mercer.[81] A similar Toronto refuge for fallen women, The Haven, run before World War I by an activist against the white slave trade, also altered its course in the interwar years, gradually redirecting its efforts to the mentally challenged.[82] The Mercer remained a key site for the reform of Ontario's prostitutes, as shown in Table 7. Admissions remained fairly constant until the mid-fifties, except for an increase in numbers in the early 1940s, which may reflect either an increase in activity or greater state vigilance in the early years of World War II. The higher numbers in the late 1950s may indicate the use of the Mercer as a 'local jail'.

Throughout this period, penal practitioners at the Mercer never stopped asking why women became prostitutes—a question that never would have been directed towards other labour that working-class women were compelled to do—because prostitution was not seen as work but as a total embrace of immoral sexual mores. The prostitute, in social discourse, *was* her work.

To begin with, bad 'home training', a lack of education in moral values, and negligent mothering were cited as basic causes of prostitution. 'This is an ignorant, inexperienced girl, with no home training', wrote Mercer Superintendent Emma O'Sullivan in the 1920s of one 18-year-old. Her foolish marriage to a 'worthless' fellow was blamed as well, though his letters to his wife indicated only a desire to reconstruct their relationship. Ignoring this, Superintendent Milne resolved to keep her away from him on release and sent her to a sister instead.[83]

To counteract a young woman's inadequate upbringing, the superintendent practised strong maternal intervention in the inmates' lives and also offered her 'superior' advice to their families. When a woman's family agreed with her suggestions for reform, promising to keep daughters away from old associates or moving her to another city, she supported them. However, if families tried to secure a daughter's release against her wishes, pleading poverty, family sickness, or their own respectability, she paid little heed. Admonishing one 'bad' mother for her failure to inculcate good morals, she announced that she was censoring the mother's inappropriate letters containing supposedly corrupting local gossip, and she was confiscating her 'totally unacceptable' presents (such as gum).[84]

Families might also explain a woman's run-in with the law by her bad upbringing or, a stock response, bad companions. Perhaps they sensed the latter explanation would excuse them, while satisfying the prison superintendent. One couple claimed that their daughter simply 'got in with bad friends' when the mother was absent in the hospital.[85] A sister who took in a released prostitute insisted that she must not 'work as a waitress again, as this provided too many temptations . . . she was associated with a wild crowd.'[86] Only in a minority of cases

Table 7
Women in Mercer Reformatory for Prostitution, 1930–1959

Year	Bawdy-House Keeper	Bawdy-House Inmate	Prostitution	Total
1930	12	11	0	23
1931	4	1	1	6
1932	9	3	0	12
1933	7	3	0	10
1934	7	3	7	17
1935	9	1	0	10
1936	19	6	6	31
1937	32	2	6	40
1938	18	5	8	31
1939	10	0	13	23
1940	33	6	17	56
1941	36	8	26	70
1942	17	4	21	42
1943	9	3	7	19
1944	11	1	5	17
1945	8	5	6	19
1946	6	1	11	18
1947	13	9	8	30
1948	3	6	4	13
1949	6	1	5	12
1950	3	1	12	16
1951	5	3	18	26
1952	9	1	13	23
1953	13	1	18	32
1954	24	3	23	50
1955	12	1	24	37
1956	17	12	50	79
1957	11	4	48	63
1958	11	6	38	55
1959	10	8	37	55

SOURCE: Ontario, *Annual Report on Prisons and Reformatories*, 1930–59.

did families and penal workers stretch their analysis of bad home training to include violence, poverty, and abuse. Debating where to send a released Hamilton woman in the 1930s, the parole assessment noted that the father was a 'drunkard who is probably responsible for her condition' and her other relatives faced unemployment and poverty so they could not take her in.[87] In another case a distraught aunt and uncle pleaded with the Mercer to release their niece, who had been terribly 'abused' as a child by her mother.[88] In contrast, a few families aided in the criminalization of their daughters, though this was far less common than with the Female Refuges Act (FRA). One stepmother 'turned her daughter in' not simply because of prostitution but also because 'she is always causing trouble between the stepmother and father' and 'was pregnant with no place to go.'[89] Another father wanted charges pressed on his daughter, 'who admitted earning $2.00–$3.00 a day as a prostitute', but he was soon demanding her release when her mother fell ill.

A recurring refrain from the Mercer keepers was also that women embraced prostitution in search of 'easy money'. Prostitutes were fundamentally lazy, but they craved luxuries; they did not want to accept the reality of hard but honest working-class labour and were aping a lifestyle beyond their prescribed lot in life. While there was certainly a modicum of sympathy in the Depression for women forced into prostitution, it was not a persisting theme after World War II, and it was the antithesis of analyses of 'call girls' forwarded in the fifties. The idea that all women selling sex craved silk stockings, however, was contradicted by one woman who admitted to occasional prostitution just to 'pay her bills'. This mother, who was caring for a sick child, admitted to the Toronto Family Court in 1931 that she sometimes 'had intercourse with the [local laundry man]'; in return, she got 'groceries and sometimes 50 cents'.[90]

In the interwar period especially, the younger charges at the Mercer were sometimes seen as naïve and pitiable, coerced into prostitution by conniving madams. A teen, 'Mary', as one sentencing magistrate claimed, was 'used by a notorious bawdy house keeper', who 'compelled her to have intercourse with all kinds of men, and go out to do soliciting on the street. . . . Under proper guidance she could become a decent citizen.'[91] The older women who 'encouraged young women into the business', however, deserved no pity. Commenting on an Ottawa woman who was also dying of cancer, supporting eight children, and on relief, the magistrate noted that 'she was suffering from diseases of turpitude, a derelict [and] morally speaking, her soul is worse than her body', for not only did she encourage her daughter to engage in prostitution, but she also was the 'cause of several young men contracting contagious diseases'.[92]

Women were thus still polarized into victims or victimizers, their character imagined as either reformable or unsalvageable. This was especially true for Native women, though few were incarcerated in the Mercer for prostitution. (Indeed, their placement in local jails reflected a view that they were unreformable.) An Aboriginal women sent to the Mercer from northern Ontario was described by the magistrate in this dichotomous fashion, with her 'Indianness' suggesting inevitable weakness: 'she is one of the Indian girls who comes in from the districts and is continually appearing on charges of this nature and drunkenness. . . . She is a menace to society . . . but her young age and a return to more desirable companionship may bring good results on her character.'[93]

During World War II, women's rejection of purity and marriage was also portrayed as an affront to the family and nation: 'she is a menace to the troops and others falling prey to her solicitations . . . [when] the soldiers here are overrun with prostitution', wrote one sentencing report.[94] When a soldier's wife was convicted in a small city, she was described as both 'thoroughly bad' and suffering from syphilis. Her 'betrayal' of her husband overseas was undoubtedly seen harshly, yet the idea that women might have obtained VD *from* their soldier partners was never remotely entertained.[95]

While feeble-mindedness was cited by many reformatory doctors in the interwar period as the precipitating factor behind prostitution,[96] it was also increasingly attributed to addiction. When Bonnie, a 23-year-old from a small Ontario town, was incarcerated in 1923, the committal claimed her real problem was addiction to drugs. After her parole she was watched by the local doctor, who informed the Mercer of her breach of parole (she went off with some men to a Marmora hotel for a few days) so that she could be reincarcerated.[97] It is small wonder that many women probably fled to large cities to escape such surveillance. Similarly, a woman widowed during World War I who turned to prostitution in the early 1920s was sent for rehabilitation, with the expectation that if she 'can get the alcohol from her system' her sexual reform will be possible.

That prostitution was one form of work available to poor women with costly addictions, or that the work may have encouraged alcohol and drug use, was little explored until the 1950s. Yet, women's own testimonies had indicated precisely this for some time. A Scottish immigrant who was a trained nurse found herself with no money in the 1930s, after her husband died, and she began to drink heavily, though her daughter was still lodged in a private school, cared for financially by others. Ostracized by friends because of her alcoholic rages, she used prostitution to survive, but she begged, when in the Mercer, to be sent to a hospital 'for her nerves', probably a call for help with her addictions.[98] By the late 1950s there were some small attempts at rehabilitative aid, including the establishment of reformatory AA groups. Prostitution is almost a 'hallmark' of addiction, argued one social worker in the fifties,[99] though penal officials could not decide which problem came first. Intensive anti-addiction programs, however, were often limited to very small numbers, not only because of resources but because few women were considered good risks for rehabilitation.[100]

In order to reform prostitutes, penal practitioners concentrated on VD treatment, work training, and moral counselling. In the former case, the treatment was intense, mandatory, and sometimes painful. Even when tests came back negative, treatment sometimes continued, an indication that the treatment was itself punishment[101] or that penal workers could not let go of their image of prostitutes as irrevocably diseased. Instruction in working-class labour was also paramount in the minds of penal practitioners. In the twenties, training women for domestic work was the first priority, though this was accompanied in the next two decades by training in factory work (for example, operating power machinery making linen and clothes for the government) and by the 1950s, in some pink- and white-collar occupations, such as hairdressing and typing.

It was not simply vocational training but the value of work itself that was lauded. With an embrace of honest labour would come new moral values, an important ingredient to salvation. When a 21-year-old candy dipper was released in the early 1920s, for instance, the Mercer superintendent noted that she would not 'lose her good intentions' like many others because she had found factory work to 'keep her hands and mind busy [so] she will take the virtuous path forward.'[102] Years later, Superintendent Milne praised a woman who found work as a stenographer because this 'aim in her life' would ensure her reformation.[103] Yet, in this case, the woman was trying desperately to hide her past conviction for fear of ostracism in her new community. This is one reason why only a minority of the Mercer files indicate that women clearly abandoned or wanted to abandon prostitution. Many of these women had already tried other kinds of poorly-paid work, and they preferred money to morality. And because of the social disapproval of prostitution, finding a new line of work was often difficult if not impossible for women already stigmatized by their arrest or incarceration. Many who did want to escape invariably moved away to a different city or even a new country.

Resisting the Norms

Even if prostitution declined *relatively* as a social issue, it remained marginalized, criminalized, and the focus of moral condemnation. Never did it entirely disappear as a policing concern. Some of the women targeted, however, resisted the attempts of legal and penal practitioners to define their work as immoral. Others simply sought ways to escape arrest and/or incarceration.

Women often tried to find a means to extract themselves from the charge, arguing that police officers misinterpreted their actions and demeanour if they were arrested on streetwalking charges or that they were entrapped on bawdy-house charges. Few such cases made their way to the higher courts, but in one appeal two Hamilton women protested that they had been inadequately represented by their first lawyer, who prevented them from testifying even though they wanted to (perhaps indicating how disinterested many solicitors were in such cases, and certainly in challenging the laws). The women had been sitting on the curb and on two occasions spoke to circling undercover detectives. One woman asked if they wanted to 'come inside for a good time . . . for $3.00', while her friend suggested they come inside for 'a good time . . . some beer and jazz'. However, because the women were (wrongly) tried together and because all three elements of the vagrancy law were not proven, the original conviction was overturned. Seldom were women so lucky.[104]

Once in court, some women pointed to their economic needs or their role as breadwinners as a strategy to secure release. One woman appearing before a Toronto magistrate in the 1930s for running a bawdy house secured probation, only 'escaping two years in Mercer because of her family'.[105] Despite the ongoing claim that women sought out luxuries, their stories suggested a practical or sometimes desperate use of prostitution to secure basic livelihood. In the interwar period, for example, some of the women incarcerated as bawdy-house keepers were widows or married women with others to support. One immigrant Russian, a 46-year-old widow, worked as a 'charwoman' besides keeping a brothel. The police in her northern community wanted to close her house down because they claimed 'drunken rows' were taking place there and that 'she was a public nuisance.' However, her polite letters back to the Mercer, returning money owed for sewing material, and her strong concern that 'her son stay in school' while she was away suggest an honest and hard-working mother who was concerned about her son's future, if not upward mobility.[106]

Other cases in Magistrate's Courts indicated husband-and-wife partnerships, or sometimes two women, running disorderly houses as a small business.[107] Often those arrested were sent to the local jail, or given the option of a fine: in the 1930s, one Toronto man was sentenced to pay $50 or spend 30 days in jail, while his female partner was given a stricter sentence of $60 or 40 days.[108] Prostitution was simply part of a larger underground economy, which could also encompass the illegal sale of alcohol or drugs. Nor did a jail sentence necessarily put an end to such small businesses. A Peterborough woman who ran a bawdy house with her husband, an elevator operator, served a short sentence in the Concord Jail Farm for Women in the early 1920s, then was released. She had little education, having been sent as an orphan to Canada at seven to work on a farm, and few job prospects, so when her husband increasingly became 'unkind and shiftless', gambling away her earnings, she became the sole proprietor of her own bawdy house. Arrested a second time, she was sent to the Concord for an indeterminate time to be treated for venereal disease.[109]

In some cases the magistrate tried to banish the woman from town, only to find that her apparent acquiescence to this proposal was quickly forsaken when she left the courtroom. Margaret Patterson, for example, gave a Native woman parole on her first prostitution charge on the condition that she leave Toronto and 'return to her people' (presumably a reserve). The woman, however, disobeyed, secured a new apartment for herself and her two children, and in a second hearing Patterson complained she continued to support her children 'by immorality'. While breadwinning with sweated labour would have been virtuous, breadwinning through prostitution was seen as 'depraved', especially since the children were exposed to it.[110]

Women used economic survival as an explanation for their choice of prostitution in the interwar period, and especially the Depression, but this remained a constant theme in later years as well. In 1940, a Windsor woman arrested for prostitution received a three-month sentence, plus another three months or a fine. Yet the sentencing report admitted that she had one young son and was 'looking after a husband and home . . . he is a carpenter out of work . . . and [these] circumstances led to this.' The admission that she was 'a good mother and good worker' did not, however, save her from punishment.[111] A minority of women were supporting children as well as spouses, though children could be taken away by the CAS if the woman served time. The more fortunate left their children with relatives. A war bride from Scotland, for instance, was divorced by her Canadian husband six years after World War II and had little means of support for herself and her young son. Employed as a waitress, then jobless, she turned to prostitution. When she was arrested and incarcerated for months, she was able to leave her five-year-old son with her sister-in-law in another city.[112]

For the most part, women's descriptions of previous work reveal insecure, seasonal, or badly paid female jobs. Younger women, who generally comprised a majority of those in the Mercer, had little education beyond elementary school, nor could their families offer economic security. In the interwar period most claimed to be domestics, or to have no occupation, though some had worked previously as waitresses or factory workers. Though a similar pattern of domestic work, waitressing, or factory work was claimed during the 1940s, by the 1950s most women were simply putting down 'no occupation', undoubtedly a strategy of resistant silence to avoid being labelled as a prostitute or to prevent future surveillance. A few women, it is true, already had jobs and were supplementing their incomes with prostitution, such as the 'inspector in a war plant' who was incarcerated during World War II.[113] And some women argued that prostitution offered them not just a job but a better lifestyle than most women could enjoy. When you are making good money and you 'have $150 a month apartment . . . and a nice standard of living', one prostitute told a journalist in the 1950s, 'what are you supposed to do, start selling stockings at $35 a week?'[114] Her cocky rhetorical question evokes Luise White's apt characterization of prostitution as 'a political economy written in women's words'.[115]

Women also tried to evade incarceration by moving across the country, or across the border to the US, though they might be deported back to Canada for entering the US for 'immoral purposes'.[116] (Deportation could also work the other way; the Canadian government deported convicted prostitutes to Ireland, the US, and other countries.) The arrest summaries of women deported from the US (sent to the indefatigable Charlotte Whitton) indicate how women used transience as a strategy to elude the law. A Windsor woman, for instance, moved to Detroit to work, but admitted that for quite a while she had actually worked as a prostitute in Detroit while keeping her residence in Windsor. In another case a group of Canadian waitresses were driven to Connecticut to work as prostitutes; the male ringleader was charged under the White Slavery Act and the women, working under aliases, were deported home.[117]

Other women simply crossed Canadian provincial and municipal borders; a significant minority of women in the Mercer, for instance, were those who had multiple criminal records in other jurisdictions, usually for drug possession, drunk and disorderly conduct, or small thefts. For these inmates, prostitution was one of a number of criminal activities pursued in a search for survival. That survival may well have been too much for some to bear. One Aboriginal woman from northern Ontario, for example, had served time in Winnipeg on theft and drunk and disorderly charges. She also served two years in Kingston for 'attempting suicide'. Like many Native women, she was unable to pay a fine to secure release, and she was undoubtedly only further alienated by her Mercer incarceration for prostitution.[118]

A few brave inmates exhibited openly defiant responses to the moralizing of magistrates and penal workers. She 'admits to earning money by prostitution and did not seem to think this was a serious offence', remarked the Mercer superintendent in the 1930s, shocked at the woman's lack of conscience.[119] Two decades later, the prostitutes interviewed by journalist Sidney Katz expressed few moral qualms about their work. He claimed one tearfully lamented the shame her parents would feel about her work, but others were more concerned with their working conditions. Although Katz claimed these women lacked any self-esteem, many expressed a strong desire for personal and economic independence. They talked of saving money to set up their own legal business ventures, and one recounted how she refused to let men mistreat her, as she 'packed and walked out on a boyfriend who beat her.' Most important, they disputed their labelling as immoral. Comparing herself to the supposedly virtuous married woman, one noted that many wives are 'phoney . . . out chippying with a boyfriend when the husband is away.' 'I hate phonies. . . . I'm not ashamed of doing business, but I would be ashamed of chippying', she announced.[120]

Finally, those women who were unfortunate enough to be incarcerated did not necessarily settle into the reformatory and embrace its reform agenda. Certainly, there were some remorseful and contrite inmates, usually the younger women. One 18-year-old wrote to the superintendent after release, repeating her gratitude for the second chance Mercer offered. She had moved to the US to stay with a sister and thanked Emma Sullivan for 'for setting her right'. 'There is nothing [to be gained] in doing wrong,' she wrote, 'for we never know the consequences [of our actions].'[121] Women like this, however, were a minority. So, too, were those who visibly rebelled, but given the intensity of the disciplinary regime, many women quickly realized that release would come more quickly through the appearance of accommodation.

Some prostitutes, though, did risk further discipline by objecting vociferously to their imprisonment. One 20-year-old domestic from Ottawa went on a hunger strike in the 1920s because she was kept in the Mercer after her sentence had expired, presumably for VD treatment.[122] Two decades later a woman involved in an attack on one of the matrons, when her sentence was extended, yelled 'they can't keep us here' as she rioted with three others.[123] One wonders, too, if the woman who asked to be transferred to a local jail, even losing her good time towards release, had no interest in the reform agenda of the Mercer, perhaps even wanting to join her friends in the jail.[124] Many women, like Rose, the bawdy-house keeper who said she was framed by the Peterborough police, did their time with few infractions, but clearly left the prison gate unreformed—or, in her case, bent on revenge. Perhaps the clearest evidence that reform was unsuccessful was the very persistence of prostitution. Throughout this entire period, the journals of public health and social hygiene, the local police reports, and the reformatories lamented their inability to vanquish prostitution. Whether they were conscious of it or not, prostitutes' daily work was a lived resistance to both the legal and social discourses criminalizing them.

The Female Refuges Act: Defining Sexual Promiscuity

The line between the prostitute and the promiscuous woman was sometimes hazy in the eyes of magistrates and judges, and always there was a fear that promiscuity led to prostitution. Early eugenic writing by C.K. Clarke simultaneously endorsed both designations for 'immoral' women and the 1919 Royal Commission on Venereal Disease and Care of the Feebleminded advocated the 'careful supervision' of feeble-minded women of child-bearing age so that these promiscuous, oversexed women who had lacked 'willpower' to control their sexual impulses would not become prostitutes.[125]

The application of laws about prostitution and promiscuity also overlapped. Although the vagrancy and bawdy-house laws were supposedly for the repeated payment of money for sex, women deemed 'dissolute' under the FRA might have bartered sex for lodging, food, or other material benefits. Magistrates sometimes seemed little concerned about which law to use and more with using *some* law to isolate the woman. In one case where a woman was incarcerated for streetwalking, for instance, the magistrate actually sentenced her under the FRA. This 21-year-old who had lost her husband in World War II, left her daughter with her grandmother in Montreal and went to work in the Ontario tobacco fields, where she was taken in by local police. The magistrate claimed he was primarily sending her away for two years 'for physical reasons' (i.e., venereal disease), but he used the FRA as the means. The clerk simply wrote down 238 (i), the vagrancy/prostitution clause, on her committal.[126] In a similar vein, Canadian women deported from the US, who are noted in Charlotte Whitton's file on the 'traffic in women', are just as often guilty of 'immorality' as of 'practising prostitution'.[127]

Judges had also wrestled with the line between promiscuity and prostitution by deliberating over who qualified as a 'mistress' and who was a prostitute. With legal precision, a key 1916 judgement quantified the answer, of course, with moral overtones. 'A woman who continues to have unlawful sexual relations with one man only is not a prostitute', the learned judges decided, 'but if she successively becomes the mistress of several men within six months, without having other means of subsistence and in such a manner as to create a public scandal in [her] locality', she can be convicted of a prostitution offence.[128]

A comparable dilemma confronted an Ontario judge in 1930, in a case revealing for its fundamentally racist understanding of promiscuity. Convicted by Magistrate Margaret Patterson on a vagrancy charge, Violet Davis appealed her indeterminate sentence of up to two years. The higher court heard that she 'wandered the streets at night, going in and out of restaurants with coloured and white men' and that she did not give a good account of herself to police. Debate centred especially on whether she had any 'means of subsistence' because she was living with a 'coloured railway porter'. To prove she was a prostitute, he mused, the law had to show she 'has to do with more than one man', yet there was only evidence of her relationship with the porter. Desperately seeking legal condemnation, the judge found his answer in a previous interpretation of 'subsistence'. Subsistence not only had to be lawful, it had to be 'reputable', not contradicting 'the moral standards of the community'. So, even though she was not a prostitute, he concluded triumphantly, it had been shown she was living with a coloured man and this was 'not the kind of subsistence that the Criminal Code' had in mind. The conviction upheld, he added that surely a *woman* magistrate like Patterson 'knows quite as much, if not more, than a man what is best to be done with a girl of this kind.'[129] For women like Violet, the maternal feminist argument that women on the bench would offer compassionate justice was surely a cruel and bitter irony.[130]

Such women were precisely those who were prosecuted under the Ontario Female Refuges Act. The Act, first passed in 1897 to regulate the Industrial Houses of Refuge that held women sentenced or '*liable* to be sentenced' by magistrates under local bylaw or Criminal Code infractions,[131] was aimed at women between the ages of 16 and 35, presumably because these were the most active sexual and reproductive years. The initial FRA allowed a sentence of up to five years for 'unmanageable and incorrigible' women but this was later amended, in 1919, to two years less a day following the coroner's inquest into an inmate's death, after she tried to escape by jumping from a window of Toronto's Belmont Refuge.[132] Accompanying this reduction came new wide-ranging powers allowing magistrates and judges to sentence 'any female under the age of 35 . . . who is a habitual drunkard or by reasons of other vices is leading an idle and dissolute life.' 'Any person' could swear out a statement about the woman's behaviour, no formal criminal charge was necessary, and hearings were in private, though written evidence was supposedly required.[133] Faced with criticisms about the Act's authoritarian powers, the provincial legislature in 1942 added an amendment to allow sentences to be appealed before the Court of Appeal—though this appears to have been little used. In 1958 these sections of the FRA were finally deleted after a campaign mounted by the Elizabeth Fry Society, though in public the government claimed that 'these sections are already dealt with adequately in the Criminal Code and other federal and provincial statutes.'[134]

Although the total numbers convicted under the FRA were relatively small, an exploration of its workings exposes the dominant definitions of promiscuity embraced by the courts. The vast majority of FRA incarcerations centred on three sometimes overlapping problems: sexual promiscuity, illegitimate pregnancies, and venereal disease. A few women incarcerated were destitute or runaways, but for the majority, 'dissolute' was equated with errant sexuality. Nor were these considered minor matters, for women often got stiff sentences: on average, they received from a year to two years, and women did not secure release easily but served the majority of their sentences. The peak of FRA prosecutions came during the 1930s and World War II, and the majority of those convicted were under 21, including many aged 16–19. Most were also Canadian-born and of Anglo-Celtic background. There was a significant minority of British immigrants, but this is not surprising given the influx of such immigrants to Ontario just before World War I and the tendency of immigrants to face economic and social dislocation.[135] Almost all the women came from either working-class or poverty-stricken backgrounds, they generally had left school by 14 or 15, and those who were gainfully employed were listed as domestics or, less often, waitresses, sales clerks, or factory workers. A significant minority had experienced state-directed care, such as a foster home, refuge, or industrial school, and many were from separated, single-parent, or reconstituted families. The 'broken family' was thus offered up as the cause of a young woman's bad behaviour, with this designation often denoting a certain moral disapproval as much as any recognition of the intense material deprivations of such families.

FRA convictions indicated deep-seated anxieties that working-class women were unruly and overly sexual, either led astray or leading men astray. For example, the sexual activity of young women often became a problem for the authorities or parents when they were perceived to have too many partners or the wrong kind of partner. One father testified before the magistrate that his 17-year-old, who had already had an illegitimate child, was 'leaving home for weeks on end' and 'she was drinking in beverage rooms and staying out late with men.' Her mother added that she could not believe her daughter was 'mentally sound', given her actions. They agreed with the magistrate that the only hope of reforming her was to offer the 'discipline' served up at the Mercer.[136]

It was not simply too many but also the wrong kind of partner that sparked use of the FRA. 'Her main misfortune appears to be truck drivers', noted one file: 'she spends nights with them and would go on drinking sprees in Chatham and St Thomas . . . she could not say no to their associates, or men she met from time to time.'[137] Liaisons of young women with men outside their social class and ethnic group were distressing for some parents, leading them to take legal action. One case—unusual because the family involved was middle class—demonstrated parents' fears of their daughters' sexual rebellion, signalled in this instance by her liaison with a non-Anglo man. A Niagara Falls minister followed his 18-year-old runaway daughter, Helen (a graduate of Whitby Ladies School), to Toronto in 1940. He secured the aid of the police in tracking down Helen, who was 'self willed' and 'keeping bad company . . . and living in a house of reported ill repute on Jarvis St.' The parents were especially distressed that they found her in the company of 'Tony, an Italian at the Fox Lunch on Queen St. West and the Casino Theatre'. She agreed to return home, but no sooner did she arrive at their hotel than she gave them the slip again. They went to court and pressed for her incarceration in Mercer, where she spent the next 18 months.[138]

The authorities probed especially for sexual guilt on women's part if they had inappropriate partners. Replicating the 'ritual of the

confessional',[139] these interviews reinforced the power of the inter-
viewer to absolve or condemn the woman involved. In one instance, a
woman had slept with her best friend's husband and became pregnant
with his child. Her blasé attitude towards the affair was taken to be a
sign of immorality, if not feeble-mindedness: 'she is very slow and
has little moral sense . . . she visits and talks freely about the parentage of her child [to her friend]', the perturbed doctor wrote.[140]

Saving such promiscuous women from a precipitous slide into
prostitution was a common rationale used by magistrates in their sentencing reports. This was the argument made by a small-town judge
concerning an 18-year-old domestic, Kathleen, a 'neglected' child
who had been fostered out by the CAS, then placed as a domestic with
'respectable' families. Kathleen chafed under the curfews and the discipline imposed by her live-in work and, after a 'wild' night away in
nearby Peterborough with friends, was brought before a judge who
warned her: 'if you persist in being the boss, we will send you to an
institution. I am trying to give you a chance. Get other friends. Stay
out of Chinese restaurants.' She was soon back in court after her
employer complained that she lied about going to Sunday school,
then took off with friends. After she admitted to having had intercourse with boys in the back of a car, the judge predicted her decline
into prostitution. He recommended more self-control, but also
claimed she needed protection from unscrupulous men. 'If you want
friends, go to Church to find them', he told her. '[D]ance halls are a
curse. If I had the authority, I would burn every dance hall in the country down. You run around with trash and these fellows only want to
associate with you for one purpose; you are like dirt under their feet;
they will tramp you into mud. . . . A good wet shingle to you wouldn't
do any harm', he concluded as he banged his gavel and sent her off for
18 months.[141]

The judge was clearly disgusted with her nonchalant view of sex
and her attempts to set her own moral and work rules. The latter
indicated wilfulness, disobedience, and a failure to know her place
in terms of both gender and class hierarchies. Kathleen's sexual
waywardness was the precipitating issue in her court appearance, but
her refusal to work at her domestic job and obey her employer was
also seen as a problem. As with other cases, there was also a somewhat voyeuristic attitude revealed as the male interrogator questioned women about their sex lives. They appeared to be
simultaneously fearful and fascinated, repulsed and attracted to
women's stories.[142] A classic question asked by police and magistrates was: how many times did you have intercourse with different

men? The legal authorities were excessively preoccupied with quantification, even egging the women on: 'how many times, would you say 50, 100. . . .'[143] One assumes that one method of rebellion for the women was to exaggerate the numbers, simply to horrify those in authority or to put an end to their questioning.

Sexual non-conformity was most often evidenced by sex out of marriage and with multiple partners. Occasionally, it was also linked to homosexuality or to interracial sexual relationships. Homosexuality, though often denied by the prison authorities, undoubtedly existed within the reformatory,[144] and it could become a rationale for further incarceration under the FRA. One 16-year-old foster child, sentenced under the FRA, came from the Ontario Training School for Girls, where she was 'considered a menace to the other girls'. The superintendent claimed she 'ran away three times' and was engaged 'in homosexual practices, pursuing the girls. . . . When they reported it to me, I interviewed her and she admitted it.'[145] Originally sent to the training school for truancy and running away, the girl was examined by psychiatrists for mental illness before being sent to the Mercer. Cases like this, highlighting homosexual non-conformity, however, were extremely rare.

Next to sexual promiscuity the two most significant factors impelling incarceration were the presence of illegitimate children and venereal disease. In the interwar period, some court officials literally used the Mercer as a home for unwed, poor mothers. A Hamilton magistrate sent a pregnant 20-year-old with no parents or means of support to Mercer under the FRA: 'this girl has no one to care for her and seems unable to look after herself. She gave herself up at the police station as she was ready to be confined.'[146] Other women were incarcerated after they had produced 'too many' illegitimate children. The angriest denunciations of these women often came from welfare authorities or CAS officials, who saw the children involved as a burden on the state. Cases focusing on illegitimacy were especially noticeable during the Depression, but not limited to it. To prevent any further progeny, local authorities sometimes tried to block these women's parole back into the community.

For some women with illegitimate children, sterilization was recommended. 'This woman has [VD] and one illegitimate child, and admits intercourse with a number of men. Her morals are nil and she is a menace to society. She should be treated and sterilized', advised one magistrate.[147] Women and their families were not always easily convinced. In the 1930s, the Concord superintendent wrote to Lena's parents repeatedly asking for their permission to have their daughter sterilized, as she had three illegitimate children. The operation, she explained, 'has been performed on several girls during the last couple of years . . . on account of these girls giving birth to so many illegitimate children . . . the poor little mites who are ushered into life in this manner are not getting a square deal, no home, no parents, no one to bring them up properly, and besides this, the girl is handicapped for life.' Although the parents agreed, they never gave their official consent and the superintendent complained to provincial authorities that their 'crafty' obstructionist tactics were evidence of the need for compulsory sterilization laws.[148]

The high number of FRA women who delivered babies while in the Mercer is striking, and the experience of being transported, under guard, to the hospital to give birth without friends or family must have been an alienating experience. Even with a nursery at the Mercer, keeping the baby was made a trial. As one woman found when she was put in solitary, contact with her baby was denied.[149] Nor did society's punishing attitudes towards illegitimacy necessarily lead to repentance. As one parent later commented, 'since [my daughter] had a baby she is even more unmanageable.'[150] Once made into pariahs, there was little reason for these young women to conform. Workingclass and poor families were more likely to adopt illegitimate children than middle-class ones, but these children might also be seen as a financial and moral burden to bear, with recrimination directed towards the woman and the child.[151] A pregnancy incurred as an accident on the way to marriage might be accepted, but premarital sex itself was not generally condoned and second pregnancies were often deeply resented. Many of the FRA women who gave birth in prison were encouraged by the CAS to give up their children, and their families did not contradict this advice. In rather chilling words, the Provincial Secretary illustrated the disparaging attitude towards both the mothers and their children: 'her father is feeble-minded, the mother dim witted. . . . I notice that she is serving two years . . . which is all the more reason . . . to *dispose* of the child.'[152]

Finally, the FRA was also used as a means of enforcing treatment for venereal disease. City solicitors, public health officials, and CAS workers all appealed to magistrates to have girls and women incarcerated if they rejected medical treatment or refused to stop having intercourse. Magistrates also routinely ordered medical examinations of women arrested for sexual offences. Presumption of VD was so strong in the case of multiple partners that women were sometimes treated for syphilis and gonorrhea even if their tests were negative. Little wonder, then, that one woman 'ran away from the

Toronto General Hospital as she was afraid of continued painful treatment for VD.'[153]

Race and Definitions of Promiscuity

Interracial liaisons, though almost always of white women and men of colour, were also used to demarcate sexual promiscuity. The police, court workers, and some working-class families perceived men and women of colour to be more sexually promiscuous and feared whites would become tainted or seduced by these lax morals (though in a few cases involving Chinese men, fears also centred on their supposed roles as pimps and drug pushers). Miscegenation was clearly a worry for some parents. In the early thirties, a 17-year-old described by her foster mother as 'boy crazy, with no regard for the truth', was found in a 'bawdy house with a Chinaman'.[154] Magistrate Margaret Patterson immediately remanded her into psychiatric care, a judgement that underscores how women's sexual non-conformity was literally equated with their insanity. In a case similar to that of Violet Davis, a young Toronto woman was arrested in 1940 on a charge of vagrancy. Though the complaint sworn out against her stated she was 'not working' and not following her 'step-father's rules', the more serious allegation was her cohabitation with 'a coloured man'. Sent first to the Salvation Army hostel, she ran away, was rearrested, and then was sent to the Mercer.[155]

Women might also be the focus of legal concern if they were sexually involved with Native men, though this was a far less common scenario in large urban centres. One young woman from northern Ontario, Mabel, was incarcerated in the 1940s after her sexual relationship with a Native man became a problem for her family and the court. Ironically, her mother was seen as a bad example as she was living common law, but she also participated in the complaint against her daughter, who she charged was 'running around with an Indian boy and would not get a job.' Mabel claimed that her boyfriend 'wanted to marry her' but became abusive 'and threatened to kill her if she saw anyone else.' The magistrate, despite his disbelief in her charges of violence, agreed that Mabel's conduct was satisfactory until she 'started seeing a young Indian boy. . . . We will put this girl in a home. We can't have her running around with Indian boys like that.'[156]

Although it was invariably the woman who was incarcerated, these cases indicate how the sexuality of non-white men was censured more stringently than that of white men.[157] They also highlight how arbitrary the hearings were, with little regard for the due process of

law. One woman who was arrested for living with her Chinese
boyfriend, after her father sought out the help of the police, recalled
how she was kept in the dark during the whole legal process. Without
counsel, she misjudged the best strategy for securing her release: 'I
was taken into a room and asked by a woman if I had ever slept with
anyone else. I felt I would have to damage my character to save my
boyfriend from blame. I said, "Yes" . . . [and] I told her I was pregnant
hoping that would help. Almost immediately I was taken to a courtroom. . . . [In court] I didn't see anyone else until the policeman [who
arrested me] spoke from behind me.' After a few curt questions from
the judge about her pregnancy, she offered to 'get married' to her Chinese boyfriend if they would just let her out. It was the wrong tactic.
She was remanded for a week in jail, then returned to court to be
quickly sentenced to one year in Belmont. Without any warning, she
was transferred to the reformatory when Belmont closed.[158]

Although relatively few women of colour were arrested for dissolute sexual behaviour, they were still perceived to be a significant
threat, both to their own community and to the white community.
When a young Chinese girl, Jennie, was apprehended in 1929, for
instance, the sentencing report claimed that she was a 'well educated,
clever and attractive Chinese girl', but 'unfortunately, she assumes the
attitude that she is Anglo Saxon and is certainly not the ordinary Chinese type. There is nothing wrong with the girl outside of the fact that
she has a desire to go out with white boys . . . the Big Sisters reported
that she was running around with young men in the evening.' Her
uncle (and guardian) had initiated the complaint, and together he and
the superintendent at Concord debated whether Jennie should be sent
to a Methodist missionary home for Chinese girls in British Columbia
or be married off to the 'proper person'. As Kelly Pineault argues, her
major crime seems to have been that 'she did not know her place',
something marriage to her 'own kind' was supposed to solve.[159]

Native women and women of colour were almost always seen to be
more prone to promiscuity, and Native women, in need of paternalist
protection. After the late 1940s, the number of Native women incarcerated under the FRA increased, contrary to the overall trend for FRA
arrests and reflecting the emerging over-incarceration of Native
women in general. Most Aboriginal women were brought before the
court by local police for alcohol-related infractions, with sexual
immorality and illegitimacy perceived to be inevitable, corollary
crimes. 'She was wandering the streets, drunk, so I . . . took her to the
station where she would be safe . . . for if I left her she would just find
more wine', testified one policeman from Kenora about a Native

woman. His claim that he was protecting her, however, revealed a more sinister surveillance, predicated partly on anxieties about her sexual relations with whites. He had also 'followed her to her rooming house', and told the judge he had seen her at the railway station and 'in cafes with white boys, . . . and there are complaints from the hotel that she is hanging around, going into rooms with men all the time.' The local Indian agent also testified that he had already tried fining her under the Indian Act to no avail, thus further clinching her incarceration.[160]

Sentencing reports for Native women also revealed the same obtuseness to the debilitating impact of women's material and social background found in many other FRA judgements: a failure to look at the damaging results of institutional and foster care; a tendency to blame the family and victim for economic impoverishment; a belief that these women simply lacked moral self-control. Immoral families were blamed for the downfall of Aboriginal women, just as they were for other FRA women, while individual women were faulted for their failure to accept the lessons of Christian schooling. Noting that one Native woman had 'spent 10 years' in a residential school, for example, the Magistrate lectured her on her failure to apply the moral lessons of her education: 'you shouldn't carry on like this. You went to Indian school for ten years . . . so you know right from wrong.'[161]

While race was clearly linked to definitions of promiscuity, the perceptions of white, non-Anglo ethnic groups were more complex. Most cases dealt with women of Anglo-Celtic backgrounds, but it is possible that non-English-speaking immigrant families were less likely to seek help from legal or welfare authorities already viewed with suspicion. The authorities were keenly interested in deporting recent immigrants, but immigrant women who became involved with the law were usually American, Irish, Scottish, or English. Ethnicity, however, was still intertwined with judgements about sexuality and morality in the pronouncements of some magistrates, police, and social workers. Significantly, the designation 'white', 'British', or 'English' was absent from the majority of case files: whiteness and an Anglo background were never considered important rationalizations for women's immorality. In contrast, if non-Anglos were involved, ethnicity was more likely to be mentioned, with the underlying implication that this might explain the presence of immorality.

Parents, Power, and Regulation

Parents initiated and supported many court actions, and those who testified against their daughters described themselves as 'nearly beside themselves',[162] near nervous breakdown, desperate, and having no other option. They lamented the disobedience of their daughters on every issue from work to clothes to sex: 'stubbornness is her special weakness . . . she insists on having her own way', lamented a typical sentencing report.[163] In ongoing, complex battles, parents and daughters wrestled for the upper hand over curfews, boyfriends, and material resources. In an attempt to curb her daughter's hitch-hiking and sexual promiscuity, one mother hid all her daughter's shoes and clothes so she could not go out; the same daughter stole money from the mother to buy forbidden high-heeled shoes to replace her hated 'rubbers'.[164]

Parents protested their daughters' failure to contribute economically to the household or to do their share of domestic labour, but the primary trigger for legal action was often their sexual non-conformity. In part, this was because parents feared for the physical safety of daughters who disappeared with men for days on end. For parents who described themselves as honest and respectable, their daughters' sexual misbehaviour was also a disgrace, an indication of their failure. Even accounting for the parents' tendency to stress their respectability before middle-class judges, their statements indicate that many working-class parents accepted sexual mores censuring extramarital and premarital sex and endorsed the idea that women needed to assume more sexual self-control than men. Only a minority, often those on the margins of the law themselves, strenuously objected to the moral interference and superiority of the authorities. Also, Native families appeared less likely to implicate their own children, though some, out of desperation, did. One single father from the north brought his daughter to Juvenile Court twice because he considered her a 'bad influence on her sister and other girls'. She had run away, had a baby, and according to the police 'was picked up at drinking parties and was involved in a break and enter.'[165]

Families sometimes tried to accommodate their sexually disobedient daughters, but then suddenly came to a breaking point, often precipitated by a lack of resources. 'Rose', for instance, was incarcerated after a second illegitimate pregnancy made her incorrigible in the eyes of Magistrate Patterson. Yet, the family initially had some sympathy for Rose, who claimed that her first child was the result of a relationship with a married man who had tricked her. The first child was adopted by Rose's mother, but the family was poor, her stepfather resented the extra mouth to feed, especially when the mother and one son were handicapped, and Rose was going from job to job. As Rose tearfully told the Mercer doctor, she had gone downtown one day to the employment bureau with some girlfriends but did not return until late. By that time, the 'angry' stepfather had called the police and a warrant was issued for her arrest.[166]

Daughters were also brought to court by parents who were trying to 'scare [them] with the threat of reform school'[167] or who sought to use the court as a weapon to separate daughters from unacceptable male partners—just as parents used delinquency laws for similar ends. Describing her daughter's boyfriend as a 'reptile', one mother pleaded with the court to intervene, as she claimed he was leading her 'weak-minded' daughter astray, getting her drunk at dances, then introducing her to other men of dubious morals.[168] Her daughter was unusually vocal, defending her right to control her own social and sexual life: 'I don't know why I'm here. I did not do anything wrong last night. . . . He is better than some around here. I phoned him up and wanted him, and that's that.'[169]

Not all parents endorsed incarceration; some sought out the help of the police, then quickly found the process moving beyond their control. Evelyn, who was described as 'mentally slow' by her parents and the authorities, was sentenced to two years, although the mother pleaded for an alternative. Despite the family's poverty, the mother was reluctant to lose her only daughter, who she claimed was 'a good girl' but was easily 'led astray' by men when she ran off to a local town. In order to keep her 'out of trouble', the mother asked for placement in an industrial school. Once in court, however, the police provided evidence that the girl had VD and the magistrate pressured the mother until she agreed to a reformatory sentence.[170]

Family conflicts also precipitated women's contact with the police, though domestic violence, often described matter-of-factly, did not necessarily command explanatory power as the reason for women's rejection of familial authority and sexual norms. In one mother's statement, for instance, she complained that her daughter 'goes out and gets drunk and comes back and her father beats her up and he is liable to be arrested for that.' It was the daughter, not the father, who was incarcerated.[171] The same insensitivity to violence was found in women's stories of rape, which were often discounted because these women had already been defined as promiscuous. Moreover, like the girls described in the chapter on incest, these women were assumed to need mandatory moral retraining after experiencing familial sexual abuse.

Ultimately, young women learned that violence was something to escape—to the streets and perhaps through sexual bartering—rather than to be confronted in the home. In the 1940s CAS officials admitted they should have removed one young woman from her home because the grandmother was psychologically and physically abusive, beating both her mother (who was an invalid) and her for 'no reason'. The girl left home at 16, but then began to hang around Chez Lui and other 'bad Ottawa bars', drinking and having sex with various men, until she contracted VD. The Judge noted the usual need for 'discipline', and added the alarming adage that perhaps she needed 'her hide tanned'. The young woman, however, offered the most pragmatic explanation of her life choices: 'I was good then [when I lived at home] and I got beaten. I'm not so good now and I don't get beaten.'[172]

Women's Responses

In response to the allegations of immorality, the majority of women agreed with the charges or remained silent. Those making no response at all may not have been consciously endorsing the court's assessment; rather, their acquiescence might be read as a realization of the power of the court. Indeed, in the court proceedings, many came to a point where they simply withdrew into passive resistance; 'I won't speak'[173] was all one young woman would say in response to questions.

A minority of women, though, rejected the label of immorality and offered alternative explanations for their behaviour, citing overbearing, excessively strict parents, unhappy foster care, or violence as their reasons for rejecting social norms. A very few women offered tales of seduction to explain their plight, such as the young woman, Rose, who dated a married man who got her pregnant. But fewer of these FRA women offered confessional tales of seduction than did the unmarried mothers in maternity homes that Regina Kunzel has studied.[174] More often, their explanations suggest using sex as barter, conforming to friends' similar behaviour, not caring about whom they slept with, or just seeing sex as distraction or pleasure with no moral verdict attached to it. While challenging the prescriptions for normal feminine sexuality, their rebellion was not a clear articulation of the right to sexual pleasure as much as an ill-formed displeasure with the existing sexual norms.

Non-conforming women offered up frank comebacks, exaggeration, and bravado, even 'boasting' in court about their misdeeds.[175] Many young women cited peer pressure as an explanation for sexual activities, but still they did so with a measure of defiance. Explaining her 'wild night' in Peterborough, Kathleen simply said she needed recreation: 'I need some friends', she shot back at the judge when he was lecturing her.[176] When one woman was offered an escape hatch by the magistrate, who wanted to know if her late nights were simply forgetfulness or wilfulness, she answered abruptly: 'Wilfulness.' She was incarcerated.[177]

Another woman also made it quite clear that she did not accept the police definition of immorality. After her release from a refuge, where she had been incarcerated for trying to elope with a married man, she returned to her small village. The local police began to receive complaints that 'she was having intercourse with different men through the village', but when a police officer went to question her, he claimed, 'I found her drunk and abusive in language. I said, I judge a lady by her language and she exposed herself and asked if I still thought she was a lady.'[178]

Women who were in court for having too many illegitimate children also challenged the verdict. Some refused to give the name of the father even if they knew it. One domestic refused to name the married 'Spadina businessman' who got her pregnant in his home; unlike him, she paid a severe price for her silence.[179] Others suggested that pregnancy was no business of the court as long as they supported themselves. A pregnant woman, already with two illegitimate children given up to the CAS, tried to point out that the latest father would support her if she could find housing, and in response to the magistrate's claim that she was 'having a high old time' sleeping with many men, she countered angrily that 'she worked pretty well every summer night and day.' The magistrate noted disapprovingly that her sister also had an illegitimate child (as if this were an inherited problem) and charged that she would become a burden on the state. The woman, however, had the last word, offering pragmatic disregard for the magistrate's standards of sexual propriety. 'Why do you continue to have intercourse with this man?' he demanded about the latest father. 'I'm already in the family way', she shrugged. 'What does it matter now?'[180]

Finally, once in the reformatory, some women continued their rebellion. Many of the women who started off at the Ontario Training School for Girls, the Good Shepherd Home, or Belmont House were transferred to the Mercer because of their attempts to run away. Despite the ill-fated Belmont woman who died jumping out of a window, others imitated her action, throwing bedsheets out the window to climb down or breaking windows. Indeed, Belmont staff complained that too many inmates refused to embrace their 'ideal of Purity': they were more inclined to 'take the line of least resistance' and return to immorality.[181] Once in the Mercer, a few FRA women again tried to escape, only to find they were punished with strapping or solitary confinement on their return. Others took a more passive route, disagreeing with the doctors who interviewed them, offering up alternative assessments of their problems, refusing the help offered by the Salvation Army. Most common were those women who simply confronted the petty rules of the prison with apathy, foot-dragging, or, occasionally, open disobedience. Sent to solitary for failing to perform her manual labour, one FRA inmate, for instance, announced to the matron that 'she never did work and never will.'[182]

How much these women absorbed the disciplinary cures of hard work, female domesticity, and sexual passivity provided within the refuges and reformatories is difficult to ascertain. Even though the majority did not return to the Mercer, some may have simply hidden their sexual activities better than before. As always, the records tell us more about the regulators than those regulated, and it is difficult to disentangle 'women's experiences from the narrative means they used to represent themselves'.[183] Nonetheless, FRA stories suggest very real tensions and antagonisms between the women whose sexuality was condemned and those who were seeking their ritual confessions and reformation.

Conclusion: Regulating Women's Sexual Non-conformity

Despite the distinctions between the FRA and prostitution legislation, there were overlapping rationales for and consequences of these laws. The FRA women were reprimanded for being wilful, disobedient to elders, overly sexual or readily engaging in sex, disrespectful of marital boundaries, lacking sexual guilt, and having no sense of appropriate sex partners. Prostitutes were similarly criticized for destroying the family and spreading disease, for their sexual assertiveness and lack of morality. Both were portrayed, at different times, as victims and victimizers, though prostitutes undoubtedly endured far more negative stigma for their sale of sexual services. Some elements of this definition of immorality resembled nineteenth-century legal and social prescriptions, but it was now articulated in an era that claimed some sympathy for women's sexual fulfilment and autonomy.

Reflecting and reinforcing hegemonic social norms concerning women's sexuality, both sets of laws worked as ideology and practice to police the boundaries of proper sexual activity for women. More-over, both the state and civil society were involved in this process: the law embraced medical, social work, and reform perspectives concerning women's sexuality, integrating them into its disciplinary codes, and the church, family, charitable agencies, and state-supported institutions were all implicated in the regulation of sexuality.

The meanings of women's sexuality constructed and applied in the courtroom in part reflected patriarchal social relations; women's reproduction and female sexual assertiveness were policed more stringently and punitively than similar behaviour of heterosexual men.[184] However, the process of censuring women's sexuality, though shaped within a culture of 'masculinist hegemony',[185] was also conditioned by the inequalities of class, race, and colonialism. The social positioning of the women arrested—who were primarily poor and working-class—had a direct bearing on how their sexual morality was regulated. Indeed, women's material impoverishment encouraged the likelihood of their arrest, and their lack of economic support was intertwined with images of dissolute behaviour. As Foucault argued, sexual control is often most 'intense and meticulous when it is directed at the lower classes'.[186]

The very definition of promiscuity, as well as the treatment of prostitutes, was also moulded by racist constructions of people of colour as more promiscuous than whites. Social codes and legal pronouncements on immorality both took into account whether a white woman's sexual relations were with a white man or a man of colour. Moreover, Native women, already vulnerable to colonial surveillance, were subject to an extra layer of sexual regulation premised on their suspected proclivity to alcoholism and immorality. Nowhere are class biases and racist perspectives clearer than in the eugenic discourses that predominated in the interwar period but lingered on after it: both 'poor whites' and women of colour are seen as limited by inherited weaknesses and pathologies, and perhaps in need of reproductive control.

Despite these overarching themes, there were some changes over this period, both in the construction of sexuality and in the locus of legal discipline. Eradicating venereal disease was used intermittently as an urgent rationale for moral regulation, and explanations for sexual deviance evolved from an emphasis on feeble-mindedness to stress psychic frigidity. Also, as the Progressive zeal dissipated in the interwar period, the police seemed to have heaved a sigh of relief and returned to segregation, regulation, and limited toleration of prostitution, which receded into more 'private' spaces. Evidence that prostitution was no longer *the* social evil, but was embedded within other social crises, was also indicated by decreasing media interest, declining arrests, and the closing of rehabilitative refuges. By the 1950s, prostitution may have been seen as a social problem, but it did not command the moral attention that the white slave trade had, nor was it yet redefined as the new social problem created by urban developers and the police (and, ironically, feminist discourse) in the 1970s and 1980s.[187]

If red-light districts across Canada were broken up after World War I, new ghettos of sexual regulation, less tied to geography and more to behaviour, took their place. If women's lack of passion was no longer a virtue, if there was new emphasis on heterosexual fulfilment, then sexual relations *other* than prostitution moved into the realm of censure. There were new borders needing policing: it was necessary to distinguish, perhaps even more clearly as sexologists advocated female sexual fulfilment, between normal and deviant sexual relationships. Not surprisingly, emphasis was placed on keeping sexual expression within marriage and on the errant sexuality and reproductive lives of working-class women and women of colour, whose supposed acceptance of casual sex had long been suspect in the eyes of middle-class reformers and lawmakers. Despite the new sexual autonomy claimed for women, 'natural' female sexuality was linked to restraint and passivity, and within the patriarchal family the wife was to be domestic and monogamous, the daughter a dutiful and chaste apprentice. The protection of these familial roles, which had both material and social power attached to them, was inextricably linked to the regulation of women's sexuality.

Women occupied more than one political and social position within this regulatory process. A few were magistrates, with more becoming penal workers, court social workers, and criminology experts. In other words, to a greater extent women were becoming those applying the standards of sexual propriety articulated by the law. On the other side were the women being policed, though in the case of the FRA, sometimes with the assent of their older female relatives. While it is extremely difficult to retrieve the voices of the criminalized, it is clear that a minority objected, resisted, and tried to escape the regulatory gaze of their better-off sisters. The tension in these encounters reminds us all too clearly that class and race, as well as patriarchy, were defining factors in the regulation of women's sexuality.

5

'Out of Control':
Girls in Conflict with the Law

If one aspect of the criminal justice system seemed to confirm Foucault's emphasis on the norm overtaking the law in modern times, it was the legal practice relating to juveniles, especially the treatment of female juvenile 'delinquents'.[1] The laws concerning delinquency offered the courts incredible latitude, power, and disciplinary potential; as American writer Roscoe Pound quipped, 'the powers of the Star Chamber were a trifle in comparison to those of our juvenile courts.'[2] Most importantly, the legal definitions of what constituted delinquency were increasingly influenced by medical, criminological, and social work experts linked to the justice and penal systems. While both legal and expert discourses on delinquency denied a will to power and punishment, stressing treatment and reform, the call for girls' rehabilitation actually created intense systems of surveillance, centring especially on the sexuality of working-class and racialized girls.

If we examine only the expert discourses defining delinquency, our conclusion might well be that sexual regulation was the crux of juvenile justice for girls and that the power of the norm had colonized the law. The story, however, is more complex. Although the juvenile justice system drew on the growing power of extra-legal experts, as well as familial systems of regulation, juridical power and the role of the state remained of critical importance to the practice of juvenile justice. Second, while sexual regulation was undoubtedly a central impetus for the surveillance of adolescent females, the discursive construction of morally pure as opposed to bad girls cannot be disentangled from the material and social context framing and provoking girls' conflicts with the law. Finally, the varied responses of girls and their families to the justice system, including glimpses of their resistance, suggest that the practice of legal regulation, though powerful, was never complete.

This chapter examines the legal, medical, and social work discourses explaining delinquency during this period, as well as the social, economic, and familial relations that prompted girls' conflicts with the law. Using government records and reports, expert and popular writing on delinquency, court testimony from Juvenile and Family Courts, and training school files of those convicted,[3] we can assess how and why girls found themselves in head-on collisions with the courts, the courts' rationale for sentencing, and finally, the reactions of girls and their families to their criminalization. While my conclusions are drawn from records centring on the Ontario juvenile justice system, the definitions of delinquency and the strategies used to alter the inner conscience of delinquent girls had a wider resonance, as well as concrete parallels, across Canada and North America.[4]

Defining Delinquency

In all aspects of juvenile justice, the federal and provincial legal regimes were closely intertwined. A child in Ontario aged seven to 16 could be sentenced under the federal Juvenile Delinquents Act (JDA, 1908) or the provincial Ontario Training School Act (TSA, 1931 and 1939),[5] though once incarcerated she was subject to the latter. Following the logic of parens patriae, both federal and provincial legislation allowed the state to step in as a surrogate parent; indeed, parents could be prosecuted under the JDA for 'contributing to delinquency' through their own immorality. According to the JDA, delinquents were those who had contravened any federal, provincial, or municipal law or ordinance or who were *liable* by reason of any act to be committed to an industrial school or reformatory, though the child was to be dealt with 'not as an offender but as a misdirected child, in a condition of delinquency and therefore requiring aid, encouragement, help and supervision'.[6] In 1924 an important amendment added another offence, 'sexual immorality or any similar form of vice', a phrasing presented in gender-neutral terms but intentionally targeted at sexually active, 'promiscuous' girls.[7]

Similarly wide-ranging and arbitrary language characterized the TSA, which stipulated that children could be brought before the court if they were 'incorrigible and unmanageable', which could be anything from violent acts to truancy or simple disobedience. Parents, as well as the police or Children's Aid Societies, could initiate complaints resulting in committal. Legally, children could be sent to

Ontario industrial and training schools under the official authority of the provincial minister responsible for the Act, though after 1939 this was done increasingly through the prerogative of the courts. Because training schools, in the tradition of earlier industrial schools for the destitute and the delinquent, were initially portrayed as welfare-related institutions, local CASs claimed neglected and abused girls would benefit from their programs.[8] When one CAS pressured a local judge to commit a girl to the Ontario Training School for Girls (OTSG), he admitted he knew nothing about its program, but, parroting the CAS, he informed the distraught girl that it was a 'fine school for [a] girl who lacked advantages . . . and needed some [work] training.'[9]

Since the JDA operated as a local option, only large Ontario cities such as Toronto and Ottawa had the resources to establish separate Juvenile Courts in the 1920s, but by World War II 23 counties had proclaimed the Act in effect. However, existing magistrates and probation officers often simply doubled as those presiding over Juvenile Courts—this was the case in Hamilton until the mid-1950s.[10] Juvenile Courts (later combined Family and Juvenile Courts) were supposed to dispense a more compassionate justice: the child was to be tried in private, shielded from publicity, and protected from testifying against herself if she did not understand an oath. Flexibility was the key to all sentencing; the courts could suspend disposition, adjourn the hearing indefinitely, offer some form of probation, including care under Big Sisters, impose a fine, or commit the girl to the care of the CAS or a foster home. Flexibility, however, did not mean lax surveillance. Once deemed a delinquent, the child could be kept under the authority of the court until she was 21 (after 1949, until 18). Surveillance was linked to a growing symbiosis of welfare/social services and the courts, as well as to the emerging 'privatized, technocratic and invisible'[11] socialized justice provided in many Family Courts by non-legal experts such as probation officers, though such programs were concentrated in large urban courts rather than in smaller centres and rural areas.

By the 1960s the emphasis on informal treatment through socialized justice at the cost of due process and children's civil rights was the focus of a mounting critique. Bernard Green, for example, argued in academic journals and the media that Ontario Juvenile Courts had created an arbitrary regime that disempowered working-class children and their families and thus reinforced many social and economic inequities in the system.[12] As legal critics in the late 1950s and early 1960s aptly noted, a child was often judged simply on the basis of 'personality and social background'.[13] The TSA's arbitrary flexibility, allowing committal through the minister and the Ontario Training School Advisory Board (TSAB), rather than strictly court committals, was increasingly criticized. Juveniles, critics noted, were tried for behaviour not deemed criminal in the adult world, and once placed within the correctional system they could be transferred to other medical, correctional, or mental institutions by their new parent: the state. Until this civil rights discourse emerged, however, the dominant rationale for the system was one of 'child-saving', which 'combined the theme of crime prevention with that of child welfare'.[14]

When pronouncing judgement, judges often eschewed discussion of the law, referring primarily to the child's psyche and familial relationships. Sentencing one girl in the 1950s, the Toronto Family Court judge lectured her mother, claiming incorrigibility often 'emerged from relations between mother and daughter; it is this relationship that lies at the back of it.'[15] His language reflected the growing presence in this period of medical and social science discourses on delinquency within Juvenile Courts. Doctors (usually psychiatrists), psychologists, and social workers provided guidance to the juvenile justice system; their knowledge, influenced by and integrated into criminology, shaped the understanding of the 'why, who, and what' of delinquency.[16] Given the immense latitude the law offered for defining behaviour such as incorrigibility, the power of these experts to designate what was delinquent became crucial: not only did the experts construct the dominant definitions of delinquency, they then advised judges on how to treat and sentence girls. Also, because of the emphasis on girls' status offences and their sexuality, these experts were arguably more pivotal to the fate of delinquent girls than to that of delinquent boys. Expert knowledges produced by these professionals certainly worked as instruments of normalization, producing 'classifications and typologies' of delinquency, 'constituting individuals as cases',[17] and exploring their actions as overt signs of covert feelings that only they could understand! Here, indeed, was the power of the norm in bold relief.

Psychology and psychiatry were sometimes seen (and used) as overlapping knowledges in the courts, though in larger courts psychologists were used to assess intelligence, patterns of normal child development, and family behaviour patterns, while psychiatrists were to penetrate into the shadowy corners of the delinquent's disturbed mind.[18] In the courtroom, law and psychiatry were often the most powerful 'double force of authority'.[19] Psychological testing of the child's mental age and IQ was nonetheless quite important: tests like these fixed, often permanently, the prognosis for the child's education, future work, and transfers to institutions for the mentally 'retarded', though by the 1950s there was some limited recognition that such tests were 'only a starting point' and were unreliable for some, such as Native girls, from different cultural and language backgrounds.[20] Social workers were increasingly used in large courts as probation officers, though in rural areas and small towns, court and CAS workers were not always professionally trained social workers but rather 'respectable' local citizens from other occupations. With trained social workers, however, they shared a commitment to methods of casework: objective investigation of the environment of the family and child through intensive interviews and observation.

While these professionals sometimes differed in their approaches to delinquency, there were some common threads in the evolving interpretation of girls' wrongdoing over these decades. In interwar Canada, the eugenic adherents of the mental hygiene movement commanded some influence in medical and social work thinking about delinquency. The influential Dr Helen MacMurchy connected juvenile crime and immorality with mental defectiveness, as did an Ontario Royal Commission of 1931, which urged sterilization as one means of preventing future criminals.[21] More routinely, experts insisted that the 'subnormal' child be segregated and trained in special classes and institutions, providing a guarantee of 'diminishing delinquency'.[22] By the 1940s and 1950s, eugenic and hereditary theories had lost some credibility. Although intelligence testing remained crucial to court assessments, experts put more stock in environmental explanations, investigative social work, and child psychology and psychiatry, including 'talking therapy' as a means of uncovering the origins of delinquency.

If there is a common faith in delinquency studies throughout this period, it lay in various forms of positivist, sociological, and scientific investigation. We need 'a scientific point of view to find the causative factors [of delinquency]', urged one major study of girl delinquents in the 1920s. 'Psychology and psychiatry are so important in this regard', the author ventured, that 'crime is no longer a legal or moral issue.'[23] By the 1940s delinquency was compared to a progressively disruptive illness that might be cured if the symptoms of 'pre-delinquency' were treated early enough.[24] The strongest, persisting theme in these theories was the focus on the 'bad environment' shaping delinquency. This did not entail a structural critique of patriarchal ideology or economic inequality—that would come in the 1970s—as much as an empirical listing of the internal, immediate problems with the family, the peer group, and neighbourhood.

Some interpretations of delinquency did change over time. Theories that stressed the ecology of crime, mapping it by neighbourhood, emerged by the 1940s (and remained in vogue until the 1960s),[25] and in the 1950s the concept of anomie or social strain was popular, though it was applied predominantly in studies of working-class male delinquency and gangs.[26] While few Canadian studies openly blamed non-Anglo immigrants for adolescent crime, a more subtle equation of bad neighbourhoods and immigrants was made by a few experts, and in smaller cities, like Peterborough, experts had no problem claiming that delinquency was minimal *because* there were so few 'foreign' immigrants.[27]

One common theme in criminological writing was inattention to girls and gender. If considered, girls might be slotted, often clumsily, into the masculine models offered.[28] In *Canadian Child and Family Welfare*, the majority of articles on delinquency focused on gangs, auto theft, Big Brothers, and industrial schools for boys.[29] Canadians drew on American studies, including the influential investigations by Sheldon and Eleanor Glueck, which argued that substandard parenting and broken homes were common denominators for female delinquents.[30] The psychiatrists overseeing the Toronto Family Court clinic would have concurred, as their reports continually lamented the 'lack of responsibility on the part of parents',[31] and scarcely a year went by from the 1930s to the 1950s when the TSAB did not offer similar assessments of the 'negligent parenting and bad home conditions' causing delinquency. The statistical categories on training schools set up by the government reflected this ideological construction, stressing, for example, 'immoral parents, no control in the home, parents separated' as 'factors causing delinquency'.[32]

Experts also argued that girls became delinquent because they had improperly absorbed appropriate roles relating to sexuality, domesticity, and motherhood. In the 1920s W.I. Thomas's *The Unadjusted Girl*, for instance, argued that a delinquent girl was not taught the 'moral code' about femininity and her 'value' as a future wife and mother.[33] In the same decade the *Journal of Juvenile Research* published a study drawing on the self-reporting of delinquent girls, who admitted to many thefts unknown to the courts or agencies, which were not the cause of their committal. The psychologist-author focused instead on girls' 'early sex stimulation', failure of the family to inculcate appropriate social values, peer group pressure towards promiscuity, and the practice of 'treating' (receiving small gifts and clothes for sex) as the causes of delinquency.[34]

In the 1950s criminologists also offered assessments centring on thwarted sexual and feminine development. Girls' delinquency, it was suggested, was more likely to emerge from severed emotional relationships, lack of love (or 'cravings for love'), inadequate feminine role models, or failure to accept their sexual/domestic role. The adage that girls were seen as emotionally disturbed and boys as minor lawbreakers was not far off the mark. As Hilary Allen argues, in legal and psychiatric discourses women are more likely than men to be defined in psychiatric terms, as 'hysterical' behaviour is part of their 'normal' psyche.[35] The rising star of Freud, apparent since the 1930s and often popularized or simplified, increasingly influenced the perception of girl delinquents by the 1950s.[36] A bad environment or social stresses, though very important, had to find fertile ground in one's psychological makeup to produce delinquency, and normality was defined according to one's progression towards heterosexual and familial maturity (sex within marriage/motherhood/femininity), which coincidentally approximated middle-class sexual norms. Delinquency could be precipitated by a warped Electra complex, by 'failure to liberate oneself from a pre-Oedipal mother', by girls' overly emotional 'feminine need to serve . . . and fear of rejection', even their sadomasochistic tendencies. Psychiatric theory, though superficially classless, took on class connotations as it was applied to girls, with individual 'neuroses' motivating middle-class girls but more deepseated 'social pathology' framing the sexuality of working-class girls. In a similar manner, of course, earlier psychiatrists had created the 'psychopathic hypersexual' label for amoral, sexually voracious working-class women.[37]

The increase in runaway girls in the fifties was also blamed on the psychiatric bugaboo of the times—'maternal dominance' in the home[38]—though, tangentially, domestic violence might be alluded to. One criminologist surmised that the runaway girl might be 'warding off the unconscious threat of an incestuous relationship with her father'.[39] Seymour Halleck's standard psychiatric text also portrayed incest as fantasy: a 'common pattern . . . is inadequate love from the mother, with the daughter turning to the father' and the close relation 'taking on a latent sexual quality'. Thus, 'to avoid incest', she turns promiscuously to other boys.[40]

Underlying all these discussions of female delinquency was the assumption that 'the predominant expression of [female] delinquency in our society is promiscuous sexual activity.'[41] Although deviant sex was sometimes noted in boys' files (and experts were concerned that they, too, evolve into normal heterosexual adults), sexuality did not assume the same central place; moreover, deviance was defined differently, with heterosexual coupling less of a problem for boys than it was for girls. This also made girls' misdemeanours more unforgivable: 'even the unenlightened know', wrote the OTSG superintendent in the fifties, 'that girls are committed to training school for "boy trouble" whereas boys are usually committed for theft, a more acceptable offence.'[42] Recently, Kerry Cannington has argued that feminist critiques of the 'sexualization' of girl delinquents[43] have in turn 'essentialized' girls,[44] ignoring other factors in their criminalization, including the connection between the welfare system and delinquency. And the latter may well have been crucial, as discussed below. However, social work and medical discourses certainly *did* concentrate on girls' deviant sexuality: to deconstruct this is not simply to reproduce it.

Delinquency, it appears, was never out of fashion as a social concern, even if the rationales, anxieties, and treatments linked to it altered over time. The sexualized adolescent culture of consumerism and leisure ushered in during the Roaring Twenties stimulated a new concern about youth depravity,[45] a concern only surpassed by the intense fears that crime would accompany the economic dislocation of the Great Depression. During the 1930s, the mass media, the police, and the Family Courts repeatedly claimed unemployment, relief, and poverty were encouraging youth crime. Even if occurrence rates of juvenile misdemeanours rose during part of the Depression,[46] the real surprise came when the prosperous war years saw even more 'youth troubles'.

These wartime 'jitters over juveniles'[47] were fed by media reports, often based on the claims of social workers and police across Canada, that there was a crisis of escalating delinquency rates. The disruption of gender roles occasioned by the war worsened these fears, as absent fathers, working mothers, and the lure of money and good times were cited as the roots of the youth problem. In 1943 a prominent female social worker warned that 'concentrations of young military men' had already led to dangerous 'sexual stimulation on the part of adolescent girls in various communities', while a Family Court judge told the Canadian Welfare Council that immoral mothers with absent military husbands were 'keeping' boyfriends on the side with their extra cash, thus also contributing to delinquency.[48] While arrest rates rose at the beginning of the war, these may have been linked to demographic changes and different policing more than to negligent mothers or oversexed camp followers. Reports on the loss of training school premises (the Ontario Girls Training School at Galt, for instance, was given to the armed forces and smaller accommodation in Cobourg secured) and the probation of more children in the community also fed the flames of panic. Without the threat of training schools, some citizens wrote to the Ontario government, children would develop 'disrespect for the law'.[49] (So much for the model of treatment rather than punishment!)

Public anxiety persisted after the war, linked in part to campaigns to reconstruct the heterosexual male/breadwinner, female/homemaker nuclear family in the face of Cold War anxieties.[50] This project of stabilizing family life was directly linked to anti-delinquency campaigns; the TSAB, for instance, called for community centres providing wholesome youth recreation and the teaching of parenting skills as solutions to youth crime. Concern was so intense that in 1954 an Ontario legislature committee began to question the dominant social work/psychiatric emphasis on rehabilitation as opposed to chastisement. While still focusing on neglectful and sexually immoral families as a major cause of delinquency, they fretted about the 'luxurious' treatment of children at training schools and considered corporal punishment as a viable option.[51]

In the 1950s, argues Mary Louise Adams, 'notions of adolescence as a sexual category' came to 'define concerns about delinquency as well.'[52] However, this linkage was not entirely novel, even if attempts to shore up heterosexual normalcy were articulated with new vigour. Nor were anxieties about youth sexuality ever gender-neutral. Just as in the 1930s, the transgressions of girls were seen as less reversible than those of boys. The 'promiscuous' girl, one social worker told a reporter in the 1950s, is 'more ostracized' than the boy who commits serious crimes like homicide. These girls, therefore, had to be 'protected from themselves'.[53]

Getting Caught

Professional discourses on delinquency, of course, were not necessarily consistently applied to the *practice* of social work and psychiatry, especially in correctional institutions. Moreover, their application cannot be separated from the material conditions and social context of girls' lives. Most experts writing on delinquency in these years assumed they were dealing with working-class and poor children, despite intermittent panics about escalating middle-class delinquency from time to time. Some experts directly acknowledged that middle-class girls were less likely to come into conflict with the law even if they engaged in exactly the same sexual practices as working-class girls; 'the labelling of female delinquency', psychiatrist Sidney Halleck admitted, 'is determined by class.'[54]

The juvenile offenders appearing in court confirmed his conclusion; social workers often noted the presence of poverty or periods of economic insecurity in their backgrounds when preparing their case files. Certainly, some middle-class families found themselves in Juvenile Court, but they were not the majority, and crucially, the funnelling process of the criminal justice system meant very few of these children ever saw the insides of a training school. The overwhelming number of girls sentenced to the OTSG, for instance, came from working-class families, and the majority of these had fallen on hard times: the parents were underemployed, unemployed, on relief or welfare, or had simply deserted. The superintendent of the OTSG justified the existence of the institution by claiming success in transforming this 'underclass' into a respectable working class: 'I know there is a curve in the living standards of our released wards. They grew up in the sordid slums and these kids now live in respectable working class districts.'[55]

Material relations are important to an understanding of the apprehension of delinquent girls, their rejection of dominant social norms, and their treatment once in the court and correctional systems; indeed, the dominant discourse of sexualization was inseparable from the power dynamics of class and race. Class selection started with the discretion exercised by the police in their apprehension of children. Policing was conditioned by an ideology that saw certain neighbourhoods, family forms (single parents), and class backgrounds reproducing delinquency. Moreover, working-class families were encouraged to use the police and courts as a means of addressing family and non-support problems because they did not have access to relatives, money, or more private treatment solutions. Especially in larger cities, Family Courts became a public resource for the more respectable working and middle classes, a means to secure counselling, aid, and professional allies to broker family conflicts, including the perennial teenage ones—breaking curfews, skipping school, and suspected sexual activity.

The method by which police, probation officers, the CAS, and welfare authorities surveyed delinquents involved tapping into neighbourhood gossip networks.[56] These were more circumscribed in affluent areas due to larger houses, physical distance of neighbours, less street activity, and different patterns of sociability. Probation officers, for example, interviewed relatives, friends, and especially neighbours about the housekeeping, hours kept, and drinking and sexual habits of family members. The latter were of particular interest. Neighbours sometimes were tight-lipped, but they also initiated some complaints or, once interviewed, told all, even commenting on those who were deceased: 'the mother is dead [but] was rumoured to be a bad housekeeper and of low mentality . . . her sister is reported to be a prostitute.'[57] Damning police testimony could also be little more than gossip. 'This girl cannot tell me one decent friend she knows,' reported one officer in a trial, 'and she is associated with someone suspected of selling tranquillizers. . . . She believes the only way to success is to become a thug. . . . The court does not know half of the situation she is in', he concluded with a flourish of innuendo.[58]

The close information networks between schools, social services, and the courts meant that families known to any one agency were more likely to be referred to the court. Truancy charges laid by the school attendance officer brought one girl to the Hamilton court in 1933, but once there, the fact that she was 'peddling candy and perfume on the street' for her stepmother and suspected of immorality helped clinch her sentence to the training school.[59] Welfare officials also passed on damning information about parents and girls to the court. If a mother was cut off Mother's Allowance for having an illegitimate child, this fact became part of her daughter's court case file. If an OTSG girl on probation got pregnant and went to a welfare office for financial aid, she was quickly turned back to the training school.

Socialized justice increasingly steered many children away from official court appearances into probation or a psychiatric clinic. In the Toronto court, occurrences, that is, problems treated out of court, far outnumbered court hearings;[60] by the early 1950s only a quarter to a third of juveniles faced court appearances,[61] with the majority directed into probationary options. Here, too, class was important. The dominant psychiatric thinking in the postwar period presumed the therapeutic approach would primarily benefit 'reflective' white, middle-class clients with 'better cognitive skills and ego strengths'.[62] This class bias would have ruled out the poorest or least articulate girls, steering them towards a court appearance.

For Native girls, increasingly before the courts in the 1950s, there was unlikely to be salvation in probation. For one thing, many girls from reserves were sentenced in smaller cities or rural areas where court probation and psychiatric services were meagre and foster homes difficult to find. Even more important, Indian agents, perhaps the same people who had testified against the girls in court, often doubled as probation officers, and their negative view of reserve life might well influence the court's decision to send the girl away from home.

Finally, the dominant racist view of Native girls as more vulnerable to alcohol abuse and promiscuity meant that judges often urged immediate isolation of the girl and her 'protection' in a training school.

If placed under probation (overseen by the court or Big Sisters), the girl and her family underwent interviews and inspections to monitor the standards of cleanliness, good housekeeping, morality, and school/work expectations laid out by the court. Families used various strategies, often at considerable sacrifice, to avoid incarceration. Some moved to better neighbourhoods or sent their child away to relatives. One 14-year-old, in charge of full-time child care and housework in her widowed father's home, had run away in 1944 and lived with an older teen for 11 days 'as man and wife'. Though this was considered serious, she was given a suspended sentence since an aunt agreed to take her in and 'look after her'.[63]

It was far easier for middle-class families and those from the respectable working class to exercise escape strategies and convince probation officers that their church attendance, participation in 'wholesome' recreation, work prospects, and homes in good neighbourhoods made them good probation risks.[64] Probation officers were impressed with the physical, cultural, and intellectual trappings of class. Probation (termed placement) officers who worked for the OTSG judged both foster parents and delinquent girls along similar lines. Good books were preferred over crime comics, tasteful furnishings over untidiness, church attendance over dance halls, and sensible clothing over 'make up and extreme dress'.[65] Finally, middle-class families and better-educated working-class families also knew how to appeal to officials to bend the rules in their favour.[66] One such father, an insurance salesman, designated by the CAS and the local police as 'the meanest' tyrant in existence, successfully lobbied a cabinet minister in the 1930s to get permission to take his daughter, who was under the care of the Juvenile Court, out of the province.[67]

The girl might also elicit the sympathy of court personnel in her probation meetings, particularly if her descriptions of family conflicts coincided with their negative appraisals of negligent and cruel parents or if she appealed to their ethnocentric or moral sentiments. A girl described as 'resentful' of her immigrant Ukrainian parents' culture might have found a sympathetic ear in the probation officer, who noted critically that the mother had endured an arranged marriage and was 'resentful and unhappy' about her life. While the mother complained that her daughter gave away the clothes bought for her, used her mother's charge card to treat her friends, and 'wore too much make up', the probation officer privately commented critically that the mother wore nothing but slacks.[68] Other girls complained of unloving families, parental fights, and step-parents they hated, even asking to be removed. Their objection to common-law step-parents might strike a chord with court workers, who had less than approving views of extramarital sex. In 1952 a suburban mother laid a charge of unmanageability against her daughter who repeatedly ran away, but the psychiatrist's report noted that Mary came across her mother and a boyfriend having intercourse one night and 'she cannot forget this disgusting scene.' Due to stress and anxiety, she was near breakdown and in need of security and counselling, he advised.[69]

Girls' conflicts with the law were also grounded in deep-seated anger, alienation, and rebellion connected to either material deprivation or contests for attention and resources within the family. Economic instability often generated geographical transience and family insecurity, exacerbating girls' rejection of social norms. Parents (especially single working mothers and fathers) left children in unregulated foster homes—with relatives or friends little able to care for them—and, not surprisingly, girls resented this predicament; some were cruelly reminded by those caring for them that they were burdens. During the Depression a father disabled by a car accident and on relief sent his daughter to her uncle's farm to be cared for. Elaine constantly wrote home, saying she was 'ill treated by her uncle' and threatening suicide, but her stories were disbelieved. Charged with vagrancy and underage drinking and suspected of being 'sexually precocious', she was sent to training school. When attempts to run back to her mother failed, she simply asked to be left alone to write poetry, perhaps her only means of working through her own perceptions of unjust treatment, which others had dismissed.[70]

Other parents who worked at low-paying jobs, such as charring or farm help, could not supervise their children properly, nor did they have adequate housing; their children often became involved in street life that occasioned problems with the law. Because social workers were convinced that broken homes caused delinquency, daughters of single parents were especially vulnerable to strict surveillance. Confined to lower-paying jobs, often seeking support payments through the Family Court, or cut off Mother's Allowance for any moral infractions, single mothers were more likely to encounter welfare or court authorities, with inevitable scrutiny of their parenting. When Joan was caught stealing petty cash from a settlement house in the early 1950s, the court deemed her mother incapable of managing her, yet the mother's major crime seemed to be her impoverished single parenthood: 'she had married a man who deserted and was a bigamist. . . . She has tried to support the family . . . and seems close to nervous breakdown.'[71]

While the contours of poverty and economic insecurity altered over these years, relative deprivation remained constant. In the Depression years, it is true, children were still found begging on the streets. One Hamilton girl, peddling door to door for her family, claimed she was raped by one man who followed her to a park. Another 13-year-old from a city in the north, sent to the streets in the late 1930s 'to sell flowers without any breakfast', was supposedly used 'as a slave' by her father, who had no job and was accused of theft. Her physical wandering quickly led to charges because she was hitchhiking and picked up by men who either forced her or paid her to have intercourse.[72]

Yet, in the more prosperous forties and fifties, pockets of abject poverty still existed: girls were removed from school to care for younger siblings, single mothers left daughters with relatives as they searched for work, and some families simply could not support their children. Poverty also overlapped with wilful neglect. One 13-year-old deserted by her parents in the late 1940s fled to her brother, but he did nothing when she went to live on a beach with two transient men. When taken in, she had not been to school for years, was physically run down and 'absolutely filthy', and had venereal disease. The real question, of course, was whether neglect should have resulted in the girl's incarceration.[73]

Parents (or teens) with steady and skilled jobs were more likely to qualify for probation and counselling, but the underemployed were less fortunate. Girls left school at an early age because they had learning problems in school, because they saw little future in education, or to help out a financially strapped family. They found jobs as part-time waitresses or maids, but the latter was isolating and poorly paid, and girls often quit, while the former was also insecure, viewed suspiciously by probation officers as leading to dangerous social and sexual contact with strangers. Parents with jobs that did not conform to a nine-to-five day (or that seemed unacceptable, as with a mother and father who worked in a bar) were also disadvantaged in the probation process. One father who charged his 16-year-old with being 'incorrigible', because she was refusing to go to work or school and was out all night, tried to tell the judge he had no way of supervising her because of his job. In response to the judge's clear condemnation of him, this working man pointed out that his wife had deserted and 'I've tried [to look after her] but I work at nights.'[74] In a cruel twist of logic, though, those who embraced the work ethic might also be penalized. One single mother whose job involved cooking at a resort near Toronto was censured for leaving her daughter behind in the city with relatives. Mothers with partners could also be chastised for working and 'not realizing how important it is to have a stable home life and a mother in the home.'[75]

Economic instability, desertion, and transience were also likely to lead to foster care. This connection between state care and later conflicts with the law—still apparent in current studies of female offenders[76]—worked itself out in many ways. In a society that idealized the biological family as the true one, foster children were sometimes made to feel rejected, or in their words, 'ashamed [and] worthless'.[77] Furthermore, foster parents were paid to do a job they could simply abandon; they were less likely to cover up a child's misbehaviour or to tolerate the torture of adolescent rebellion. Court and training school authorities constantly lamented the shortage of foster parents for teenage girls. Unless they were going to do domestic work, fostering was seen as a source of potential trouble. Moreover, once girls were enmeshed in a cycle of rejection and marginalization in foster homes, it was difficult for them to see any benefit to conforming with good behaviour. Is it any wonder, one psychiatrist asked, that a girl who had been in 15 homes in seven years was 'impulsive, rough, boy crazy and insolent?'[78]

Though children certainly found love and care in foster homes, they were sometimes abused. Seldom, however, were their stories believed. One young girl who felt her foster mother had 'no affection' for her had to 'work on the farm every day for long hours before and after school.'[79] Others claimed they were assaulted or sexually abused. The outward respectability of foster parents impressed CAS workers, who later sometimes admitted that children were not even given enough to eat. In addition, the signs of respectability to social workers could be oppressive to teenage girls, one of whom begged the court to send her to training school, which seemed preferable to a strict foster regime in which she was 'never allowed out except to go to church.'[80] The social workers' faith in foster parents' religiosity as a sign of their good parenting was tragically displayed when one OTSG ward became pregnant by a well-respected 'church going' fundamentalist foster father who also admitted to hitting the girl. Even though the foster father acknowledged the blame for the pregnancy, the CAS and the OTSG decided not to prosecute him, knowing that the girl's supposed sex delinquency would discount her testimony in court.[81]

The physical, spatial, and sensory experience of economic instability cannot be underestimated as a stimulant to disobedience and disregard for the law. Some working-class children and certainly the very poor had little money for recreation, making temptations of petty theft attractive. Even the smallest amount of money could be fought over, causing a child to run away: one girl, who was taken to court in the 1930s by her foster mother for being 'incorrigible' and 'unstable', had fought with her foster mother over one dollar.[82] Even in the more prosperous fifties there was a gap between the advertised world of teen consumption—clothes, makeup, and restaurants—and the reality that many teens had scant resources for such consumption. Girls charged with theft were seldom hoisting cars or doing break and enters; they usually pilfered clothes, candy, jewellery, or cash from employers, family, or neighbours.

For those who were very poor, despair and resignation became inscribed indelibly on their psyches. Parents who faced obstacles to daily survival had trouble offering children any hope, including hope that conforming to social norms would bring prosperity or happiness. Girls' rebellion against school, work, and sexual abstinence was interpreted by court workers as anti-social behaviour, immaturity, or a lack of intelligence or ambition, but sometimes hopelessness just made sense. As one child commented, why should I 'grow up when all adults are unhappy. . . . I do not know one good marriage. Look at my mother', she added: 'illness, one child after the other', and death from tuberculosis.

Poverty also accentuated physical problems such as illness or disability. These left parents even poorer, and angry and frustrated—as with one embittered father, confined to the home, jobless after an accident, who kicked his daughter furiously whenever she walked by. Disabilities left children isolated and hostile, too. One teen with a hearing problem and speech defect accused of sexual immorality was criticized for not holding a job and running away. Yet, her stories of sexual abuse by her brother, of feeling she was 'not good enough for anybody', were dismissed. It took *nine* years after she was designated a 'problem' by the CAS, and great pressure from the training school on the penny-pinching government, to get a hearing aid for her. 'She is not crazy, though a little paranoid', commented the psychiatrist reasonably, 'due to the fact she can't hear.'[83]

Many girls from poor and working-class families were also expected to take on work responsibilities never demanded of middle-class girls. As one psychologist admitted, some girls laboured under such 'heavy responsibilities' at home, caring for children, sick relatives, and disabled or alcoholic parents, that it was understandable they wanted to claim 'excitement' and adult pleasures at night.[84] Girls might also feel that adult pastimes of drinking, sexual liaisons, and partying were the reward for the daily grind of early wage work. When Marilyn quit school in 1942 at 14 to help her single mother by working in a chocolate factory, she assumed the payoff was to stay out all night with boys. Her mother, supported by the Juvenile Court judge, thought differently.[85]

One reason that girls judged to be delinquent and removed from their homes found it difficult to sever ties with families designated inadequate or immoral, even though this was encouraged, was that they felt kinship with parents and 'their many hardships in the home'.[86] The young girl sent out to sell flowers at 13 excused her father, saying he was 'punished for not getting relief, sick, unable to do the best for [us]'.[87] Hearing that her father was in jail, another OTSG ward on placement abandoned her job as a domestic and hurried home to another city to care for younger siblings. 'It is certainly upsetting,' said her placement officer, 'however this is nothing new and does not excuse her irresponsible attitude towards her employer.' In another cruel twist of logic, the girl was chastised for embracing the ideology of familial care often portrayed as the salvation for delinquents.[88]

Court workers and judges also tended to see the material and cultural background of Native girls from reserves as more likely to lead to immorality and delinquency. Girls who lived in cramped, substandard housing, who spent much of their time outside, and who avoided school or who drank were fingered as problems by the Indian agent, CAS, or local police—and sometimes by relatives as well. Once before the court, material deprivation was blamed more on culture and the 'lackadaisical' nature of Indians than on the legacies of colonialism. Since reserves were portrayed as impoverished, degenerate, and culturally backward places with high rates of immorality and alcoholism, it was assumed girls could not be reformed there.[89] One 14-year-old found intoxicated in a community near the reserve was sent to training school after this one misdemeanour. 'She has to be protected from alcoholism, if she is drinking at fourteen', reasoned the judge. Yet, the same crime might have won a more affluent, white child a suspended sentence and probation.

A typical story of an urban committal in the 1940s illustrates how definitions of sexual immorality could be linked to poverty and neglect. Donna was brought to Juvenile Court at 13 for incorrigibility, primarily because she had intercourse with an older man in his car, and 'possibly' with others. Also of concern was the fact she and her siblings had 'been caught begging' on the streets and neighbours complained they ran 'wild' when left alone to fend for themselves on weekends while their mother was away with her boyfriend. Fears of Donna's delinquency expressed by the CAS were closely linked to her mother's poverty and immorality. Deemed 'unintelligent and illiterate', the mother was cut off Mother's Allowance for having an illegitimate child with her boyfriend (who could not marry her because his own wife was in a mental hospital) and was cut off welfare after being pressured by the welfare authorities (unsuccessfully) to give him up. The children were 'neglected, had lice' and were temporarily removed by the CAS, though later returned to her. Donna's incarceration was actually aided by her mother, who agreed with the judge 'she could not control her' and wanted her to get some educational 'training' to secure a better future for her. Donna could not escape her contradictory feelings about her family: internalizing the training school morals, she felt 'disgraced' by them, but knowing only too well the material and social circumstances beyond their control, she missed them and 'worried about them'.[90]

Sexualizing the Delinquent Girl

For a small number of girls like Donna, the end of the line of juvenile justice was training school. Though far fewer girls than boys were brought to Juvenile Court, girls were more likely to be placed under court supervision (in some cities this meant more frequent visits and assessments than for boys) and they were more likely to face institutionalization. Girls were more liable to be sent to training school, after only one or no court appearances, while boys were offered more second chances. In Ontario, it was usually the case from the 1930s to the 1950s that more than 50 per cent (and as high as 73 per cent) of girls were sent away after initial contact with the juvenile justice system, while for boys it was less than 50 per cent and sometimes as low as 21 per cent. The ratio of boys to girls brought to the largest Juvenile Court, in Toronto, was about 10:1, but girls were two to four times more likely to be incarcerated than boys (see Table 8 and Figure 8).[91]

Statistics are not unambiguous,[92] but they are supported by cases in which court authorities articulate the urgency of isolating girls from society. The reason lay in the different charges boys and girls faced. In the 1940s and early 1950s, for instance, more than half of the boys before the Toronto Family Court were charged with theft, while, on average, only 20 per cent of the girls were. Truancy was an important reason for apprehending girls until 1944; after that, incorrigibility—often linked to promiscuity—accounted for 40–50 per cent of girls' charges. Figures 9 and 10 show these gender differences for

Table 8
Dispositions of Children Brought to Court, Toronto, Selected Years

	1928		1933		1938		1943		1948		1952	
	Boys	Girls	Boys	Girls	Boys	Girls	Boys	Girls	Boys	Girls	Boys	Girls
Adjourned indefinitely	1,961	66	679	42	389	27	534	67	212	12	249	23
Supervision of court	84	0	84	3	92	16	162	8	223	31	185	18
Supervision of Big Brothers/Big Sisters	113	10	319	25	295	35	196	41	83	7	71	14
Other supervision	0	0	0	0	32	18	93	55	34	9	34	19
Foster care	40	5	0	0	50	10	80	2	9	2	14	1
Training school	19	4	15	6	30	3	65	13	43	18	55	24
Fined	90	4	14	0	29	0	126	3	13	1	17	1
Dismissal	36	2	27	2	28	0	52	3	11	0	25	1
Withdrawn	0	0	0	0	14	6	45	21	11	12	33	16
Suspended sentence	72	6	1	0	0	0	0	0	2	1	1	0
Returned home	0	0	0	0	0	0	11	5	3	2	3	1
Totals	2,415	97	1,139	78	959	115	1,364	218	644	95	687	118

SOURCE: Toronto Family Court, *Annual Report*, selected years.

Figure 8
Percentages of Girls and Boys before the Toronto Court
Sent to Training School, Selected Years

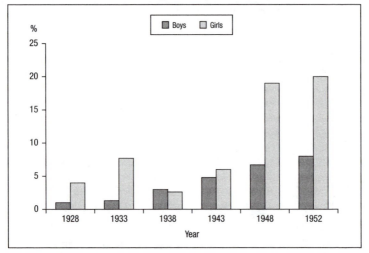

SOURCE: Toronto Family Court, *Annual Report*, selected years.

selected years in regard to property offences and incorrigibility/
truancy offences. The courts were influenced by the social work/
psychiatric discourses that saw sexual immorality as more dangerous
to a girl's future, and possibly to the community. We had better send her
to training school, noted one judge, 'before she is ruined in body and
soul'.[93] Boys who were arrested for the theft of bicycles, cars, sporting
goods, or even guns could presumably stop stealing or repay their victim; girls' loss of virginity, however, spoiled 'the goods' forever.

Even if sexual behaviour was not the first reason for contact with
the Juvenile Court, it could easily take centre stage. Faced with a
break-and-enter charge, a London judge asked the mother: 'is she
fond of boys . . . out at night . . . immoral . . . have you had her examined [by a doctor]?'[94] Making girls submit to gynecological exams
was a standard means of resolving the gravity of the situation; if the
doctor proclaimed she was not a virgin, the need for reform was especially urgent. Suspected immorality was also a reason to keep the girl
in training school as long as possible. The mother of Diane, a 16-
year-old who was convicted of stealing a ring from her employer,
tried to secure her daughter's release, telling the Attorney General the

Figure 9
Property Offences as Percentage of Total Offences for
Girls and for Boys, Toronto, Selected Years

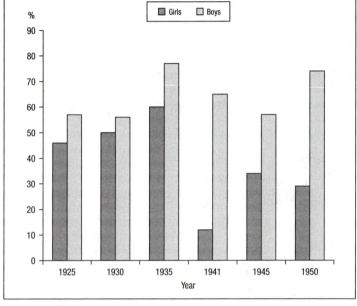

SOURCE: Toronto Family Court, *Annual Report*, selected years.

sentence was 'only to be three months' and that because Diane's 'younger sister has a heart condition' she was needed at home. However, the CAS had pressed the training school to keep Diane, who was described as 'simple and easily led'. Their concern: she had stayed out 'all night last year' and 'after police investigation it was found she had intercourse with two men in a house.' She was also 'hitchhiking to other cities with a friend' and, in the view of the CAS, a sexual risk due to 'lax discipline' in her home.[95]

Most often, concerns about sexual activity came within a package of accusations: incorrigibility, running away and immorality. Like the young women arrested under the FRA, delinquents were considered risks when they engaged in sex with too many or unacceptable partners, such as older men. Girls who ran away were courting disaster, for they might be pressured or coerced into sex by men who, as one judge warned a 13-year-old, 'will use you then kick you out when

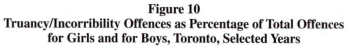

Figure 10
Truancy/Incorribility Offences as Percentage of Total Offences
for Girls and for Boys, Toronto, Selected Years

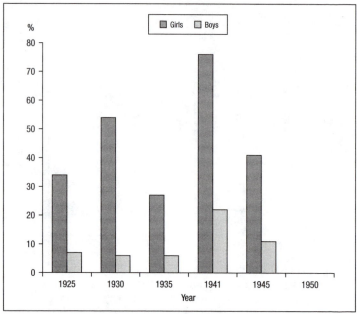

SOURCE: Toronto Family Court, *Annual Report*, selected years.

they are through. If you remain on the street, you are headed for a life
of misery . . . kicked from pillar to post, with no home, no friends, the
worst life in the world.'[96] Such concerns with runaways were not all
illusory, for many girls had little sexual knowledge and only their sexuality with which to barter food, lodging, and transportation. Those
who ran away with steady boyfriends, however, were also considered
at risk, and those who protested that they slept in parks and cars—
without men—were either little believed or perceived to be irrespon-
sibly flirting with sexual danger.

A girl's attitude towards her sexual misbehaviour was crucial to
her fate. If she rejected her parents' authority to set curfews and bar
unacceptable boyfriends, or the court's authority to do so, she was in
trouble. Girls deemed irrepressibly 'boy crazy', those who would not
renounce their sexually aggressive ways through counselling and probation, positively invited isolation in training school. During World

War II, this had a new twist, with soldiers the lure of danger. 'She is soldier crazy', complained the police to one judge during World War II, 'she waves at them all, is hitchhiking to other places, going out in cars with soldiers.'[97] Yet, this was an age group generally curious about sex, a fact that intensified once boys became prohibited. As the OTSG superintendent admitted privately in the 1940s: 'There is hardly a girl over 13 who is not interested in boys after several months' incarceration in the school. . . . If we are to keep all potential sex problems in school until they are 16, we will need room for 300.'[98]

A girl's lack of guilt was also cause for concern, even though some younger girls did not even know what the word 'immoral' meant or why they were appearing in court for having intercourse.[99] For Native girls coming from different language groups, the search for 'guilt' was undoubtedly difficult, since there was often no equivalent word in some Native language groups. Assessing remorse was essential to the confessional screening the girls encountered in probation or later in the OTSG: the 'unabashed recounting of sexual experiences', noted one doctor, indicates the 'seriousness' of this girl's mental problems.[100] Boasting about sexual deeds was especially worrisome because it was feared girls might contaminate and encourage the unexperienced. The Training School Advisory Board urged that one girl, who 'confessed' to 'sexual abuse [by her father] and immorality' in her own home, not be fostered out with young children unless she had separate sleeping arrangements, presumably for this reason.[101]

The CAS, court psychiatrists and psychologists, and probation workers were especially aghast when girls displayed little emotion, regret, or even interest when describing the sexual acts (and especially those such as oral sex) with boys or men they barely knew, sometimes in return for small gifts. One such girl readily volunteered a list of her encounters, and that of her sister, for which she was usually paid a dollar. 'This condition of affairs is shocking', noted the Crown attorney who was also charging the men. 'There are women old enough and willing to do that sort of thing without having little girls doing that.'[102] Consent was a legitimate concern for the court. Some of the younger girls, at 11 or 12, described being raped without even knowing the word yet. They did not have a strong sense of their rights and were fearful of voicing their own feelings. One girl 'thought if she refused [the boys who wanted sex with her] she would be seen as a coward'; her psychologist then added approvingly, 'so her sex delinquency was more acquiescence than aggressiveness.'[103]

A racially inappropriate partner (though not a frequent concern) was also a sign that the girl had not internalized the appropriate sexual norms, with concerns focused primarily on white girls involved with Afro-Canadian boys. One CAS worker lectured a 15-year-old white girl who twice spent the night with a 'coloured boy in a car', warning her that 'these coloured boys are like tom cats that chase alley cats.' The judge agreed she did not understand the 'seriousness of the situation'.[104] Parents also brought daughters to court for transgressing racial lines. One Toronto mother was so worried that her white daughter was 'socializing with coloured in dance halls . . . [and that] she will have a black baby' that even the court workers found her obsessive. Yet racism was conveniently ignored when the very few Afro-Canadian girls in the OTSG complained of prejudice: 'her main problem is not accepting being coloured; she looks for slights when there is none', said a training school official dismissively.[105] Concerns about transgressing other ethnic or religious boundaries were not common, though in a small number of cases ethnicity was offered as a factor in delinquency. Some social workers assumed working-class European immigrants were less able to teach daughters 'social skills'[106] and moral values, that they drank too much, or most often, that these daughters would act out in opposition to their parents' Old World values. In the 1930s there were occasional suspicions of the inferior cultural values of the few 'foreigners',[107] but over the next two decades ethnicity was not constructed as a significant explanation for delinquency.

It was not simply the girl's sexuality but her family's sexual history that was scrutinized by the courts, and sadly, some children recognized full well that 'they were being punished for their parents' misdemeanours.'[108] Pre-sentencing social work and psychiatric reports commented on the existence of other illegitimate children in the family and parental sexual misbehaviour. Girls, it was assumed, would simply 'imitate their mothers' or 'follow in the footsteps' of other immoral relatives.[109] Insisting that one girl charged with truancy and theft be removed from her family, the Hamilton CAS concentrated on the mother's sexual morality and housekeeping as the reason for sending her to the OTSG: 'The mother is agency prone', they argued, and immoral, for 'she had an illegitimate child after the father's death . . . giving birth the same time as her son had a baby [a fact considered somehow in bad taste] and the house is filthy with mouldy wine glasses everywhere.'[110]

Definitions of the morally lax family incorporated the inescapable effects of poverty. Families were criticized for 'children sleeping together in one room' and for taking in too many strange boarders.[111] Physical neglect could also be used to reinforce charges of sexual immorality. The Hamilton CAS brought a mother to court, reporting that her 'seven children were parked in various places and not cared for, looked after ever. If the mother does not have one man, she has another, so the children camp out here and there while the mother is in hotels.' Her 15-year-old daughter admitted to sex with a '43-year-old man who gave her a coat and some money',[112] both of which the impoverished child needed.

Definitions of the immoral family altered over time, though only in small ways. In the 1930s, alarm was voiced over sexual exhibitionism at school or masturbation. One woman tried to persuade the court that her stepdaughter was a delinquent because she was teaching her own daughter and others how to masturbate.[113] By the postwar period, concerns focused almost entirely on promiscuity, though sometimes this still meant little more than a girl 'admitting to intercourse with her boyfriend and a few others'.[114] Both venereal disease and illegitimate pregnancies were potential signs of immorality, though by the postwar period in particular, the latter might be excused as a singular mistake, especially for the better-off, and VD could be treated in out-patient clinics. Although deemed an emblem of 'delinquency', unwed motherhood was by the fifties a distinct sexual problem, requiring other kinds of isolation/treatment.[115]

Attitudes towards common-law unions also changed very slightly. Parents (especially mothers) who lived common-law were morally suspect and could be forced by the CAS and the courts to choose between their partners and custody of their children. Indeed, the 'contributing' sections of the Juvenile Delinquents Act offered the means of charging parents deemed immoral, and in the 1930s social workers allied with the Canadian Welfare Council pressed for more precise and stringent legal condemnation of adults corrupting their children by living in adultery.[116] Their efforts were only partially successful and were ultimately sidelined by unsympathetic judicial decisions. By the 1950s, some court personnel, certainly in larger urban areas, were less uniformly condemning of common-law unions, particularly if the partnership closely resembled a 'respectable' marriage.[117]

Interpreting and Resisting the Norm

Many parents shared the Juvenile Courts' alarm over their daughters' sexual immorality, yet girls' delinquency was still interpreted differently by the experts, judges, parents, and the children themselves. Probation officers and OTSG staff occasionally betrayed lingering preconceptions that delinquents had simply inherited a bad character:

'another example of bad heredity or bad environment', commented one OTSG placement worker when her charge did not behave.[118] Finding it difficult to jettison their middle-class moorings, they wondered how very poor families, in substandard housing and living conditions, could bring up moral citizens, though some were forced to admit that parental love and dirt could coexist. The mother in a very poor rural family was described disparagingly as 'slovenly, dirty and repeatedly pregnant', but the home 'seems close', a placement officer conceded, with the older 'children helping the younger ones.' 'As unkempt as it is, she has a strong tie to the home', the OTSG superintendent admitted when the girl ran away to her mother.[119]

Ironically, the family was seen as both the cause of delinquency and its cure. Court and penal workers often had an image of the ideal family: a strong male head of household/earner and a mother caring for the family (or, if need be, a virtuous, labouring single mother); sex within marriage; wholesome family activities such as church-going, not drinking. The same image characterized the government inquiry into delinquency in 1954, which claimed the 'real cure' for delinquency was a 'desirable home life with its family gatherings, religious teaching and proper parental example'.[120] Yet, many families did not approximate this ideal, and this contradiction followed the girls through Family Courts and training school and into foster homes and their work placements. It was a no-win situation for the girls, who were presented with this familial ideology even though they constantly experienced its cruel contradictions. Not surprisingly, the sexual containment of marriage, even at 16 or 17, was seen as the 'best thing that can happen' to a delinquent girl, as long as the husband was respectable. Indeed, with 'overly developed, sexual girls . . . if marriage is put off too long, there might be complications', penal workers warned.[121]

Judges shared court and penal workers' image of the bad girl/ideal family and used the courts to defend and promote it, delivering their verdicts with paternalistic authority. Offering the supreme ideological rationale for the system of juvenile justice, they chastised, warned, lectured, and also cajoled girls and their parents.[122] In first court appearances, Juvenile Court judges often used informal conversation and simply issued a warning. Even when passing a training school sentence, a judge might couch his verdict in supportive words, telling the girl she had 'the ability to be a fine young woman . . . there are many nice things about you, but you are on the wrong track.'[123] Addressing a girl who ran away from her foster home with a man to a hotel, he warned, 'there is nothing wrong with sex, but there is proper place for it in our lives and you have not found the proper place. Don't cheapen yourself. You will look back on this and worry about these escapades when you have found the right man . . . you will thank us.'[124]

Judges did, however, display displeasure with girls who were saucy and insufficiently apologetic, and whose actions had betrayed temperate, respectable parents: 'I don't think you appreciate what your parents have done for you, the embarrassment they suffer coming into this court with you',[125] a small-town judge told one teen. 'You can't get away with that stuff in here', a York County judge thundered at a girl who talked back to him, declaring angrily that her Big Sisters worker was 'prosecuting' rather than helping her. His sympathies clearly lay with her hard-working Polish immigrant parents, who deferentially pleaded with the court for help so they could sleep at night because they were 'worrying constantly about her' being out all hours of the night.[126] Parents could also be subject to shame. Even when neglect was not an issue, they were chastised for being inadequate: 'you have failed', said one judge in his rebuke. 'Do you want shame and disaster on your doorstep?'[127]

Parents' wishes do sometimes overlap with CAS and court strategies; they wanted the troublesome child reformed or possibly removed from their home. Rather than stressing their own failure to approximate an ideal family, though, parents spoke of their fears for their daughters' safety and future and of the disruptions they were causing in family life. One mother approached the court through Big Sisters because she wanted her second daughter 'to avoid the fate of her sister', who had 'an illegitimate child, an early marriage and much unhappiness'. Because the girl was avoiding school, 'staying out late at nights, running with a tough, boy-crazy crowd in search of excitement', the mother feared her daughter would follow her older sister's path.[128]

Parents also used the court to pry daughters away from unacceptable mates. A teen went to visit a former neighbour, 28 years older, and apparently, with her consent, they ran away for 'three months and lived as husband and wife'. Although the parents did not favour training school, the judge saw it as the only way to effect their wish to have her isolated from the man and to teach her 'the error of her ways'.[129] A decade later, in the late 1950s, the suburban parents of a 15-year-old went to court to secure her isolation from a 'no good', ex-convict, older boyfriend. Even though she only admitted to 'having sex a couple of times', her 'respectable' parents impressed upon the judge the dangerous obsessiveness of her attachment, explaining she had even 'climbed out of a window when they were asleep [in order] to see him.'[130]

Daughters, parents also feared, might be seduced by an older peer group or gang, encouraged to drink, stay out late, and then become sexually active. And they were not always wrong. Moreover, other siblings had to be protected from a life of crime. One girl, supposedly of low intelligence, had enlisted her brother in her forgery and theft schemes. Her mother told the judge, 'I don't know anything about the [training school] but I will take your advice. . . . I feel it is not justice to the other children for Mona to be with them.'[131]

Even if the parents' aim was to protect daughters or scare them into better behaviour, the judicial process could move beyond their control—just as parents found with the Female Refuges Act. One sole-support mother asked that her wayward daughter who was out on the streets all night with soldiers be 'put in a good Christian home' because she worked from seven to seven and could not afford to send her to high school, which would have entailed paying for school books and other fees as well as additional clothing purchases. The judge sent the daughter to the OTSG.[132] Determined to pursue their own agenda, the court authorities often tried to make parents take ownership of the sentence, persuading them that 'it was in the best interests of your daughter', though if this failed, they just railroaded reluctant parents. The physical and social arrangement of the court, with the judge sometimes listening on a raised dais, the experts relaying inside information about family intimacies, and the parents, apprehensive or ashamed, created a space of 'subtle coercion' that reinforced the judge's power, despite claims that he was dispensing paternal understanding.[133] For the few immigrant or Native families needing translators, the process was even more alienating.

To have any say, some working-class parents instinctively knew they should construct themselves as a respectable family. One mother tried to tell the judge she '*used* to go to Church three times a day', though he was rather cynical about her claim; another tried to downplay her part-time job in a dance band as this was seen as a bad substitute for church-going.[134] Others pleaded, 'We are poor, but I try my best',[135] invoked their ethnic stature as good 'British citizens', or got other local respectable people to intervene for them.

Some parents simply refused to acknowledge their own immorality or endorse the moral interference of the court. 'Well,' commented one mother sarcastically to a social worker about her daughter's sexual liaison, 'they've had their nights together [as an unmarried couple] so why don't you just leave them alone?'[136] Parents might hide daughters' pregnancies and sexual affairs from probation officers, or take issue with judgements about their morality and parenting. One father, who was living common-law with his housekeeper, was blamed by a judge for his daughter's sexual immorality.' I am not the start of this trouble', he countered in anger.[137]

Some Native parents and grandparents did lay complaints against their daughters for drinking, sexual immorality, and truancy. However, once in court, their wishes were often dismissed with a measure of racist paternalism—unless they agreed with the court's prognosis. One RCMP agent pushed for a sentence after underage drinking charges were laid against a girl, even though the father thought he was only in court to 'discuss the problem'.[138] Another father who worked as a school janitor reacted angrily to the Indian agent's testimony against his daughter, first pointing out that he needed his daughter's help in his daily work since he had arthritis, but also disputing her immorality: 'there are so many rumours about her, that to be true, she would have to be a woman of 50.'[139] He, too, was ignored and his daughter was removed from the home.

Nor were protesting girls a match for the power of court. Deciphering girls' attitudes is extremely difficult given their silence in the courtroom. Though they often claimed culpability, they were clearly cowed by a legal process they did not always understand, language beyond their grasp, and sheer fright of being removed to an institution. Once adults had testified against them, they sometimes changed their plea to guilty or gave no response. As naïve as some were, *they* understood the power of the law. As one child in the Toronto court told an observer, the judge seemed 'like a god'.[140]

However, in interviews with court workers and in the psychiatric confessional, girls were more likely to lay out their side of the story. Some girls protested their designation as delinquent, claiming they were wrongfully accused of activities such as underage drinking or that parental and court suspicions of bad behaviour were exaggerated. Faced with violent or alcoholic parents, or even poverty, some girls declared they wanted to be sent away and later claimed the regimentation of a training school was a welcome relief, 'a better place than home'.[141]

Girls instinctively knew that denial of sexual wrongdoing was important, so they laid claim to their virginity, as with the girl who reassured the court that she avoided intercourse, only letting her boyfriend 'put it between my legs'.[142] A minority also maintained that sexual activity was their own business, rejected the moral norms prescribed by the court. One teen admitted to having intercourse with many boys and that she could not shake her desire to 'pick up boys' even after incarceration. She later tried to suppress her feelings by joining the Salvation Army, but as her social worker noted, this, too, became a venue for seeking out sexual excitement: 'the spirit for improvement is willing, but the flesh is weak', admitted the young woman herself.[143] Girls who were prosecuted after running away with an older man or boyfriend sometimes claimed they were 'in love' as a means of excusing their behaviour. Others claimed sex secured them affection, linked it to their peer culture, or even declared the court hypocritical for punishing them for something adults did all the time. A few girls defiantly declared sexual promiscuity would punish parents they disliked; when she feels 'rejected by her mother', Jane told the psychiatrist, she 'goes out to have intercourse to hurt her.'[144]

Court and penal workers questioning girls were often looking for singular, rational decisions about sex. Girls, however, were curious, ambivalent, unsure or became caught in a series of events over which they felt they had little power. Sexual activity was a strategy to explore new pleasures, but it could become a means of survival. One young Oshawa teen with a record of disobedience and incorrigibility was sent out on an errand and, to her mother's distress, was not found until three months later in Toronto. She explained that she was hanging around with a gang involved in theft and was threatened by them after she had been indiscreet about their crimes. Claiming she feared this gang, she hitchhiked to Toronto and was kept by a truck driver in his apartment. She claimed to dislike him, but also that she did not try to leave. The judge was horrified with her admission of 'constant' sexual acts with this man; what she exhibited, presuming her rendition of events was true, was just plain confusion.[145]

Such confusion also characterized girls' attitudes to running away, which often precipitated their surveillance by the court. The authorities deemed running away childish and immature, but to some girls it seemed the only way out of a difficult situation. Girls ran when faced with violence in the home or foster home, when forced to live with families they did not like, or because they felt unloved and rejected. Sometimes, they ran away to avoid punishment they knew was coming. Running was also a means of cementing ties with boyfriends or female peer groups; it could combine escape from unhappiness and a desire for adventure. One foster child was confined to the CAS shelter after her mother was sent to jail for 'sexual offences' and she was rejected by a number of foster homes. Returning from one 10-day escape from the shelter, she promptly offered the staff a long list of men she had sexual intercourse with. Yet, her bravado also masked long-standing anger and pain. Claiming her uncle had first sexually abused her, that she had 'no one to love her', and that CAS staff 'picked on her', she probably felt she had little to lose by running; many runaways like her also found that sex could be bartered for shelter when they were on the run.[146]

If girls came from homes where there was little material benefit to staying, running made all the more sense. Girls can't have been completely immune from the romanticized images of neglected orphans seeking their fortune or of the smitten girl eloping. Who is to say the girl who climbed out of her window to meet her boyfriend did not see herself as a wronged Juliet? Children's rationalizations of their running were often disregarded as fabricated stories, yet subsequent events sometimes proved their claims of abuse, rejection, or loneliness had validity. A very few girls also used the opportunity to find jobs, new lives, and relationships. One mature 15-year-old protested vigorously when she was brought back from Saskatchewan, where she had established herself with a steady waitressing job. Even though she was pregnant, she still wanted to live away from her family and support herself and the baby. Given her age, her determination was seen as destructive rather than as positive, especially by the superintendent of the OTSG who thoroughly detested her because 'she thought she was smarter than others.'[147]

Court and penal workers expressed some understanding of girls' desire to run from sexual abuse, though in comparison to current discourses these problems were underemphasized in their explanations for delinquency. About 12 per cent of all the girls examined in OTSG files claimed incest, and others told their psychiatrists of 'ill treatment' by male relatives or referred to 'shocking sex experiences',[148] suggesting the numbers might have been higher. 'Gwen is another one of our many cases of incest',[149] noted the superintendent of an inmate in 1953, and in a magazine interview with June Callwood that year the prevalence of sexual abuse was noted again.[150] Why, then, was abuse downplayed in explanations for delinquency?

As Chapter 2 detailed, the medical and sociological discourses in this era analysed incest as an aberrant, deviant behaviour, uncommon except among the very poor, lower classes. Lingering eugenic preoccupations meant that incest was equated with intercourse, not always the form of sexual abuse girls endured, and a girl's story might be rejected if a medical exam proved her hymen intact. In one such case, the girl repeatedly ran away and was sent to the OTSG for incorrigibility, with the CAS claiming 'she was as much to blame as her father' for tension in the family.[151] Experts were also influenced by the Freudian image of incest as unconscious, possibly a fabricated response of girls to difficult relationships with mothers and fathers. The language in doctors' case notes often implied the girls were complicit, as they 'confessed' to 'bad relations with father',[152] and some social workers separated incest out as one unfortunate incident in the past without considering its long-term effects on the girl or the fact that abuse was rarely a one-time occurrence.[153] One or two girls were incarcerated after incest was discovered, for training schools were seen as a means of removing them from the home, secluding them from the community, and inculcating new moral values. But isolation was understandably experienced as a form of punishment, especially when fathers and brothers went free.

When abused daughters came into conflict with the law, they had often run away from home; they were brought before the courts, sometimes by their own fathers, for being incorrigible. If there was no conviction against the father or stepfather in place, she might also be returned to the home. Overlapping with running was many girls' rejection of the dominant standards of femininity and sexual purity. Girls' resistance to incest became integrated with a 'more general youthful rebellion' that encompassed illicit sexual activity with other boys and men. By rejecting their proper roles as obedient and passive daughters (which had kept many *in* abusive situations), they embraced aggressive, sexually active roles, which also got them into trouble.

This link between abuse and delinquency confounded the courts. In one case before the Ottawa Family Court in the 1950s, the psychiatrist's mental health report on 16-year-old Mary Ann clearly said that she 'traced her problems to five years ago when her father had sexual relations with her.' The father was rejecting, the mother cold, commented the doctor, and 'cases like this one with incest superimposed on rejection have a dim prognosis.' After reading this report, why did the Family Court judge ignore the questions of abuse and violence and ask the girl and her parents only about her drinking and runs from home? Moreover, when a Toronto Family Court doctor examined her later, he suggested her promiscuity was pursued in a 'rather vengeful manner with males' and that institutionalization was probably the only solution for she would 'run away from a therapist'. Apparently, the father never faced charges himself.[154]

In the same way that incest was sometimes discounted, girls claiming they were sexually assaulted were disbelieved if they were already designated promiscuous or their families immoral. Moreover, subsequent sexual activity with the same or different men after a rape immediately discredited the girl's story. Police did sometimes prosecute

older men for carnal knowledge of young girls, but they also abandoned cases in which the girl's story stood in simple opposition to the
man's, especially if his class or race status made him a 'respectable'
character. A young Afro-Canadian woman claimed she was raped by a
group of boys in the club room of a downtown church. She was dismissed as a wild storyteller; after all, said the psychiatrist, 'this is
probably a fabrication [otherwise] the minister [whom she told] would
have investigated.'[155]

Girls might also run away to escape physical and emotional abuse,
although the connections between violence and delinquency were
more complex. It was sometimes difficult for the court to decide
where the line between corporal punishment (still accepted as a
parental right) and violence should be drawn. In postwar Toronto, a
father brought his daughter to court, charging her with incorrigibility;
he claimed she didn't attend school and was going over to a house of
'DPs at night and not coming home'. Yet, it was later admitted there
'was considerable corporal punishment [of her] and drunken quarrels
between parents' at home. When she was paroled later, she, too,
became violent, attacking her mother with a knife.[156] One father
'badly beat his daughter' for staying out all night and disobeying her
probation orders. He was given six months' probation; she was sent
away to training school. Perhaps his rage was excused because she
was disobedient and immoral, and it was thought best to remove her
from his physical reach, but girls were well aware that their isolation
signified a punishment that male relatives escaped.[157]

Violence was most often encountered by girls from a male relative, but mothers were not always blameless, and because women's
violence was harder for social workers to believe, it could be hidden
for some time. Pamela, born out of wedlock when her mother was
very sick, later became the brunt of her mother's frustration and
anger. Her mother sent her to live in the unheated part of the house,
she was told to eat by herself, and she was 'also beaten so badly that
she had a scar on her face'—all of this later admitted by the father.[158]
Emotional abuse was also difficult to substantiate, and a few girls perhaps exaggerated their stories of emotional rejection in the hopes that
this would excuse their delinquent behaviour. Yet, case files unfold as
histories, and court personnel sometimes admit their initial faith in
parents was misplaced. In the late 1950s a probation officer admitted
that a teen, previously disbelieved, had presented an accurate picture
of her mother's dislike for her: 'The mother', previously commended
as a good housekeeper and churchgoer, 'lied to us' about her daughter's behaviour. 'She never accepted her back into the family and only

gave good reports in the hopes of early release, then she was going to make her leave home.'[159]

The cruelty of parents should not be dismissed as one cause of girls' alienation and subsequent criminalization. Worn down by worries, injured by their own experiences of violence, full of despair, some parents used their children as scapegoats for their own anger. What was lacking in the indictment of parents by the experts, however, was any analysis of the structural patterns of inequality and power that encouraged violence and abuse. Finally, it must be acknowledged that children could respond to their parents with derision and cruelty. To argue that criminalization was an ineffectual response to girls' sexual exploits, running away, and petty theft is not to deny that rebellious, rude, and inconsiderate teens did exist. Some simply hated authority, every last ounce of it. 'Is intolerant of everything that curtails her desire to be independent', noted one file very truthfully.[160] Teens could assault other siblings or lash out at parents who, through no fault of their own, could not provide them with the time or material goods they desired. 'Acts as if her mother is dirt beneath her feet', wrote one CAS worker of a girl who claimed to resent both her mother's poverty and her decision to remarry.[161] One can hardly blame parents with such painful problems for seeking the help of professionals.

For both girls on probation and the minority of girls sent to training school, the best strategy to secure release from the court's surveillance was a measure of accommodation, at least on the surface, to the project of character reformation advanced by the juvenile justice system. Girls had to seem to disown the past, acknowledging 'out of control' sexual activity to be dangerous, breaking ties to past friends and sometimes even to families. Sexual fantasies were to be redirected into familial dreams of marriage and motherhood, and aggressive, boisterous, tough, or rude behaviour was to be moderated by a more subdued femininity. Moreover, aimless, undisciplined girls had to be transformed into those appreciating good work habits. In short, a girl's sense of self was to be transformed, creating a new citizen, a new subjectivity, through the acceptance of values mirroring proper femininity, restrained sexuality, and the work ethic. While most court and penal workers optimistically believed that girls could change their behaviour, they saw a few as too morally corrupted and 'pathologically' promiscuous to change. Some penal staff were often more pessimistic and could not refrain from dividing the girls into polar images of 'good' and 'bad'. There are the 'bewildered, confused unhappy girls who want our help', commented a training school superintendent, and then there are 'those only interested in sex, smoking and jiving . . . those [who can't be] helped by mental health professions. . . . Not all delinquents come from broken homes . . . some are just born that way.'[162]

Conclusion

At first glance, Donzelot's claim that modern juvenile justice was increasingly colonized by the rule of the norm, by non-legal experts of the mind, seems an apt way to describe the treatment of girls before the courts. Psychiatric and social work knowledges helped determine what judges saw as the most dangerous behaviour—they offered scientific categories and sociological typologies to diagnose female delinquency, and they advised judges on how to sentence delinquent girls. Circulated and reaffirmed as irrefutable knowledges, these discourses led to more probationary surveillance and to the 'preventative' incarceration of working-class girls to correct their immorality. The influence of experts was also closely connected to the expansion of the state's role in juvenile justice and correction. Over these four decades, the Ontario government assumed more control over juvenile correctional institutions, replacing older philanthropic efforts and often drawing on and integrating medical and social work professionals directly into its policy and administrative efforts.

At the same time, we should not overemphasize the triumph of the experts and their attempts to govern the soul. Although the courts drew on these new knowledges, they also retained some control over how they were used, and it was ultimately the judge, commanding supreme juridical authority, who decided if and how such assessments would be used. Second, within this system, power was also exerted by parents, who, embracing similar images of female sexuality and the family, used the police and the courts in efforts to manage and reform daughters they believed were out of control. Third, there was often a gap between the official discourses on delinquency that stressed 'welfare and treatment' and the actual solutions, including punishment, used on girls. Certainly, once incarcerated, girls were less 'overmedicalized' and psychoanalysed than they were simply ordered about in a strict institutional regime bent on behaviourist control.[163] Finally, the experts' views and the judges' pronouncements did not go completely unchallenged by parents and girls in court. A minority of parents and girls resented and rejected the moral intrusion of state officials into their lives, offering up their own interpretations of girls' conflicts with the law. Parents pointed to their poverty, work problems, or lack of familial support in raising daughters; girls complained of the abuse inflicted upon them, their alienation, and frustrations with school and families.

Exploring the dominant discourses about female delinquency does have the great benefit of stressing the social construction of criminality. The medical and sociological models describing and explaining delinquency were simultaneously moral constructions, reflecting and reproducing ideologies of sex difference and class inequality. Girls were criminalized for sexual offences that boys and adults were not, and they were dealt with quite severely because of fears of their moral contagion. Girls were pressed into the task of creating sexual purity, maintaining the family, indeed, even helping to contain male heterosexuality within marriage. In one sense, girls were profoundly sexualized within the juvenile justice system. While an emphasis on sexualization should not stand alone, neither should this feminist insight be totally abandoned.

At the same time, we should not be misled by the official discourses dominating the historical record. Because the records we draw on—particularly those of the experts—so strongly emphasize themes of sexual regulation, we are apt to forget that delinquency also encompassed crimes against property and that sexual regulation cannot be separated from the material and social context of girls' lives. The socialized justice meted out by the courts was, after all, differentially experienced according to class and race. Court and penal workers defined a good family with moral meanings attached to wage work, sociability, and sexuality: churchgoing was preferred over beverage rooms, respectable jobs over relief, monogamous marriages over common-law adultery. Both poor and racialized groups were seen as more likely to be promiscuous, undisciplined, or immoral, and thus less promising probation risks. The overwhelmingly working-class and poor population who ended up at training school indicates how class overdetermined the outcome of girls' conflicts with the law. Similarly, escalating numbers of Native girls sent to the OTSG by the 1950s underlines how racism and colonialism overdetermined their conflicts with the juvenile justice system.

When one examines the difficult conditions of delinquent girls' lives it might make sense to ask why they *would* conform. The reality of profound alienation, conditioned by factors such as transience, poverty, underemployment, ill health, foster care, anger and violence, is striking. Girls before the courts had often seen the dark side of family life or had rebelled against familial controls, yet they were offered the unrealistic ideal of family reconstitution or reconciliation as a solution to their problems. One delinquent girl, noted a penal worker, talked incessantly about her remaining relative, a grandmother, not because the grandmother had cared for her well, but just because she was desperate to have a family.

There is no doubt that abuse, violence, and neglect within the family led girls to the street and to trouble with the law. However, we need to understand the family not simply as a contained psychiatric problem but in terms of the power relations it embodied and how these relations blended with the 'social space'—the laws, institutions, and strategies of governance—making up the juvenile justice system. A materialist and feminist understanding of the anti-social family, buttressed by insights concerning normalization effected by expert knowledges, offers a different picture. The family acted simultaneously as the shock absorber for the oppressive social relations created by capitalist economies, colonialism, and masculinist ideologies; it was a 'grid' of power relations, based on age and sex. Expert knowledges that explained the out-of-control delinquent girl evolved as strategies to regulate adolescent conduct, but their power derived from their fundamental harmony with the underlying structures of material inequality and social and cultural alienation shaping the lives of girl offenders.

6

Native Women, Sexuality, and the Law

In the early 1930s a young Ojibwa woman, Emma, living on a north-western Ontario reserve was sentenced to two years in the provincial reformatory for vagrancy. All the evidence against her centred on her supposed sexual promiscuity—including graphic evidence of her most recent sexual liaison—and the fact she had two illegitimate children. Although the Indian agent and RCMP appeared at the trial, the complaint appeared to have been made by her relatives and other community members. A petition was presented by the Indian agent, with the signatures of her cousins, aunts, uncles, grandfather, and others, asking that 'in the interests of the morality on the Reserve and the accused, she should be sent to a Reformatory.' Later, when parole was discussed, the agent claimed that opinion was not favourable among her family because of her 'reputation' and he suggested that Emma be released into another community.[1]

In one sense, Emma's fate was not unusual: in mid-twentieth-century Canada, and especially after World War II, the numbers of First Nations women incarcerated in local and provincial correctional institutions increased steadily. While women like Emma were supposedly incarcerated for sexual offences, the most fundamental reasons for their conflicts with the law and subsequent imprisonment were material and social deprivation, cultural alienation, and systemic racism, combined with escalating social stresses on reserves and the increasing urbanization of Native peoples.[2] At first glance, Emma's apprehension at the insistence of her community also suggests that some First Nations were willing to use the powers of the Indian agent and Euro-Canadian law, even to criminalize their own members, implying some 'acquiescence' to the process of colonization.[3]

Although this is far too simplistic a characterization, this case does indicate the importance of probing the complex ways that Native women's sexuality was regulated, both through received Euro-Canadian law and also through its partial absorption into the social practices of First Nations peoples.

This chapter explores attempts to discipline the sexuality of Native women, examining the means and rationale for legal and moral governance, the interplay of customary Native law and Canadian law, and the resistance and responses of Native women, families, and communities to the imposition of new standards of conduct. The sexual regulation of Native and non-Native women alike was part of a broader project of nation-building: the creation of moral families, based on Western (largely Anglo) middle-class notions of sexual purity, marital monogamy, and distinct gender roles of the female homemaker and male breadwinner was an important means of creating moral and responsible citizens, the 'bedrock of the nation', as legal authorities never tired of saying.[4]

Yet, historically, the rights and representation of citizenship have also been linked to race, and nowhere is this more salient than in the operation of the law. As legal scholars have demonstrated, Canadian law played a significant role in constituting and reproducing racist ideology and sanctioning discrimination, exclusion, and segregation in public policy, statute law, and judicial interpretation. In the early twentieth century, for instance, Asian women did not qualify as potential citizens, while Afro-Canadian women encountered second-class citizenship through the process of educational and social segregation.[5] Race was socially constructed through the law, with a racial hierarchy of white superiority clothed in rationales of necessity, progress, and even science sustained both by subtle ideological consent and by repressive coercion.[6] Race was also an integral ingredient of colonial relations articulated through the apartheid and paternalism of the Indian Act, which equated citizenship with disavowal of Aboriginal life and assimilation to the 'white' nation.

As we have seen, the sexual regulation of Native women sometimes intersected with that of poor and working-class non-Native women.[7] Both were drawn into the orbit of the Female Refuges Act, for instance, when they were presumed to overstep the boundaries of promiscuity, illegitimacy, or venereal disease. By the 1950s, more Native girls were also subject to the moral and sexual surveillance of the Juvenile Delinquents Act and Training School Act, though this, ironically, emerged from concerted attempts by bureaucrats and social workers to offer Native girls *equal* social citizenship—that is, equal rehabilitation akin to poor and working-class girls.[8] The complex process of reforming the underclass and the colonized thus sometimes overlapped, claiming common goals—such as the inculcation of sexual purity and domesticity—and purporting a common familial model of citizenship.[9]

While recognizing intersection and overlap, we also have to acknowledge significant differences based on race and colonialism. Those differences are highlighted in this chapter, with particular emphasis on those women subject to the Indian Act. Attempts to remake First Nations sexual codes in a Euro-Canadian mould had long predated the twentieth century, but they assumed new legal and political dimensions over time. They were sometimes direct and coercive; they were also subtle, indirect, and ideological in nature, seeking to reshape the consciousness, conscience, and subjectivity of Native peoples. As the 'cutting edge of colonialism',[10] the law was one crucial site of sexual regulation. While recognizing the many semi-autonomous spheres of formal and informal regulation—such as the overlapping assimilative projects of the missions and schools—the power associated with the Criminal Code and the Indian Act cannot be ignored.

Certainly, the 'normalizing power' of the law was never absolute, for the 'disciplinary project'[11] of colonialism was fraught with ambiguity, as indigenous peoples ignored, inverted, or attempted to manoeuvre within new, imposed forms of legal governance. Lingering systems of 'illegalities'—that is, non-observance, resistance, rejections of Canadian law, and alternative means of conflict resolution—existed in the cultures of Native peoples, but the power of new 'legalities'[12] imposed by the state and its apparatus was, by the twentieth century, more difficult to evade. After more than a century of physical encroachment and cultural belittling, Native peoples could be drawn into acceptance of some aspects of Euro-Canadian law. By erecting the boundaries of debate and shaping the definitions of crime and immorality, Euro-Canadian practices of justice gained some ground and were constructed upon existing social practices and forms of authority in Native cultures.

This complex process was experienced differently by Aboriginal women and men. For example, both Native women and men were subjects of an ongoing Euro-Canadian project to transform the Aboriginal family, an enterprise that implicitly challenged existing gender and sexual relations, portraying Native conventions as less civilized than white/Anglo ones. However, Native women were also perceived through a Euro-Canadian lens as 'wild women' symbolizing sexual excess, temptation, and conquest,[13] and thus they became the particular focus of white, masculine concerns about sexual control. Attempts to encourage conformity to a middle-class Euro-Canadian ideal, to restructure the moral conscience of Aboriginal women, were thus shaped by the race and class relations of colonialism and simultaneously by related patriarchal images of sexual purity.

Colonialism, Customary Law, and Canadian Law

In twentieth-century Ontario, colonialism—that is, 'geographical incursion, external political control, social dislocation and the ideological denigration based on race'[14]—remained the defining characteristic of Native/non-Native relations. While colonialism has many faces, its dynamic often includes attempts to redefine the sexual codes and family relations of indigenous populations. Since the pathbreaking writing of Franz Fanon, modern writers have wrestled with the oppressive yet contradictory sexual dynamics of colonial relations, exploring colonizers' attempts to alter kin and productive relations through sexual control, and also the more controversial cultural, psychological internalized anxieties and fantasies shaping sexual practices and desire in colonial encounters.[15]

Some of this research has granted an important place to ideology and hegemony as theoretical guideposts in discussions of the law. Jean and John Comaroff, for example, warn that colonialism is not a completely 'contingent text' but rather an 'economic, social and cultural' revolution, the inevitable handmaiden of 'industrial capitalism and imperialism'.[16] They nonetheless devote serious attention to cultural conflict, including colonialist attempts to reshape indigenous religion, families, and sexuality. This tradition of inquiry, strongly represented in anthropology, urges us to locate the 'actor perspective'[17] of the colonized and sees contests over familial and sexual relations closely intertwined with the political economy of colonialism. Drawing on Gramsci, the Comaroffs argue that culture provides a space within which both domination and resistance occur. The hegemonic ideas of the dominating, colonizing group often have the power to homogenize, rationalize, and silence sexual and domestic alternatives as 'unthinkable',[18] though certainly the possibility of resistance allows for the remaking of ideology over time.

In more recent, Foucauldian-inspired, explorations of colonialism, sex plays a more prominent, if not dominating role. Drawing on Foucault, though challenging his Eurocentrism, Ann Stoler argues that Foucault's European 'bourgeois sexual order' was constructed first in colonial contexts and that the racialization of sex central to colonial endeavours was imported back to Europe, redrawing European discourses on sexuality—a theme promoted also in Ann McClintock's culturalist interpretation of colonialism.[19] Stoler's exploration of Foucault, sex, and colonialism argues convincingly for new attention to the centrality of race to modern 'biopower', including attempts to manage certain populations deemed sexually 'deviant'.[20] Indeed, eugenic fears pinpointed by Foucault in his discussion of sexual regulation were inextricably connected to fears of intermixed, interracial colonial 'blood'. Stoler also highlights the way in which colonialism came to represent a contested cultural terrain of sexual order/disorder, which was reflected in the power struggles between the colonizers and the colonized and sometimes within those groups as well.

Such reinterpretations of Foucault, in which race is integrated with his explorations of the discursive construction of sexuality and the creation of sexual subjectivities through power relations, have offered new angles of interpretation for sexual regulation and colonialism. Many, however, rest on historical evidence drawn from white-minority colonial possessions (unlike the Canadian example), and we should be wary of the theoretical homogenization of all colonial societies over time. In addition, despite claims that sexual discourses and political economy are both addressed,[21] as is resistance, some of this scholarship remains ensnared within the cultural meanings of colonialism and the construction of the 'bourgeois' sexual self, 'ignoring the human agency [especially that of the colonized] within the structural processes' of colonialism.[22]

Related theoretical issues characterize debates concerning customary law.[23] The sexual regulation of Native women must be contextualized not only with attention to the broad picture of race and colonialism, but also with regard for the more precise, evolving relationship between Native custom, customary Native law, and Euro-Canadian law in Canadian history. Over the past two decades, Native peoples have embarked on the retrieval of customary practices of law and justice, sometimes encouraged by federal and provincial governments, that were prodded both by First Nations' demands for self-government and by an awareness that the criminal justice system has resolutely failed Aboriginal peoples, as victims and as defendants.[24] These efforts have encountered difficult questions: how does one historicize customary law, exploring its evolution over time, its relationship to power, domination, and resistance, its changing ideological purposes? How can one avoid 'freeze-framing' culture, extracting it from its material and historical moorings, and also avert its reinscription in new forms that disadvantage less powerful members of the Native community?

How can we discover, to begin with, how the sexual codes of conduct/misconduct in First Nations cultures changed over time, especially when Aboriginal cultures varied across Canada, when many of the sources used to uncover past practices, including accounts by colonizers and anthropologists, are partial and invested with ideology, if not themselves entangled in colonialism. Oral tradition and testimony, often reflecting the fluid, social, pedagogical nature of Aboriginal law, may be used, but they are far more likely to be denigrated by Canadian courts, with their Eurocentric bias as to what is considered a valid historical source.[25]

Moreover, looking to Euro-Canadian courts to decide customary law has its own ironies and dangers, especially for women, as these courts have sometimes interpreted First Nations customs through the lens of patriarchal ideology and racial bias, for example, excusing violence against Native women as 'more natural' in Aboriginal cultures.[26] As Jo-Anne Fiske argues, having Canadian courts 'fix' a definition of Aboriginal customary law, especially if women are marginalized in this debate, may work against the interests of Native women.[27] Other national histories carry many warnings of the sexist and patriarchal misuse of customary law against indigenous women by European/white courts.[28] For Native peoples, in other words, customary law is currently an important 'political resource',[29] an integral part of identity creation that has potential for decolonization, but also for divisiveness.

The dominant theme in many current accounts of Aboriginal customary law is the cultural dissonance between European and Aboriginal concepts of social order and dispute resolution.[30] Aboriginal law is described as process-oriented, rather than concentrating on rules and rights; the means of social control in Native cultures apparently included shaming or ostracism, at worst banishment, though mediation, reconciliation, and payment of compensation were also used to restore peace after a transgression of the social order. The important goal was community harmony, not punishment of the offender. Individual autonomy was protected, as well as community peace, with the established order a fine balance between the two. The teaching and control of elders were crucial to social order, and those lessons were gender-specific, as women's and men's roles were distinct, though a symmetry of equality is also implied. Indeed, some recent accounts, stressing the 'matriarchal' nature of some Native cultures, in which 'women were considered and treated as equal, respected, revered as lifegivers',[31] suggest the ideological influence of a highly politicized 'maternalist' discourse within the contemporary Native women's movement.[32]

While the evidence showing some cultural divergence between Aboriginal and Euro-Canadian justice is indisputable, such accounts also risk reifying law in the realm of culture. Historical eras and changing social circumstances are conflated and tradition is presented as unmediated, creating a static, essentialized, and homogenized description of Aboriginal law. More historicized explorations of First Nations conflicts with Euro-Canadian law suggest that cultural dissonance was not the overriding theme in all periods or for all crimes.[33] Indeed, Native cultural survival went hand in hand with changing legal practices and political ideologies. Historians of colonial law in other countries have long argued that customary law is a *process*, in which custom is altered by indigenous/European colonial contact, by ongoing material and social crises, and by changing productive and kin relations. Most importantly, it is shaped by the relations of power and hegemony endemic to colonialism, including contests for power within indigenous groups.[34]

Establishing what constitutes 'tradition' is inherently ideological: this expert knowledge creates new hegemonic interpretations of society that can be used or abused by those exercising power. Any new 'inventions of tradition', argue some committed to Aboriginal forms of justice, must be carefully scrutinized for their impact on existing gender or age power imbalances. The counsel of Patricia Monture-Angus, that Aboriginal justice is best seen as a 'process not a concept', is well taken.[35] If we see customary law as historically constructed, framed by colonialism, shaped by material, social practices, a fluid cultural product embodying both domination and resistance, we can better understand Native women's encounters with Euro-Canadian laws governing sexual morality in the twentieth century and their attempts to accept, resist, or negotiate with them.

Managing Sex through Regulation of the Family

Attempts to regulate sexual and kin relations in order to assimilate, convert, or subjugate First Nations peoples have been noted in Canadian research on early contact and the fur trade, in discussions of Christianization and residential schools, and in explorations of state and mission attempts to reorder the domestic sphere of women on reserves.[36] As Karen Anderson has argued, this involved both direct coercion and the indirect 'colonization of the soul', with the colonized literally coming to discipline themselves.[37] Feminist writers have often gravitated towards the early history of egalitarian Native societies, exploring the decline in women's status and the assault on women's sexual autonomy occasioned by colonialism, although recent research suggests the story is more varied and more complicated than a simple linear decline over time.[38] Nowhere is the example of reordering of kin relations more blatant than in the Indian Act, designed to create a patriarchal family unit in First Nations societies that already had a variety of kinship systems, including many matrilineal and matrilocal ones.[39]

The use of the law to regulate Native sexuality was achieved on more than one front: it was facilitated by the broad powers of the Indian Act, the reserve system, and the assimilation promoted by missions, schools, and the state. Sexual regulation must also be seen in the light of the increasing social and material marginalization of the interwar and post-World War II period. White settlement was encroaching further and further north in the province, causing the flight of some Native peoples to urban centres, though the majority of Native peoples remained on reserves.[40] Traditional means of subsistence were undermined, particularly with a decline in fur prices in the postwar era, and as a result social supports in Native communities were under stress. The reserve system eroded people's wage-earning possibilities and created a new reliance on treaty payments; it also unsettled the social organization of some Native peoples unaccustomed to such close, sedentary living.

The effect of Christianization was also a factor shaping Native culture. Despite the initial resistance of many communities to conversion, by the early twentieth century Christian imperialism had made deep inroads into Native societies.[41] Both Catholic and Protestant missionaries stressed the evils of premarital and extramarital sex and the damnation of those who abandoned monogamy and marriage, proclaiming this message from the pulpit and in the classroom. Residential schools also tried to inculcate sexual morals, stressing virginity before marriage, sexual purity, domesticity, and motherhood for girls.

Church and state efforts were directed by a deep-seated paternalism and a racist conviction that acculturation to Euro-Canadian values would benefit Native peoples. Similar premises shaped the Indian Act, though the precise contours of state assimilation changed over time, and as early as the 1920s assimilation was seen as almost infeasible by some bureaucrats. Admittedly, the Indian Act was contradictory, offering assimilation through segregation, advancing cultural denigration, but also creating a focus for Indian identity; it was also variously applied, ignored, or modified in different regions and by local Indian agents. As a study of two Ontario agencies also shows, Aboriginal peoples tried to subvert or manoeuvre around parts of the Act they found unacceptable.[42] However, its assimilative intent and its *potential power* to control Native peoples' lives cannot be denied. For example, Indian agents could act as justices of the peace or magistrates, prosecuting, trying, and convicting reserve inhabitants for infractions of the Act and the Criminal Code, a concentration of power quite unparalleled in Canadian law.

The agent's duty to monitor and record marriages and legitimate births was also mandated by the Indian Act (and was necessary to secure official Indian status). Federal Indian policy over the years also gave him a more general goal: to encourage Native families to assimilate to the image of the middle-class Anglo/white family. Marriage, adultery, sexual activity, and illegitimacy were all linked in the view of Indian Affairs; the surveillance of 'proper' marriages should theoretically police illegitimate births and also control the problem of adultery and sexual immorality. Both parsimonious motives and Christian moralism shaped the department's policies regulating the family. While the federal government clearly wished to limit those 'legitimate' status Indians eligible for treaty support, sexual control was also central to their overall policy of cultural assimilation, for monogamous, lifelong unions were seen as signs of sexual order/civilization, while deviations from this model were a sign that Native peoples remained attached to sexual disorder/primitive endurance.

The regulation of marriage was the first line of defence for the federal Department of Indian Affairs in its quest for sexual order. From the late nineteenth century on, Indian Affairs bureaucrats had to be continually reminded by the Department of Justice of the *Connolly v. Woolwich* case, which had accepted Native customary marriage as valid in 1867. While contemporary legal writers have cited this case as evidence of respect for customary law, the story is more complex. Customary unions were accepted because they were deemed similar to (the superior form of) Christian marriages, not out of respect for Native practice; the measuring stick of exclusive sexual coupling, monogamy, and a lifelong union led to court approval. As Department of Justice officials reminded Indian Affairs, customary unions were *only* legal 'where they were voluntary unions for life to the exclusion of all others, where there is cohabitation and normal marital duties.'[43] Euro-Canadian values remained dominant, setting out the boundaries of which sexual relations were 'normal' and 'legal'.

Also, there was an underlying ambivalence expressed by the Indian Affairs bureaucracy with this legal decision, and as a result there was debate over which forms of marriage should take precedence. Policy on Indian marriage was laid out in circulars by 1899 and was revisited regularly after the 1920s, particularly when World War II sparked debates about which Native soldiers' dependants were legitimate and could receive dependants' benefits.[44] However, the responses of agents to policy directives indicate that some viewed customary marriage suspiciously, as less genuine in commitment than Christian marriage. Agents, for example, worried that customary marriage would lead to 'barter in women' and 'desertion'.[45] Officials in Ottawa also thought more stringent legislation was needed so that 'there could not be any loopholes for avoiding mutual marital obligations . . . marriages must be mutual and exclusive unions.'[46] Jail and hard labour for six months was the solution proposed by one Indian agent for husbands who deserted. Such harsh treatment was presumably to correct people less socialized to Euro-Canadian ways. If they leave any marriage, said the Kenora agent in the 1920s, 'the parties should be punished, to teach the rest of the band they cannot act in this manner without being punished.'[47]

In one policy circular, Indian Affairs urged its agents to prevent all separations: 'every effort should be made to put an end to this evil. Agents must impress on Indians a proper view of marriage relations and damage done to individuals and the community [with the] prevalence of immorality. There should be punishment of those guilty of offences. Indians guilty [of leaving their marriages] should be punished and the injured parties receive compensation.'[48] Treaty payments, rations, or relief might be cut off if 'a woman . . . leaves her marriage . . . without any justification'. If the wife was deemed upright and the husband errant, she might be rewarded; the agent could (and some did) transfer the treaty payment of the adulterous husband to his wife.

The suspicion expressed by the department and its agents that Natives treated marriage too cavalierly did not disappear easily. Indeed, waves of panic came and went over this entire period. 'Promiscuous and irregular cohabitation is increasing', wrote one agent in 1944; marriage is seen as 'trivial', just 'loose cohabitation'.[49] The basic reason for such attitudes, according to a western agent during World War II, was that 'Indians, [though they were] like the Irish in the way they make a living . . . lacked moral fibre and religious conviction the white races had developed. Perhaps we expect too much of them', he concluded, characterizing their customary marriages as 'not spiritual unions'.[50]

Some agents sought informal ways, including lectures, to preach the superiority of Euro-Canadian (i.e., Christian) forms of marriage; it was presumed Christian unions were taken more seriously, and thus adultery and desertion would be less likely. 'I have stressed since taking over the importance of legal marriage with the Indians; I have stressed the attitude of the Department. I hope they will gradually cooperate and protect their rights with legal marriages', noted a northern Ontario agent in the 1940s.[51] Agents also felt they knew best when a 'proper' customary marriage had occurred; again, their evaluations were shaped less by intimate knowledge of Native cultures than by Euro-Canadian standards. In a case indicating how the spheres of legal and non-legal regulation often overlapped, a residential school principal wrote to the agent, claiming a young man was sleeping with a student and they were 'living immorally'. The young man was 'tried by the Agent' but it appeared that the usual marriage customs—speaking to her parents, coming to an agreement with them—had been followed. Although he could not pursue the case, the agent, concerned about the girl's age, could not resist moralizing: 'I felt I must dismiss the case but I lectured him about not marrying an Indian girl until she had finished school.'[52] Priests and ministers might also try to enlist the aid of an agent to encourage church marriages and the Christian baptism of children. Failing this, they could apply their own pressure—for example, refusing to grant sacraments to a dying man until he renounced his second wife and illegitimate children![53]

Punishment could be even more draconian than financial penalties: if unmarried partners lived together, charges of immorality were brought forward under the Indian Act and jail terms could result. This was especially true in the interwar period. In northern Ontario, 'Mary P, a treaty Lac Seul', was brought before Agent Edwards and admitted to 'living as a wife, when she is not married'. Because she was ill, she did not serve her jail sentence but her male partner did get one month in jail—a strong reminder that such discipline could be levied against men as well.[54] Another woman in the same agency also tried the route of pleading guilty 'to living with John S' to her RCMP inquisitors, but mercy was not the result. She was remanded and 'taken into Kenora' with her '2½ year old child, not yet weaned', presumably to serve her sentence.[55]

Agents might also use their power to define who had the right to live on the reserve in order to break up illicit relationships. If one partner was not a status member of the band, he or she could be banished from the reserve. In one report of 1943, an agent who was 'asked to come and settle troubles' by the chief of one reserve mediated complicated charges of adultery and counter-adultery. When Nancy, an orphan from another reserve, finally admitted to her affair with a married man, the agent told her to 'stop the lies' or they would 'throw her off the reserve'.[56]

By the 1940s there is less evidence of jail terms for common-law relations—though some jail sentences were meted out for immorality. The department, noted Kenora Agent Edwards, finally rescinded its earlier advice; regulations advocating the 'prosecuting of immorality', he noted, 'had sent some to jail, then they were cancelled because we found we did not have the right to imprison treaty Indians for things [living common law] that others [whites] could legally do.'[57] As with other Indian Affairs policies, implementation of directives on marriage was uneven. Some agents decried and others defended customary marriage, though even those who defended the practice only did so if the relationships were lifelong. Edwards, a northern agent in the field for many years, eventually tried to tell Ottawa that 'immorality . . . resulted from discouragement of customary marriage', and he urged Ottawa to pass legislation giving 'Agents the power to marry people' (as in some Western provinces) because it was both financially and logistically impossible for Natives to go into urban centres, wait the three days required for licences, or find ministers to marry them.

Other agents were upset with the churches for complicating the issue by refusing to recognize customary marriage. One agent was furious with a Roman Catholic priest who married a man to a second wife, even though he had already been in a customary union for almost 20 years. The agent was concerned that the first wife and child would not receive financial support, but he was also irate that the Catholic Church was promoting the message that customary marriages could be easily dissolved. The wife was far more practical and less moralistic, indicating that the man should do as he wished, as long as she and their child were 'provided for'.[58]

Despite these variances, however, an underlying thread was apparent. Customary marriages were applauded if they looked exactly like Christian ones, if they were lifelong and monogamous, if husbands undertook their roles as providers, wives their roles as domestic caregivers. In the eyes of most agents, customary marriages might positively act as 'bulwarks against the raw passions and promiscuity'[59] of the Natives. Christian and 'legal' marriages were still better because they represented a more thorough internalization of prohibitions against extramarital sex and serial partners. Similar attitudes concerning common-law marriages characterized the moral regulation directed at non-Native poor and working-class women as well. Common-law unions were feared to be less binding and serious, and in the 1930s the Canadian Welfare Council (CWC) pressured the state to ensure legal mechanisms so that children could be removed from households tainted by adulterous 'immorality'. While the goal of encouraging sexually respectable families may have overlapped, the means of enforcement were distinct: the Indian Act offered the state and its agents more arbitrary, paternalist means of enforcing morality (whether they were successful or not), at least on reserves. On the other hand, the CWC never secured the prohibitions against adulterous and 'immoral' parents that it sought, in part because the judiciary was unsympathetic to such sweeping powers.[60]

Finally, it is revealing that only half of Native custom was embraced; divorces, which had also been part of many Native cultures, were forbidden. This created enormous problems for those wanting to sever customary marriages, since they had no option of doing so as tradition had allowed, and if they did create a new union they could be charged with bigamy. Of the Native women sent to the Mercer Reformatory on bigamy charges during these years, one may well have been punished for such actions.[61] Ottawa was unequivocal when responding to one agent, who asked what to do when a woman left a 'husband who abused her', escaped to a large city, and married another man. 'Use the provincial authorities and the Criminal Code', the Department of Indian Affairs replied. 'Indian marriages are legal and binding and the guilty party should be punished.'[62]

Many Native women and men, especially in more remote areas, continued to practise and defend customary marriages, defining them as the courts originally did, as lifelong exclusive unions. They expressed regret and dismay if others abandoned the commitment made to these marriages. In one instance, a mother wanted the agent to intervene to help her daughter, who had been 'promised' in such a union, was pregnant, and had just found out that the father refused to marry her and was with another woman. 'Please help me with the law', she pleaded.[63] In other situations, band councillors tried to impress on young people the importance of marriage, customary or Christian, and prohibitions against sex before marriage. One band sent a resolution to Ottawa, via their agent, asking for the power to enact the following rule on the reserve: 'young people are not to run after each other unless they want to marry.'[64]

In one long exchange over the marriage question, a slightly different view came from the Six Nations Reserve during World War II. Longhouse men, reported the agent, were 'incensed' when it was implied that their customary marriages were 'common-law' marriages. They took this as a great insult, presumably because the term 'common law' impugned their customary marriages as examples of immorality. The exchange would seem to suggest, at some level, internalization of the view that such common-law unions were immoral.[65]

The primary challenge from reserve inhabitants to the imposition of Euro-Canadian laws centred on the notion that marriage must be lifelong. Some used a variety of forms of marriage to move from one partner to the next, a practice facilitated by the hierarchy of marriages (some being perceived as more 'legal' than others) set out by the church and some agents. For example, they married in a church or civil ceremony the second time, claiming the first marriage was customary and did not count, using the Euro-Canadian denigration of customary unions as a rationale, almost as a form of informal divorce. They also reversed the strategy, going from church to customary marriage, in both cases, always infuriating the agent by subverting the law with its own murkiness. Their actions indicated the continuing non-observance of the Euro-Canadian ideal and ongoing 'illegalities' within Native cultures, as well as the desire within Native cultures to shape their own practices with regard to sexual and domestic relationships.

Sexual Immorality

If couples were able to support themselves and their children, leaving no one destitute, serial monogamy might be reluctantly accepted. The agents' disciplinary ire, however, was often focused on a more 'extreme' problem: promiscuity. Indeed, the fact that the Indian Affairs filing system designated a whole category for 'Immorality on the Reserves', with almost all the complaints centring on sexual misbehaviour, indicates the importance of the agent's role as custodian of sexual morality. And the resulting persecutions and prosecutions reveal, most strikingly, the contradictory nature of sexual regulation on Native reserves.

Some of the cases of immorality that the agent pursued were classified as adultery; clearly, the policing of marriage and the prevention of promiscuity (or 'profligacy', the word used in the Indian Act) were closely intertwined goals for the agent and for some prosecuting magistrates. The agent might act on his own accord or in concert with others on the reserve. Agents, of course, sometimes claimed to be paternal protectors of Indian women, especially young women, against 'lewd' white men or Indians ready to 'exploit' them.[66] In one such case in the 1950s, an agent wrote to a white railwayman in northern Ontario: 'It is [*sic*] been brought to my attention that you are spending a good deal of time with Mrs. X, before the death of her husband after. Your time is obviously spent drinking and carrying on. . . . If brought to my attention again, I will ask the OPP to investigate with a view to arranging a charge against you and Mrs. X.'[67]

While the Indian agent might initiate legal proceedings against immorality, he might also be prodded to act by the band council or chief when they suspected crimes such as incest and sexual assault or, more often, when they objected to sexual immorality. The witnesses against one woman accused of 'profligacy' under section 101 of the Indian Act in 1933 were the chief and four councillors from her reserve. The RCMP and agent simply concurred that she 'had been carrying on in an immoral manner' so she received one month in the Kenora jail.[68] The case of Emma, which opened this chapter, was also typical. Band councillors and reserve residents took up petitions, went to the agent or other authority figures such as the school principal with their complaints, and demanded action. As Robin Brownlie concludes succinctly about two Ojibwa Georgian Bay reserves in the interwar period, 'a woman charged with immorality had more to fear from neighbours and clerics than [from] the Indian Agent.'[69]

In another instance, a band councillor complained to a bureaucrat in Ottawa that the agent was ineffectual when it came to policing sexual immorality. He pointed out that the agent should have used treaty time (the once-a-year treaty payments) and other economic sanctions to punish these people. His letter is worth quoting at length as it sets out the complicated nature of these complaints, which reveal dissension within the community:

I have just got back from X Reserve and found out that Joe A, widow Mary (Simon's wife) are going together although they have been told many times not to. Councillor Stephen found them sleeping together. Also that Will L has run away with Jane, wife of Pierre. Here, at M, Charly P, single, lives with the wife of WK. I have told the Indian Agent and nothing is done. If the first [couple] were punished we would not have the subsequent 3 couples living this way. I am a councillor and have all the Indians with me who revoke these misconducts. . . . Please keep order among the Indians for if this continues there will be murdering done by these husbands who are losing their legitimate wives. The Indians are disgusted with these 3 couples. The Indian Agent just tells them to be good and they only laugh and say they don't care. I tried to part

Charly P and WK's wife but Charly took a big flashlight and threw it at my eye.[70]

The agent was called on the carpet by Ottawa and, indignant at the charge that he was ignoring immorality, suggested that the government make customary marriages easier and more binding.

Similar attempts by band councillors to maintain marital fidelity are described in some band council minute books. A Georgian Bay council had a Mrs K 'charged with insulting [the] Chief with bad language when advised by him to return to her husband.'[71] Oral histories completed in the 1970s of Northern Ojibwa also recorded efforts to keep marriages monogamous and intact. 'The Chief and Council and the Agent tried to make people stick to their marriages', remembered one woman, illustrating with her own experience: 'One day I had a quarrel with my husband and I ran away from him. The chief and all three of his councillors . . . talked to me and told me to go home again. . . . But if people really couldn't get along, the man or woman would just leave the house and not come back.' Some older people look back nostalgically on these early systems of control, contrasting them to the youth of today: 'the young people of today just shack up with anybody, much younger than before . . . it was kind of a crime to have a baby without a definite father.'[72]

Councils and chiefs, of course, were not autonomous from the agent's authority; they were often kept in a state of tutelage or were chosen for their acquiescent posture to the government. Their participation in sexual and marital regulation must be seen in this light. In some cases it was also the result of their ties to Christian missions. But individuals often called on the agent to intervene as well, to bring home relatives who had abandoned marriages and gone astray, to correct immoral behaviour of daughters and wives. 'I need help from you', wrote one grandmother to an agent, 'about my daughter, X, I don't like what I hear. My sister-in-law was in to visit me a while ago. It is awful what my daughter is doing. When a car goes through the reserve, she just jumps in and leaves her boys alone. . . . I don't want her to fool around and go to town . . . please give her a good talking to.'[73] Another mother told the agent that she would accept her daughter's committal to a Toronto training school 'until she is of an age when she is able to work. . . . I'd like her to be there for her own good, and before she gets deeper into trouble.'[74]

Some band councils also took a dim view of women's illegitimate offspring, passing resolutions that 'no illegitimate children be adopted into the band'.[75] And the department periodically reminded agents never to register any illegitimate children, in part (like the bands) for financial reasons, but also because Indian Affairs claimed this would 'place a premium on immorality'.[76] Again, financial penalties were one way of chastising such mothers and warning others. After Mother's Allowances were made available to Ontario Native women, the monthly allotment was administered through the agent, who substituted as the province's moral investigator, cutting off the allowance if a woman had an illegitimate child.

Whatever band councils said, some families still welcomed and cared for illegitimate children and even tried to secure their status. Occasionally, too, chiefs and even agents 'intervened to plead for'[77] women with illegitimate children, asking that they be returned to the reserve and aided by the community. However, strains of negative moralism existed and, indeed, increased over time. Those families and communities who expressed reservations about taking in illegitimate children may have been influenced by the churches' moral lectures, but the reality of increasingly scarce resources on reserves was probably also crucial.[78] By the 1950s, Indian Affairs faced a new problem with illegitimacy: how to respond to Native women who now refused to have illegitimate children registered with the band because they were 'ashamed' of them. A social worker tried to get a stubborn Indian Affairs bureaucracy to change the policy, allowing women choice on this question. She noted that a Native woman she was advocating for 'was ashamed of her pregnancy . . . and fears condemnation if her parents and community know [and] this is not an isolated case.'[79]

The Long Arm of Racism

Charges of immorality levelled against women on reserves might also lead to an appearance before a magistrate and a jail or reformatory sentence. In the early 1940s a young Native woman from southern Ontario was brought before the court by the Indian agent and local RCMP for drinking and 'dissolute' sexual behaviour and was subsequently sentenced under the Female Refuges Act to a term in the Mercer Reformatory. Though she listed her occupation as a 'domestic' who was looking after her father, the RCMP officer testified that 'she is transient, has no work', and had been convicted on many alcohol charges, including 'brawling with white men'. While incarceration might be couched in paternalist rhetoric, the image of these women was undoubtedly racist. 'Have you been in the habit of getting drunk, have you? have you?' intoned the magistrate. 'I hope that by removing you, my girl, from unscrupulous white men and Indian soldiers you will start a new life. It is too bad that such a good looking Indian like you should throw yourself away', he concluded condescendingly.[80]

As Chapter 4 indicated, the number of Native women incarcerated under the FRA increased in the 1940s and 1950s, and Indian agents could play a central role in the sentencing process. One 23-year-old woman living on a reserve was first incarcerated under the vagrancy statute, though the court was told she had also been charged with intoxication and 'was acting as a prostitute' near the reserve. The agent's report pronounced her a 'troublemaker on the Reserve' with a 'violent temper and [using] foul language', though he added that a 'large portion of blame' for her situation was the fact she had 'no proper home to go to'. Three years later, she was incarcerated in the Mercer for the third time, now under the Female Refuges Act; although concerns with her 'dissolute' behaviour remained the same, her sentence was longer. The Indian agent now recommended parole to a sister in Toronto instead of returning her to the corrupting influence of her home on the reserve.[81]

Even when the official charge did not relate to sex, the committal form might offer warnings, often lurid and voyeuristic ones, about sexual immorality. When a young woman was sent to the Mercer after incurring many alcohol charges, it was reported that she was 'an outlaw on the Reserve' due to her immorality. 'When she gets drunk, quite often she is usually found in the company of different, disreputable men, sometimes with no clothes on. She will take on any man that happens to come along', the magistrate wrote in explaining the sentence. Police and legal authorities often saw intoxication and sexual immorality as inextricably linked for Native women, and their fears of Native women's weaker willpower precipitated the decision to incarcerate. She is 'loose in character, highly sexed, and particularly so when she is intoxicated', noted a typical committal for a northern woman sent to the Mercer Reformatory.[82]

While many of these convictions were for women who came from reserves, the long arm of the law also touched women far from the authority of the Indian agent. Linda, only 17, was convicted under the Female Refuges Act in the 1920s when she was 'living with a man not her husband'. She was found sleeping on a railway platform with him and was reported to have been travelling around the country, and was subsequently incarcerated.[83] To some extent, the sexual regulation of women like Linda resembled that imposed on non-Native women over this period. Many shared previous experiences of impoverishment, addiction, ill health, violence, and family dissolution. Some had also been in state care. Many were indicted by the 'immorality' or criminal records of their families. 'Her family history is a bad one', noted a sentencing report for a Native woman that could easily have been written for countless inmates, 'her father is living with a woman not his wife and . . . her mother is possibly worse than her, and certainly partly at fault for her behaviour.'[84]

However, the treatment of Native women differed in one important regard: the courts were influenced by racial stereotypes of Aboriginal women as weaker in moral outlook and more sexually promiscuous. Once incarcerated, they were often perceived to be less likely candidates for rehabilitation.[85] Also, Native women might become the disciplinary focus of fears concerning interracial sex. Even if anxieties concerning miscegenation were far less intense than in the nineteenth century, they could still be a factor in Native women's incarceration. As Jean Barman argues, the ideological outcome of a century of colonial efforts to 'tame' Native women's sexuality was the heightened 'sexualization' of all aspects of their lives, making them the inevitable target of legal and social regulation by the twentieth century.[86]

The issue of interracial sex was raised, for instance, in the case of an 18-year-old dishwasher, Anna, sent to the Mercer in 1942 from a northern city. Her trial also showed how, even when Native women moved to the city, the Indian agent from their 'home' reserve might be called in to testify against them. Anna's agent claimed she had appeared before him on the reserve three times for intoxication, and he had used the Indian Act to 'fine and warn' her. He further added that 'a doctor had informed him' Anna was now pregnant. The police chief also offered second-hand gossip: 'we hear she is in the family way. . . . Other stories that we hear around town are that she is drinking all the time. . . . [It is] not hard to believe [that] she is going into men's rooms.' The police constable who followed her, however, was very specific about who she had sex with: '[I] noticed her a regular at the train station with white boys. . . . I've seen her in cafes with white boys, coming in and out.'[87] The magistrate was critical of the 'heresay' evidence offered against Anna, but not critical enough: she was sent to the Mercer for 18 months.

Despite increasing urbanization, therefore, Native women could not always escape the surveillance of the Indian Act. Nor could they shake the colonialist, racist stigma of 'primitiveness' associated with the reserve. 'She is one of the young Indian girls that have moved to this city and whose conduct during the summer is disgraceful to say the least', noted one magistrate during World War II. Concerns that she was 'hanging around' the military barracks and engaging in sex with the men were articulated, and he added fatalistically, 'she is an Indian girl and probably will never stay away from the drink.'[88]

Tragically, incarceration for sexual immorality could simply become the first step in women's future conflicts with the law. One young woman, first convicted off the reserve for sexual immorality and sleeping with white men, later returned to the reformatory again and again, on charges of intoxication as well as sexual immorality and 'idleness', a synonym in her case for increasing poverty, addiction and destitution.[89] And tragically, women might also blame themselves, encouraged to admit their 'guilt' because of the potency of dominant definitions of morality. 'The surroundings' in the training school, wrote one young woman to her agent, 'will help me to better myself into the kind of girl my town would want me to be.'[90]

Indeed, the records of Native women who were imprisoned in the provincial reformatory, as well as of those sent to the training school, reveal families and communities themselves condemnatory of immoral sexual behaviour. Not only could Native relatives and communities play a role in turning a woman over to the police, but sometimes they also asked that a woman not get parole or at least not return to the reserve. 'She has been refused care by her own community', it was noted of one imprisoned woman accused of immorality and prostitution. 'Her sister does not want anything to do with her, as she sends men over there and her sister says she does not want to live this kind of life.'[91]

Some families, however, were still less interested in debating or contradicting the designation 'immoral' for these women and more concerned with trying to secure sympathy or mercy for their relatives. Explaining her sister's downward spiral with alcohol and subsequent incarceration for immorality, a Native woman remarked to the authorities: 'her problems started after her first [illegitimate] child was born [because then] she had no self respect.'[92] Families thus tried to place the charge of immorality in the context of a woman's deprivation, alcoholism, or family dissolution. One sister, for example, wrote to the prison, pointing out that her sister was abused as a child, then was not allowed to marry the man she wished, as an explanation for her behaviour. However, it is revealing that direct denial of charges of sexual immorality came less frequently than rejection of the legitimacy of other convictions, such as those for alcohol infractions, indicating that, at some level, a colonialist project of 'colonizing' the sexual soul had been successful.

Colonizing the Soul

How then do we explain this process of sexual regulation, aimed at all Native peoples but more bluntly at women? First, the inordinate disciplinary power invested in the Indian Act and also the agent must be acknowledged. His job was to survey his subjects, to 'normalize' certain behaviours through a system of punishments and rewards, lectures, and advice.[93] Indian agents, as Robin Brownlie points out, were intermediaries with white society and the state, acting as both social workers and arbitrary, paternal rulers over people considered childlike. It was precisely the agent's combination of roles, encompassing necessity, aid, and repression, that solidified his power.[94] Though agents' aspirations to enforce sexual and marital morality varied from one community to another—as did their successes—knowledge of the agent's far-reaching *potential* to discipline, abetted by missions and schools, should not be ignored. Moreover, the Indian Act's patriarchal provisions concerning treaty rights, stipulating women's loss of status if they 'married out' (a provision finally removed from the Act in 1985), made women especially economically vulnerable to the agent's control.

Denied aid on reserves or simply searching out new lives, Aboriginal women might join the increasing numbers of First Nations people moving to urban centres. Even if they could escape the agent's purview—as Anna could not—they could not avoid the widespread racialized and gendered view of Aboriginal women. The long-standing European view of Aboriginal women in a 'dialectic of denigration and desire',[95] as sexually licentious and in need of 'conquest', meant they were the special mark of regulation by police and the courts.

The power of the law, of course, was tempered by women's attempts to elude or evade it, and on reserves by the outright rejection, at least by a minority, of the agent's moral authority. These people persisted in creating their own 'illegalities', leaving marriages, changing sexual partners, ignoring pronouncements about illegitimate children. Others resisted the incursion of outside welfare and penal experts into community life. When a young woman who had been incarcerated in the Ontario Training School for Girls was released on parole, she returned to her reserve and became pregnant by the son of her neighbour. The placement officer sent out to retrieve her for reincarceration (as was the policy) was confronted by adamant relatives of the boy, who insisted that they would adopt the child, that the girl was not ready to settle down and marry yet, and that she should not be returned to the OTSG. We will 'settle things our own way', they argued, 'in the long house tradition; we will do what is right.' In a rare recognition that they might be right, the officer left the families to work out a solution.

Significantly, though, this case was unusual. Moreover, it may be a mistake simply to equate Native communities' rejection of some Euro-Canadian laws with their embrace of Native custom; the story is more complex. Recognition of the changing nature of colonialism and its particular character in this later era of 'advanced colonialism' is important. Early contact accounts of some First Nations often stress women's sexual autonomy, the ability to divorce, and fewer prohibitions against non-marital sex. However, by the late nineteenth century, life histories and ethnographies emphasize lifelong marriages and premarital chastity as the ideal—evidence of Christian missionary successes.[96] Even the Iroquois 'traditionalists', notes one author, 'stressed marital fidelity' as a shared community value.[97] Descriptions of Ojibwa and Cree communities in the early twentieth century emphasized the importance of marriage as a cement to kin relations and community harmony, as a co-operative partnership in the battle for survival.[98] Few such accounts discuss sexual relations, though elders from a number of Native language groups referred to the existence of sexual taboos, prohibitions on extramarital sex, and the monitoring of such activity by the community, by elders, or (in some cultures) by shamans—a Foucauldian form of discipline, though certainly one distinct from that of the colonizers.[99]

By the mid-twentieth century, communities might be aware of the negative impact of Christian morals, but they were still deeply influenced by them. Edward Rogers, an anthropologist who worked for years with Ojibwa people in northern Ontario, noted in the 1950s that 'chastity and adultery, for *men* previously of little concern, now due to Christianity, are condemned. However, the Chief cannot command obedience to the "new ways". . . . He wanted to intervene with a married woman having an affair, but the relatives said no.'[100] Traditional and Euro-Canadian/Christian morality overlapped as 'conflicting systems', he argued, but the latter could be overwhelmed by the former. Previously, for example, 'there was little concern if a girl was pregnant. They simply asked the father to marry or support the child. . . . But the Christian taboo on premarital sex and the knowledge that pregnant girls will be hurt by European morality have led to recent concern with teen boys seducing girls.'[101]

In the interwar period some anthropologists went further, suggesting the internalization of patriarchal norms, claiming, for instance, there were signs of 'men feeling they have a sexual "right" to women.'[102] A controversial account of Ojibwa women in northern Ontario, Ruth Landes's *Ojibwa Woman*, described a culture in which women were valued less and subject to male violence and sexual control, a view that contradicted other anthropological accounts.[103] As a reinterpretation of Landes's work suggests, however, her own background and the intent of her female informant to relay stories of women's courage and hardship may have allowed Landes to 'hear' stories missed by other observers.[104] If sexual conflict and control existed, continues Sally Cole, this cannot be separated from the 'hard times'[105] increasingly affecting these communities, that is, declining resources, few opportunities for wage labour, and increasing government control.

In such circumstances, frictions were inevitable between older means of community control stressing mediation, reconciliation, and teaching of lessons and newer controls offered by Canadian law and the state. The increasing incursion of the state into Aboriginal communities also provided the possibility of some groups using the agent's power to exert or reassert theirs. As Tina Loo has argued in regard to British Columbia Aboriginals, 'some native peoples brokered the extension of the European state',[106] drawing on legal powers outside of their traditional communities as possible levers of control within their communities. The hegemony of Canadian law offered the possibility of exerting moral governance over neighbours who were seen to be violating community sexual norms, with these norms an amalgam of Native and European tradition.

The similarity to legal contests in other colonial contexts is striking. As Martin Chanock demonstrates in his study of African customary law, the efforts of African male elders to reassert their status and power over women and youth in the face of worsening economic prospects and social crises occasioned by colonialism, such as rural depopulation, shaped how the elders (re)interpreted 'custom' as 'customary law' for British agents attempting to authenticate a fixed legal code of 'traditional' law. When the band councillors, noted in the example opening this chapter, asked for the imprisonment of Emma to enforce morality, therefore, they were not simply enforcing custom but customary law as *they* saw it, with the latter already influenced by the lived experience and pressures of colonialism. Their attempt to regulate morality may have overlapped with the traditional power of elders teaching the young; they may have reflected the views of those who had absorbed Christian ideas; they may have represented one group establishing status over another; and they may have also represented the transfer and internalization of patriarchal values so strongly promoted by the colonizers—or all of the above.

Moreover, the community's exercise of moral regulation cannot be separated from the debilitating material effects of colonialism. On Ontario reserves, for example, the social consequences of so-called immorality were perceived to be worsening an already difficult situation: marriage desertion was linked to abandoned children and destitute wives, both real problems in the midst of increasing poverty. Moreover, as with the case of Emma, communities who urged that women be removed to the Mercer Reformatory may well have believed that the reformatory would actually *help* these women, even if we now know that the opposite was true.[107] Finally, it is revealing that a number of cases I have described involved elders monitoring the young. Similarly, one US study of a tribal court argues that the majority of adultery charges were levelled at people under 25: 'the enforcement of white man's morality was taking place in an old way; in effect, an elder was attempting to shape the conduct of his grandchildren.'[108] However, one crucial difference in the Ontario case was that such regulation was aided by outsiders from the Canadian state and that sexual behaviour was becoming more stringently disciplined, and in a more alienating manner. It might also be criminalized, with women removed from their communities to prisons and reformatories where they were isolated, marginalized, and misunderstood.

Conclusion

The sexual regulation of First Nations women was thus fundamentally shaped by the social construction of 'race' through the law and by the politics of colonialism. Although Native and non-Native women alike were perceived to be pivotal to the broader nation-building project of creating 'moral' citizens and families, their encounters with the law also diverged, in part because Native women confronted a different legal regime and racialized surveillance, in part because Native communities drew on distinct cultural traditions as they grappled with the economic and social stresses of advanced colonialism.

As a 'cutting edge of colonialism', the law was used as a central instrument of the state's attempts to assimilate Aboriginal peoples and reshape their cultures in a Euro-Canadian and middle-class mould. The Indian Act, government policy, and Indian agents were used to encourage nuclear, monogamous families that did not separate and in which men were protectors and earners, and women were sexually restrained, domestic, and a good moral influence. The Criminal Code, provincial courts, prisons, and reformatories might also be used, as a last resort, to refashion sexual morality and marital and family life. Both direct pressure—from financial penalty to imprisonment—and indirect proselytizing were part of this regulatory process. Indeed, ideological efforts to redefine public morality, to rerepresent images of sexual order/disorder, to re-inscribe the sexual subjectivity of Native peoples—to colonize the soul—were critical to this project.[109]

As the cultural values of Native peoples were denigrated, the possibilities of articulating a distinct social-sexual code became more difficult, especially since schools, clerics, and missions often supported the agents. Indeed, the state was never the sole agent of regulation, as other powerful institutions, such as the Protestant and Catholic churches, prescribed influential discourses of sexual and familial moralism. Moreover, state officials, educators, and religious leaders employed existing internal family and community mechanisms of sexual and marital regulation in this process, and conversely, some Native leaders and community members incorporated the Canadian law and the power of the agent into their attempts to secure community stability and order.

Regulation was never uncontested, complete, or uncomplicated. Clerics might oppose the policies of Indian agents on marriage; agents' own efforts to police morality varied widely; and Native communities and cultures responded with degrees of acceptance, negotiation, or resistance to these efforts. The latter is a critical point: the new legalities articulated by the state always overlapped with some lingering practices of non-observance or 'illegality'. Some Native women and their families rejected the imposed morality, though they could not always escape the consequences of this rejection, which, at worst, meant women's incarceration.

The context of colonialism and the hegemony of patriarchal Euro-Canadian laws thus frame the picture of sexual regulation, even if cultural persistence and individual resistance were part of the inner design. Within First Nations cultures, domination and resistance both existed, but not on equal terms. In colonial contexts, premised upon unequal social power and an ideology of racism, indigenous values were often more fragile, while the hegemony of those controlling legal knowledge was more authoritative.

Subversion of dominant ideologies always remains possible, and recently has become far more probable given the cultural renaissance and political organizing of the First Nations. However, in this ongoing debate over new forms of Aboriginal justice there is a troubling history to contend with: past colonial successes, the domination of Euro-Canadian law, and the overlap of Aboriginal and Euro-Canadian sexual regulation. Even if justice was process- rather than punishment-oriented at one time, by the mid-twentieth century colonialism had created new stresses, inequalities, and repressions within Aboriginal societies. The articulation of customary law and the reinvention of tradition on reserves, argues Carol Laprairie, is now complicated by the 'contemporary political economy of reserves', faced not only with poverty but by new inequalities based on age and sex, and 'these may be in conflict with attempts to create new, ethically rooted participatory practices' of justice.[110] Attempts to construct new forms of 'popular justice' in post-colonial societies, though laudable, have in the past been jeopardized by the lingering, deeply entrenched legal ideologies of the previous colonial state.[111] Reinventing traditions will thus mean contending with and challenging a colonial past in which women's sexuality was prescribed and regulated, both by the colonizers and later within Native cultures, a process that created the power imbalances that Native women are now struggling to overcome.

7

Conclusion

Although the moral politics of recent anti-prostitution campaigns reflects current discourses, legal strategies, and connections to the state, the existence of moral politics, expressed through and constituted by the law, has a much longer history. In trying to understand how legal regulation relating to women, sexuality, and the family operated in twentieth-century Ontario, I have drawn on the most basic premises of critical legal thinking: the plurality of law, the need for constant cross-examination of its fabrication and meaning, and the idea that law is only comprehensible in its social, economic, and political contexts. Moreover, the law was never a monolithic text but rather a combination of discourses, practices, personnel, and strategies designed to guide, rule, aid, and punish those deemed 'under the law.' Looking at the sexual rules and penalties that girls and women faced under the law, it is especially clear that legal, social, and sexual regulation was an overlapping process, crossing the boundaries from state to civil society, drawing heavily on the prestige of formal institutions such as the courts, but also linked to informal governance through the family, churches, schools, penal institutions, and medical and social science discourses.

However, assessing the 'how and why' of these plural processes also entails making generalizations, identifying persisting structures of inequality, and locating concentrations of power, not simply exploring its infinite circulation through the social body. The current theoretical dilemma, as some legal theorists have suggested, is how we negotiate our way between legal imperialism on one side and the 'expulsion' of law from modernity[1] on the other, between universalizing theories and moral relativism, between the doctrinaire embrace of foundational categories and the embrace of none. My compromise has been to encompass, on the one hand, a skepticism about the law's claim to truth and justice and a deconstructive method that starts with the everyday, particular, local, lived experiences of the law in women's lives. On the other hand, I also assume that a feminist analysis speaks from some standpoint, and mine clearly favours materialist-feminist approaches, an emphasis on multiple sites of empirical reconstruction, and a persisting investment in the concept of 'truth claims' such as justice and equality.

If the law was plural, it was also an arena of contest and struggle. Although the weight of this book tips the balance towards regulation and acquiescence, the examples of sexual and familial regulation explored here also disclose disagreement, negotiation, and resistance. During the era surveyed, organized feminism seldom mounted a sustained critique of the law's masculinist double standard, nor did most men and women appearing before the courts offer trenchant political critiques of the class, colonial, and gender biases inherent in the criminal justice system. Rather, resistance was more often expressed in partial, sporadic, everyday rejections of the courts' presumptions, as well as in complaints about its failures to live up to lofty promises of aid and fairness. Though perhaps not well organized or consistently articulated, resistance was more than an automatic reflex, a reactive impulse to the exercise of power. It emerged in the disjuncture women sensed between the law's claims to justice and the injustice they felt, through women's displeasure with moral judgements applied to them, through their consciousness of and disagreements with a criminal justice system unbalanced by the inequalities of class, race, and colonialism.[2]

Women who attempted to use the courts to secure peace and security from domestic violence sought, first and foremost, inclusion in the justice system. They wanted their stories to be heard. They wanted to use the police, or the moral power of the magistrate or judge, to establish their claims to justice in order to escape violence or end it. Most women came to the courts only after makeshift strategies such as shaming their partner, or taking refuge with relatives and friends, bore no results. Many only sought formal legal remedies, with their attendant costs and public visibility, when poverty and non-support issues, fear for their children, or their own emotional and physical breaking point convinced them they had little choice.

Women invested considerable faith in informal and socialized justice, hoping that the modern offerings of the Family Court, including the private solutions of probation or counselling by experts, would end the violence in their lives. Yet the irony of modern solutions was that they could be refurbished past practices. Family Courts, like Magistrate's Courts, could easily translate legal problems into moral and therapeutic issues, with the battered woman on trial as much as the man. Some of the barriers women encountered to having their complaints taken seriously, or finding remedies, remained problems in the 1950s as much as in the 1920s. Given women's lack of economic and social alternatives in both work and family life, given an entrenched ideology of masculine paternal authority and feminine domestic passivity, women found escape hatches from wife-battering difficult to secure. Indeed, the ideological construction of an 'ideal victim' not only remained a constant, it seemed more confining in a post-World War II culture of Freudian familialism.

Married women dealing with wife-battering were much like the few children who had their cases of incest heard in court. In both situations, the courts were often a last resort, and violence was never understood simply through the letter of a prohibitive law. Rather, powerful social knowledges, based in medicine, psychiatry, social work practice, and—in the case of incest—eugenics, combined with the law to create the process of regulation. For both wife-battering and incest, sexual regulation was also related to class and social status, with the criminal justice system more likely to patrol the working class and poor, whose families were suspected of more deep-seated pathologies. Finally, the failure of the law to offer protection from violence does not necessarily suggest that we should uniformly condemn all such regulation as perfidious or dangerous, though it should result in our asking in whose interests regulation has operated, why, and whether and how that can change.

Despite courageous attempts to use the courts to gain redress, victims of violence could find that the judicial process exacerbated their alienation. Incest was considered even more unbelievable than wife-battering; it was extremely difficult to prove, given the court's obtuse indifference to the intimidating structures of power that victims, more than defendants, faced on trial. It was also ultimately difficult for survivors to escape, physically, emotionally, and psychologically. A patriarchal family politics of surveillance and domination, the reality of women's economic and social vulnerability, and the reluctance of those with legal authority to open up the Pandora's box of familial sexual abuse—other than to fret over the reproductive consequences of incest—meant that girls were often disbelieved or their cases put aside.

Many girls ultimately adopted other strategies of resistance to sexual abuse, acting out against social norms or running away from home. Even after some girls were incarcerated for sexual 'immorality', they persisted with a strategy of personal resistance, telling their version of sexual abuse in the counselling confessional, although the dominant medical discourses, like the law, had tremendous difficulty matching survivors' stories with their psychiatric suppositions. The experiences of these girls and women also exposed one of the contradictions of legal regulation focused on the family. Legal discourses, government policy, and judicial pronouncements all spoke of the need for state intervention in and public control over violence within the family, usually to save children or protect women. Indeed, over this period, more resources were put into courts designed to aid such families. But in reality, those applying the law often clung to notions of familial privacy, and they remained committed to the protection of gender roles associated with the heterosexual, nuclear, male-headed, hierarchical family, as well as to the notion that women were the (always blameworthy) moral guardians of children. Without alternatives to this familial model, as well as transformation of the material deprivation limiting many women's choices, a public crusade against the private terrors of the family was likely to falter.

This image of the ideal family was also linked to the regulation of women considered promiscuous, teenage delinquents, and Aboriginal women, as well as women who made their living by selling sex—in other words, women who did not embrace the dominant familial norms of sexual purity, marital fidelity, or youthful sexual innocence. If victims of violence were discredited for not fulfilling these norms, these women were chastised for directly flouting them. It was also inevitable that economically and socially marginalized women were those least able to realize sexual and gender norms expected of them. Women and girls often faced a double bind: to avoid conflicts with the law, secure mercy, or obtain probation, they were urged by court and penal personnel to embrace honest working-class labour and 'normal' family life. A normalized ideal of the 'good mother' and 'good daughter', therefore, was deeply embedded in the operation of the law. Yet, many girls and women had already seen the family's darker side through the alienations occasioned by violence, economic insecurity, and emotional estrangement; their rejection of the class and gender contract, then, made sense in light of their own experiences.

The final familial contradiction, of course, was that many of the female offenders described in this book were brought to the attention of the state by families themselves; indeed, the state encouraged the family to use the legal apparatus to re-establish its internal order and social respectability. This was especially the case for minors, but sometimes also for adult women whose relatives accepted some of the dominant ideals of female/male sexual difference, including the need for female sexual restraint within marriage. Their consent to the law was organized around the reassurance that young women would be protected from sexual harm and the family preserved, reasoning that resonated reassuringly with men and women often coping simultaneously with distress, deprivation, and social marginalization. The same internal regulation also occurred in Aboriginal families and communities, which, despite their alienation from the Canadian state, had absorbed elements of the dominant Judeo-Christian ideology concerning sexuality and the family.

When it came to sentencing and penal solutions, there were variations in the courts' perception of women who violated familial and sexual norms. Delinquents, representing the future of the nation, might still be remoulded into moral, feminine, hard-working citizens. Prostitutes, however, were seen as more dangerous to family life and, at some periods of history, to the health of the nation. Though the view of Aboriginal women was distinct again, shaped by racist suppositions of Native culture and reserve life, they, too, were seen as dangers to the nation, or at least to the colonizing mission of the nation. First Nations peoples, supposedly clinging to 'primitive' sexual practices, had to be assimilated into a new Euro-Canadian middle-class sexual order. Even if the rhetoric of Indian agents and courts claimed to offer paternalistic protection to morally weak and childlike First Nations women, this attempt to refashion their sex and family lives was shaped by systemic racism and colonialism.

For these offenders, exclusion from the power of the law, not inclusion in its reach, was usually their goal. They, too, might voice dissatisfaction and disagreements with the law's assumptions and its effects on their lives. Whether it was prostitutes who continued to work after promising to leave town, Aboriginal couples who refused to abandon customary marriage, teenage girls who disputed their designation as delinquent, or promiscuous women who would not name their partners or even acknowledge their own immorality, women voiced unhappiness with a system that controlled their sexuality, usually in a manner more censorious than the regulation of men.

The sexual regulation of these women was the product of the law and the disciplines acting in concert, although certain issues and cases could spark friction and disagreement between judges, penal workers, probation officers, and psychiatrists. In general, legal and non-legal personnel, discourses, and practices worked to reinforce the sexual/social order, not simply by offering up correctional strategies to erring women but by defining the very nature of sexual 'order' and 'disorder' against which women were measured in the criminal justice system. The prescriptions of acceptable sexual behaviour laid out by the law also created a locus of discipline that cast its net far wider than the legal and correctional system. As Foucauldian scholars have emphasized, penal punishment becomes part of a broader system of moral regulation within the larger cultural formation by normalizing some behaviours, pathologizing others, and setting out definitions of 'good/bad, abnormal/normal' for all of society. These definitions of women's sexuality, given authority by the legal system, 'permeated all social groups, so much so that punitive powers of moral enforcement were dispersed throughout all of civil society, ordering self repression for all, even by the repressors themselves.'[3]

We may be justified in looking back critically on the alliance, for instance, of judges and psychiatrists, particularly the gender norms that experts wished to inculcate in criminalized women. But it is also important to remember that, at the time, many medical, social work, and legal professionals perceived themselves to be a progressive vanguard, bringing new scientific theories to bear on the problem of criminality. Indeed, the entire 1920–60 period could be characterized as optimistically modernist: there was immense faith in the power of medical and social science experts to study, treat, and alter criminal behaviour and the suffering associated with it. Advocates of the Juvenile Delinquents Act, for instance, believed they were creating a more humane and reformative youth justice system by stressing the alteration of girls' inner character rather than simply punitive incarceration. Yet, these transformative goals, as we have seen, brought broadened definitions of delinquency that condemned offences of character, family, and morality and wove a wider net of informal forms of surveillance.

Furthermore, an image of innately pathological female deviance, even the need for pure punishment, was never completely vanquished from this modernist world view; this was particularly true in penal institutions, even if penal workers claimed publicly they were offering maternal rehabilitation. The threat of reformatory or training school never disappeared from the legal arsenal; invocation of such a sentence was precisely the point at which juridical power was bluntly manifested—when discipline had to be re-established, when surveillance became incarceration.[4] Moreover, this tactic was primarily used against poor, working-class, and racialized women and girls, precisely because the dominant definitions of immorality were associated with class and race.

Justifying the use of the law were two prescriptions for reform. On the one hand, experts offered rehabilitation of the woman's abnormal psyche or arrested character development, drawing, for instance, on psychology and psychiatry. On the other hand, they condemned the social pathologies—such as dysfunctional families—perceived to be at the root of her criminality. Over these decades, strictly biological explanations for crime generally (though not completely) made way for psychogenetic ones, stressing women's adherence/non-adherence to socially prescribed (but still 'natural') feminine roles. In the post-World War II era, both psychoanalytic categories and social-psychological explanations, delving into women's gender socialization and their role in the family, were influential in explaining their rejection of sexual norms.

By the 1970s a more decidedly structuralist view of law, and a critique of the criminal justice system influenced by both feminism and Marxism, directly challenged the concept of the individual deviant and the reigning faith in positivist modernism. What is defined as a crime, it was argued, reflected economic, political, and social contests for power, and often the triumphant hegemony of capitalist and/or patriarchal ideologies, even if these worked to mask, mystify, or reinterpret the law as neutral or benevolent. The letter of the law might differ from whom it actually protected or prosecuted, though popular consent to the apparatus of the criminal justice system was understandably built around its very claim to offer justice and fairness.

This book has obviously drawn on these critical traditions and on the materialist, Gramscian, and feminist frameworks underpinning them. The word 'promiscuous' used repeatedly in legal judgements to categorize and punish women, for instance, worked as *ideology*, translating, explaining, and rationalizing concepts of 'moral' and 'normal' womanhood. These concepts in turn reinforced colonialism and the social construction of 'race', reproduced inequalities between men and women, and separated the well-placed middle-class experts from those with marginal social status who were being judged. Our analysis of female delinquency, I have also argued, must recognize the way in which material and social deprivation was intrinsically linked to discourses about 'promiscuous' or immoral girls and was directly implicated in their prosecution, sentencing, and punishment.

Post-structuralist and Foucauldian analyses have challenged the political and theoretical perspectives of materialism and feminism on a number of levels, offering insight into the intricate processes of the regulation of women's sexuality. Delinquency and deviance, as Foucault so eloquently argued, are themselves products of power/ knowledge: those whose expertise and status gave them claim to power controlled the 'conditions of possibility'[5] of knowledge production. There is little doubt, for instance, that expert definitions of delinquency, forged in the medical and social sciences, were extremely influential in the classification and treatment of girls in conflict with the law. The symptoms of delinquency—from defiant dress and makeup to public and frequent sex and ultimately to rejection of a feminine and familial future—were, in a sense, invented by the experts, then uncovered and diagnosed by their trained eyes.

Both girls and their families were subject to normalization, which drew on the disciplinary strategies outlined by Foucault, and this process undoubtedly extended beyond the state, traversing the social body through the schools, the family, the church, the psychiatric clinic, the court, and the prison. These institutions were not always of one mind, though they might overlap in moral intent: the 'medical model' of treating criminals, which some assume to have triumphed over the course of the century, actually drew on and incorporated Judeo-Christian moral precepts, even as society was becoming increasingly secular.

Both the sexually 'abnormal' and 'normal' women were defined within the bounds of this broader moral culture, and the hierarchy of sexual practices thus formulated insinuated its way into the internal consciousness of women themselves, underlining how, in more than one sense, their bodies became sites of power. Women's own embrace of the prohibitions on sexual conduct takes us back to questions of consent and consciousness, though these are often dissected in post-structuralist terms as 'subjectivity'. The paradox of modernity, as Foucauldians point out, was that girls, women, and families appeared to be governed not simply through an all-powerful, coercive state but through their own 'freedom'. Married women accepted the advice of the Family Court probation officers to cure domestic violence by sleeping with their husbands; girls learned to monitor their inner urges through the lessons of probation; Aboriginal families accepted the 'colonization of the soul' prescribed by the colonizers. This subtle governance was facilitated not only by the courts but by allied institutions and experts who promoted these 'technologies of the self'. Admittedly, families also used the courts for their own purposes, and the consciousness of women caught up in the criminal justice system could be fractured by contradictory, reluctant sentiments: this was not a linear avenue of one-way control. I have no doubt that teenage girls who nodded to their probation officers left the room to disobey their orders.

Furthermore, this 'government at a distance' should not be equated with the exercise of 'freedom': whether one is talking about the prostitutes, delinquents, or battered wives, women often faced a very limited set of choices over which to exercise their agency. Our analysis of sexual regulation must also circle back to the material context and relations of power that framed this regulation over time. However brilliantly the process of normalization is revealed in Foucauldian terms, one also needs to ask why certain expert discourses, rather than others, were promoted as the norm. Why did some moral guidelines and sexual practices assume dominance? Why and how did the disciplines and law combine to incarcerate differentially the poor and marginalized? Why was incest policed very little, but youthful promiscuity monitored so closely? Why were Aboriginal women incarcerated for living common-law when white women were not?

In the spaces and silences left by Foucault, who did not take up questions of race, colonialism, and women's oppression, subsequent scholars have probed these questions. Disciplinary practices, as many feminists argue, are thoroughly gendered; normalization reproduces 'censures of hegemonic masculinity', that is, asymmetrical power relations between men and women. The condemnation of promiscuity, so important to the thinking on delinquency and to the use of the Female Refuges Act to control young women, as well as the measure of sympathy extended to victims of violence, was not a neutral insult directed at men and women. Rather, it was located in historical, social, gendered power relations that reflected patriarchal ideals and sanctioned the legal punishment of non-conforming female heterosexuality.

In the case of First Nations women, sexual denigration went hand in hand with economic disinheritance, social marginalization, and an ideological construction of race that naturalized middle-class, supposedly 'white' familial forms as superior. Colonialism directly shaped the image of the 'sexually primitive Indian' that underlined Canada's Indian policy well into the twentieth century, and the operation of these laws, layered with paternalist surveillance, was highly centralized, allowing marginal spaces for resistance. While invisible and subtle forms of governance were important to this process, blunter forms of coercion also served to constitute race and colonialism in law.

Furthermore, these constructions of women's criminality/immorality took precedence precisely because they translated, interpreted, and legitimized the gender order, political economy, and culture of Canadian society. Discourses on sexuality, laden with power, constituted class, gender, and race as they were lived out by women in conflict with the law. Censures of sexuality may have been subject to human agency, redefinition over time, or negotiation and contest, but these contests were highly sensitive to the dominant relations of class, gender, and colonial power.

For that reason, material determination and attention to the influence of the state should remain in our theoretical sights, and we should be wary of an overly deterministic trajectory in which the state becomes progressively degovernmentalized over the twentieth century. Whether it was the Ontario government ignoring calls to repeal the FRA or dictating the leisure activities of girls in the OTGS, whether it was the higher courts tightening restrictive prostitution laws or the federal Department of Indian Affairs issuing national orders defining Indian marriage, the state and its apparatus maintained and in some cases extended considerable dominion over the operation of the criminal justice system. While acknowledging the plurality of law and the complexities of the modern state, we can still identify concentrations of power that both unobtrusively and more vigorously protected dominant ideologies and interests.

Socialized justice did increasingly rely on non-legal experts and other social welfare institutions, from the CAS to the psychiatric clinic, from the welfare office to the Indian agent, and the justice system was deeply indebted, in its analysis of crime, to medical and social science knowledges. At the same time, the state's most authoritative spokespersons—judges and the courts—maintained some control over how this expertise would be used. In ideological terms, the law and the courts commanded and imposed the supreme claim to final truth, reminding us of Carol Smart's corrective rejoinder to Foucault: with respect to women and the law, 'juridical power is still formidable.'[6] Rather than an invasion of the law by the disciplines, the law and the disciplines joined forces to produce regulation, the essence of which censured non-conforming sexuality, though this was always differentially applied according to gender, class, and race. This does not negate the possibility of ideologies changing over time, of regulation possibly taking feminist forms, or of resistance to repression or oppression: it simply reminds us that these may be difficult, uphill battles.

This should also prompt us to balance the story of regulation and 'colonization of the soul' with divergent accounts of disagreement and dissent, to emphasize the inevitable reciprocity, and tensions, between our historical subjects and structures of power and authority.

Women's subordination under the law was lived out as a complex ensemble of accommodation, escape, denial, self-destructive behaviours, and self-affirming actions. Despite the focus of this study on regulation and the power of the law, it does acknowledge moments of transgressive disagreement when women queried whether they were really on the receiving end of 'justice'. However partial their insights or preliminary their questions, our project is to develop them more fully, both in historical reconstruction and in contemporary political practice.

Note on Sources

The primary sources used for this book include social work journals, government documents, and prison files. However, since court and penal records, often catalogued very differently, comprise some of the sources used, a brief note is in order.

When I began this research almost a decade ago, many local courts had not deposited their records in the Ontario Archives. My use of court records was therefore geographically limited by what was available. This was particularly true of the chapter on wife assault, for which deposited Magistrate's and Family Court records were scant for the province, and, unfortunately, there were no comprehensive records from the north at that time. I also used court records as they came into the Archives so they were unprocessed and uncatalogued, even by date. Thus, some of the records in the York domestic case files had no numbers and were arranged only by the name of the person. For these, I have simply listed the box number with 'anonymous case file'. I have listed all Toronto and York records under one designation; three groups of records are involved, with different transfer numbers: (1) Transfer 74–454 (22–5836) comprised of Toronto Juvenile and Family Court records from the 1930s on; (2) Transfer 80–531 (22–5829) York Country Juvenile and Family Court, including the 1930s and 1940s; (3) Transfer 73–430 (22–5833) Metro Toronto Family Court, 1950s and 1960s.

Two jail registers for Peterborough and Kenora were also examined, as were records from the Mercer Reformatory for Females and the Ontario Training School for Girls, later called Grandview. These latter two groups of records are not always complete, nor do they consistently contain the same information, but a large sample does allow one to draw important conclusions about women's backgrounds and their treatment in the justice system. My Mercer sample (400) was primarily of those women charged under the FRA and prostitution laws, but the OTSG sample (350) was not selected by charge but randomly over time. In both cases, these files only tell the stories of women in conflict with the law who were incarcerated, a biased sample in some respects. However, these records are useful in detailing those girls and women seen to be most 'at risk' and therefore in need of rehabilitation or punishment, and they also help to reveal the prevailing construction of 'bad' versus 'good' women. Unlike court records, they also draw in women from across the province, from rural and urban areas, as well as from First Nations reserves. This was one of the major reasons I drew heavily on them.

In the case of youth, most children were able to escape the most punitive arm of the law—incarceration—through the net of socialized justice. However, the records of those sent to training schools are one of the only means of gaining access to Family and Juvenile Court records from across Ontario. Due to the nature of Juvenile Court hearings, many records were destroyed; others have not been deposited in any archives, and provisions of the Young Offenders Act make them difficult to access. The OTSG records have the virtue of including pre-incarceration material, such as court transcripts, school and probation reports, psychiatric clinic records, and sometimes correspondence with family. The dates cited for such institutional records note the time at which girls or women came into the institution.

Some similar information on delinquents was also gleaned from federal Indian Affairs records, which were also used for Chapters 4 and 6. Except for the Criminal Assize Indictments, the York County General Sessions, and York County Court Judges Court, records required special Freedom of Information (FOI) research agreements and thus carried confidentiality provisions. No actual names are thus ever used for FOI records.

Primary Sources

Archives of Ontario (AO)

Annual Report of the Inspector of Prisons and Charities (later, Prisons and Reformatories)
Annual Report upon Ontario Training Schools
Annual Report of the Toronto Industrial Refuge

Ministry of Correctional Services (Dept. of Reform Institutions), RG 20, Administrative records

Ministry of Correctional Services, RG 20, D–13, Mercer Reformatory for Females (Case Files and Prison Register)

Industrial and Training Schools, RG 60, Ontario Training School

Department of Public Welfare, RG 29

Attorney General's Papers, RG 4

Attorney General, Criminal Assize Indictments, RG 22–392

Attorney General, York County Family Court Files, RG 22

Attorney General, Crown Attorney's Records, Peterborough County, RG 22

Attorney General, Welland County Family Court Records, RG 22

Attorney General, York County Court Judges Criminal Court, RG 22–5870

Attorney General, York County General Sessions, RG 22–5871

Report of the Royal Commission on Public Welfare, 1931

Report of the Royal Commission on the Treatment of the Feeble Minded and Venereal Disease (Hodgins Commission)

Cape Croker Council Minutes

Cambridge City Archives

Grandview Information Files

National Archives of Canada (NAC)

Canadian Council on Social Development Papers (Canadian Welfare Council), MG 28 I 10

National Council of Women Papers, MG 28 I 25

Department of Indian and Northern Affairs, RG 10

Dorothy Flaherty Papers, MG 31 K 25

Metro Toronto/City Archives

Annual Report of the Chief Constable of Police

Annual Report of the Toronto Family Court

Dept. of Public Welfare, Series 100

Peterborough Museum and Archives

Grand Jury Report, 1916

Elizabeth Fry Society of Toronto Library and Archives

Minute books, annual reports, clipping files, correspondence

Professional Journals and the Popular Press

American Journal of Orthopsychiatry
Canadian Child and Family Welfare
Canadian Congress Journal
Canadian Journal of Corrections
Canadian Journal of Mental Hygiene (later *Mental Health*)
Canadian Welfare
Chatelaine
Globe and Mail
Journal of Juvenile Research
Journal of Social Hygiene
Journal of the American Medical Association
Maclean's
Peterborough Examiner
Psychoanalytic Quarterly
Saturday Night
Toronto Star

Notes

Chapter 1

1. Alexandra Highcrest, 'When protection is punishment', *Globe and Mail*, 14 Aug. 2000.
2. Such rhetoric may not actually reflect public opinion. Anthony Doob, 'Transforming the Punishment Environment: Understanding Public Views of What Should Be Accomplished at Sentencing', *Canadian Journal of Criminology* 42, 3 (2000): 323–40.
3. Early works in criminal justice history often employed quantitative methods or drew on social control and class analyses. See, for example, Harvey Graff, 'Pauperism, Misery and Vice: Illiteracy and Criminality in the Nineteenth Century', *Journal of Social History* 11 (1977): 245–68; Elizabeth Langdon, 'Female Crime in Calgary, 1914–40', in L. Knafla, ed., *Law and Justice in a New Land: Essays in Western Canadian Legal History* (Toronto, 1986). Some works accept the dominant definitions of criminality. For example, see D. Owen Carrigan, *Crime and Punishment in Canada* (Toronto, 1991); Peter Oliver, 'To Govern with Kindness: The First Two Decades of the Mercer Reformatory for Women', in Jim Phillips, Tina Loo, and Susan Lewthwaite, eds, *Essays in the History of Canadian Law* (Toronto, 1994), 516–71. Others are more critical (though not Marxist), such as John Weaver, *Crimes, Constables, Courts* (Montreal, 1996). Research has often taken a 'law and society' focus: see the volumes of *Essays in the History of Canadian Law* published by University of Toronto Press. Feminist studies have been numerous, including excellent overviews of women and the law, such as Constance Backhouse, *Petticoats and Prejudice: Women and Law in Nineteenth Century Canada* (Toronto, 1991), and thematic explorations, such as

Karen Dubinsky's analysis of women and violence: *Improper Advances: Rape and Heterosexual Conflict in Ontario, 1880–1929* (Chicago, 1993) and Carolyn Strange's study of incarceration, 'The Velvet Glove: Maternalistic Reform at the Andrew Mercer Ontario Reformatory for Females, 1874–1927', MA thesis (University of Ottawa, 1983). Only a few (usually nineteenth-century) studies examine the criminal 'underclass' with gender as a focus. See, e.g., Judith Fingard, *The Dark Side of Victorian Halifax* (Porters Lake, 1989); Mary Anne Poutanen, 'The Homeless, the Whore, the Drunkard and the Disorderly: Contours of Female Vagrancy in the Montreal Courts, 1810–42', in K. McPherson et al., eds, *Gendered Pasts: Historical Essays in Femininity and Masculinity in Canada* (Toronto, 1999), 29–47. Recent studies are more likely to embrace discourse analysis and/or draw on Foucauldian ideas: see, e.g., Carolyn Strange, *Toronto's Girl Problem: The Perils and Pleasures of the City 1880–1920* (Toronto, 1995). Other authors are exploring the intersection of working-class culture and homosexuality. Steven Maynard, 'Through the Lavatory Wall: Homosexual Subcultures, Police Surveillance and the Dialectics of Discovery, Toronto, 1890–1930', *Journal of the History of Sexuality* 5 (1994).

4. The 'underclass' is used as a metaphor for social transformation and reflects ongoing constructions of the 'deserving' and 'undeserving' poor. See Michael Katz, *The Underclass Debate: Views from History* (Princeton, NJ, 1993), 3–26.

5. Terry Eagleton, *The Illusions of Postmodernism* (Oxford, 1996), 69; Teresa L. Ebert, *Ludic Feminism and After: Postmodernism, Desire and Labor in Late Capitalism* (Ann Arbor, Mich., 1996), 23.

6. Many excellent studies end by the 1920s. See, e.g., Ruth Rosen, *The Lost Sisterhood: Prostitution in America, 1900–1918* (Baltimore, 1982); Barbara Hobson, *Uneasy Virtue: The Politics of Prostitution and the American Reform Tradition* (New York, 1987); Timothy Gilfoyle, *City of Eros: New York City, Prostitution and the Commercialization of Sex* (New York, 1992); D. Nilsen, 'The Social Evil: Prostitution in Vancouver, 1900–20', in Barabara Latham and Cathy Kess, eds, *In Her Own Right: Selected Essays on Women's History in B.C.* (Victoria, 1984); Constance Backhouse, 'Nineteenth Century Prostitution Laws: Reflection of a Discriminatory Society', *Histoire sociale/Social History* 18 (1985): 387–423; Lori Rotenberg, 'The Wayward Worker: Toronto's Prostitute at the Turn of the Century', in Janice Acton et al., eds, *Women at Work: Ontario* (Toronto, 1974), 33–70.

7. Bradford Morse, 'Aboriginal Peoples, the Law and Justice', in Robert Silverman and Marianne Nielsen, eds, *Aboriginal Peoples and Canadian Criminal Justice* (Toronto, 1992), 56.

8. This term from Susan Hirsch and Mindie Lazarus-Black, eds, *Contested States: Law, Hegemony and Resistance* (New York, 1994). On this issue I have also been influenced by John Comaroff and Jean Comaroff, *Ethnography and the Historical Imagination* (Boulder, Colo., 1992); Sally Merry Engle, *Getting Justice and Getting Even: Legal Consciousness Among Working-class Americans* (Chicago, 1990).

9. For discussion of such case files, see Linda Gordon, *Heroes of Their Own Lives: The Politics and History of Family Violence* (Boston, 1988), 13–17; Steven Noll, 'Patient Records as Historical Stories: The Case of the Caswell Training School', *Bulletin of the History of Medicine* 69 (1994): 411–28; Regina Kunzel, *Fallen Women, Problem Girls: Unmarried Mothers and the Professionalization of Social Work, 1890–1945* (New Haven, 1993), 5–6. For the argument that they can help uncover client views, see Lykke de la Cour and Geoffrey Reaume, 'Patient Perspectives in Psychiatric Case Files', in Franca Iacovetta and Wendy Mitchinson, eds, *On the Case: Explorations in Social History* (Toronto, 1998), 242–65. On women's use of narrative in the courtroom, see Joan Sangster, 'Pardon Tales from Magistrates Court: Women, Crime and the Courts in Peterborough County, 1920–60', *Canadian Historical Review* 74 (June 1993): 161–97.

10. Engle, *Getting Justice and Getting Even*, 180.

11. The literature on criminology and women is vast. For a few different examples, see Carol Smart, *Women, Crime and Criminology: A Feminist Critique* (London, 1976); Smart, *Feminism and the Power of the Law* (London, 1989); Pat Carlen, *Women, Crime and Poverty* (Philadelphia, 1988); Lorraine Gelsthorpe and Allison Morris, eds, *Feminist Perspectives in Criminology* (Philadelphia, 1990). For Canadian examples, see Ellen Adelberg and Claudia Currie, eds, *Too Few to Count: Canadian Women in Conflict with the Law* (Vancouver, 1987); Karlene Faith, *Unruly Women: The Politics of Confinement and Resistance* (Vancouver, 1993). For a review essay, see Dorothy Chunn and Shelley Gavigan, 'Women, Crime and Criminal Justice in Canada', in Margaret Jackson and Curt Griffiths, eds, *Canadian Criminology: Perspectives on Crime and Criminality* (Toronto, 1995), 141–84. Historical studies examined the nature of women's crime, how women's crime was perceived by society, and women's treatment by the courts and correctional institutions. See note 3.

12. Colin Sumner, *The Sociology of Deviance: An Obituary* (New York, 1994), 288.

13. J. Hagan, J. Simpson, and A.R. Gillis, 'The Sexual Stratification of Social Control', *British Journal of Sociology* 30 (1979): 25–38; J. Hagan, 'Class in the Household: A Power-Control Theory of Gender

and Delinquency', *American Journal of Sociology* 92, 4 (Jan. 1987): 788–816.

14. On the latter two approaches, see Otto Pollock, *The Criminality of Women* (Philadelphia, 1961); Otto Pollock and A. Friedman, eds, *Family Dynamics and Female Sexual Delinquency* (Palo Alto, Calif., 1969).

15. Albert Cohen, *Delinquent Boys* (New York, 1955), 14. In the Ontario Training School for Girls, for example, an EEG study looking for abnormal brain waves in the girls was conducted alongside the more dominant approach, psychotherapeutic interviews concerning girls' family history and personality.

16. Alan Hunt, *Explorations in Law and Society: Toward a Constitutive Theory of Law* (New York, 1993), 253.

17. One example was Sidney Harring, *Policing a Class Society: The Experience of American Cities, 1865–1915* (New Brunswick, NJ, 1983). The recent suggestion that a 'conspiratorial' analysis is all the Marxist perspective amounted to is simply untrue. For this characterization, see D. Owen Carrigan, *Juvenile Delinquency: A History* (Toronto, 1998), 144.

18. Colin Sumner, *Reading Ideologies: An Investigation into the Marxist Theory of Ideology and Law* (London, 1979), 247–8.

19. Hunt, *Explorations in Law and Society*, 252.

20. Poulantzas quoted in Sumner, *Reading Ideologies*, 262. Douglas Hay, ed., *Albion's Fatal Tree: Crime and Society in Eighteenth Century England* (London, 1974); E.P. Thompson, *Whigs and Hunters* (New York, 1975). For comment on the Marxist tradition in regard to women, see Shelley Gavigan, 'Marxist Theories of the Law: A Survey, with Some Thoughts on Women and the Law,' *Criminology Forum* 4, 1 (1983): 755–90. For a review of Canadian works, see Brian Young, 'Law in the "Round" ', *Acadiensis* 16 (Autumn 1986): 155–64. For a comparative view of Marxist and Foucauldian interpretations of punishment, see David Garland, *Punishment and Modern Society: A Study in Social Theory* (Chicago, 1990).

21. Robert Williams, *The American Indian in Western Legal Thought: The Discourses of Conquest* (New York, 1990). Despite the emphasis on discourse, the notion of ideology is employed: 'The Doctrine of Discovery [in law] was nothing more than the reflection of a set of Eurocentric racist beliefs' (326). See also Ron Bourgeault, 'The Struggle for Class and Nation: The Origin of the Metis in Canada and the National Question', in Bourgeault et al., eds, *1492–1992: Five Centuries of Imperialism and Resistance* (Halifax, 1992), 153–89. See below for a discussion of critical race theory.

22. Pat Carlen and Anne Worrall, eds, 'Introduction', *Gender, Crime and Justice* (Philadelphia, 1987). See also Mary Eaton, *Justice for Women?* (Philadelphia, 1986).

23. Hilary Allen, *Justice Unbalanced: Gender, Psychiatry and Judicial Decisions* (Philadelphia, 1987).

24. Faith, *Unruly Women*; Pat Carlen, *Women, Crime and Poverty* (Philadelphia, 1988); Pat Carlen, 'Out of Custody, into Care: Dimensions and Deconstructions of the State's Regulation of Twenty-two Young Working-class Women', in Carlen and Worrall, eds, *Gender, Crime and Justice*; Dawn Currie, 'Feminist Encounters with Postmodernism: Exploring the Impasse of Debates on Patriarchy and Law', *Canadian Journal of Women and the Law* 5, 1 (1992): 63–86.

25. Pat Carlen, 'Virginia, Criminology and the Antisocial Control of Women', in Thomas Blomberg and Stanley Cohen, eds, *Punishment and Social Control: Essays in Honour of Sheldon Messinger* (New York, 1995), 213.

26. For some examples, see Anthony Platt, *The Child Savers: The Invention of Delinquency* (Chicago, 1977); Eric Schneider, *In the Web of Class: Delinquency and Reformers in Boston, 1810s–1930s* (New York, 1992); Susan Houston, 'The "Waifs and Strays" of a Late Victorian City: Juvenile Delinquents in Toronto', in Joy Parr, ed., *Childhood and Family in Canadian History* (Toronto, 1982), 129–42.

27. Nicole Hahn Rafter, *Partial Justice: Women in State Prisons, 1800–1935* (Chicago, 1985).

28. Andrée Lévesque, *Making and Breaking the Rules: Women in Quebec, 1919–1939* (Toronto, 1994). These examples of how social control was actually employed by historians indicate a variety of applications and research conclusions. Some historians who offer critiques of social control add important qualifications, but then circle back to similar arguments. For example, see David Bright, 'Loafers Are Not Going to Subsist Upon Public Credulence: Vagrancy and the Law in Calgary, 1900–14', *Labour/Le Travail* 36 (1995): 37–58. Social theory critics tend to overgeneralize about historical works using social control terminology. Allan Hunt, for example, claims it always ignores 'human agency'. Hunt, *Governing Morals: A Social History of Moral Regulation* (Cambridge, 1999), 18–19.

29. For the definition of critical (or revisionist) social control theory, see Stanley Cohen, 'The Critical Discourse on "Social Control": Notes on the Concept as a Hammer', *International Journal of the Sociology of Law* 17 (1989): 347–57. See also essays critical of social control in Stanley Cohen and Andrew Scull, eds, *Social Control and the State: Historical and Comparative Essays* (Oxford, 1983).

30. For an excellent feminist critique of social control, see Dorothy Chunn and Shelley Gavigan, 'Social Control: Analytical Tool or Analytical Quagmire?', *Contemporary Crises* 12 (1988): 107–24.

31. Ibid. See also Linda Gordon, 'Family Violence, Feminism and Social Control', *Feminist Studies* 12, 3 (Fall 1986): 453–78.

32. Mary Odem, *Delinquent Daughters: Protecting and Policing Adolescent Female Sexuality in the United States, 1885–1920* (Chapel Hill, NC, 1995).

33. See Cohen, 'The Critical Discourse'.

34. Rafter, *Partial Justice*, 157.

35. Adrian Howe, *Punish and Critique: Towards a Feminist Analysis of Penality* (London, 1994), 64.

36. Phillip Corrigan and Derek Sayer, *The Great Arch: English State Formation as Cultural Revolution* (Oxford, 1985); Douglas Hay, 'Time, Inequality and Law's Violence', in Austin Sarat and Thomas Kearns, eds, *Law's Violence* (Ann Arbor, Mich., 1992), 141–73. For sociological examples, see Stephen Brickey and Elizabeth Comack, eds, *The Social Basis of Law: Critical Readings in the Sociology of Law* (Toronto, 1986).

37. Hunt, *Explorations in Law and Society*, 276, 253.

38. The best-known work was Smart, *Feminism and the Power of the Law*.

39. Kerry Carrington, *Offending Girls: Sex, Youth and Justice* (Sydney, 1993), 107, 88. For the earlier views on sexualization she is criticizing, see Meda Chesney-Lind, 'Girl's Crime and Woman's Place: Toward a Feminist Model of Female Delinquency', *Crime and Delinquency* 35, 1 (Jan. 1989): 5–29; Steven Schlossman and Stephanie Wallach, 'The Crime of Precocious Sexuality: Female Juvenile Delinquency in the Progressive Era', *Harvard Educational Review* 48 (1978): 65; Gloria Geller, 'Young Women in Conflict with the Law', in Adelberg and Currie, eds, *Too Few to Count*; Indiana Matters, 'Sinners or Sinned Against?: Historical Aspects of Female Juvenile Delinquency in British Columbia', in Barbara Latham and Roberta Pazdro, eds, *Not Just Pin Money: Selected Essays on the History of Women's Work in British Columbia* (Victoria, 1984).

40. Nikolas Rose, 'Beyond the Public/Private Division: Law, Power and the Family', in Peter Fitzpatrick and Alan Hunt, eds, *Critical Legal Studies* (Oxford, 1987), 66, 73–4. For another attempt to develop a 'feminist-pluralist' analysis, in contrast to the so-called 'ideological indoctrination' of Marxist-feminist analyses, see Faith Robertson Elliot, 'The Family: Private Arena or Adjunct of the State', *Journal of Law and Society* 16, 4 (1989): 443–63.

41. Rose and others claim that feminist theories rest on notions of false consciousness, but this has been answered by those who point out that materialist and feminist works attempted to understand 'multi-faceted ways in which power was manifested, while never ignoring the "centrality" of state formations'. Susan Boyd, '(Re)Placing the State:

Family, Law and Oppression', *Canadian Journal of Women and the Law* 9, 1 (1994): 47.

42. Howe, *Punish and Critique*, 83. This is all the more ironic since Foucault is reported to have noted that 'they [his commentators] don't understand what I am saying.' Quoted ibid.

43. This definition draws on Hunt, *Governing Morals*, ix; also Mariana Valverde, 'Introduction', in Valverde, ed., *Studies in Moral Regulation* (Toronto, 1994), v. There are still important differences between authors claiming to use Foucault. An early British contribution, R. Dobash, R. Dobash, and S. Gutteridge, *The Imprisonment of Women* (Oxford, 1986), draws on Foucault but still uses the idea of social control.

44. Michel Foucault, *Discipline and Punish: The Birth of a Prison* (New York, 1977), 177; Foucault, *History of Sexuality*, vol. 1 (New York, 1980), 144. For some feminist reinterpretations of Foucault, see Sandra Lee Bartky, *Femininity and Domination* (London, 1990); Susan Bordo, 'Feminism, Foucault and the Politics of the Body', in Caroline Ramazanoglu, ed., *Up Against Foucault: Explorations of Some Tensions between Foucault and Feminism* (London, 1993), 179; Irene Diamond and Lee Quinby, eds, *Feminism and Foucault: Reflections on Resistance* (Boston, 1988); Jana Sawicki, *Disciplining Foucault: Feminism, Power and the Body* (London, 1991); Carol Smart, 'Disruptive Bodies and Unruly Sex: Historical Essays on Marriage, Motherhood and Sexuality', in Smart, ed., *Regulating Womanhood: Historical Essays on Marriage, Motherhood and Sexuality* (London, 1992); Mary Louise Adams, *The Trouble with Normal: Post-War Youth and the Making of Heterosexuality* (Toronto, 1998).

45. Nancy Fraser, 'Michel Foucault: "A Young Conservative"?', in Susan J. Hekman, ed., *Feminist Interpretations of Michel Foucault* (University Park, Penn., 1996), 26.

46. Alan Hunt and Gary Wickam, *Foucault and Law* (London, 1994).

47. Quoted in Linda Alcoff, 'Feminist Politics and Foucault: The Limits to Collaboration', in Arleen Dallery et al., eds, *Contemporary Crises in Continental Philosophy* (Albany, NY, 1990), 75.

48. Michel Foucault, in Colin Gordon, ed., *Power/Knowledge: Selected Interviews, 1972–77* (New York, 1980), 98. See also Ladelle McWhorter, 'Foucault's Analysis of Power', in Callery et al., eds, *Contemporary Crises in Continental Philosophy*, 119–26.

49. Kate Soper, 'Productive Contradictions', in Ramazanoglu, ed., *Up Against Foucault*, 31; Bordo, 'Feminism, Foucault, and the Politics of the Body', 179–202.

50. Karlene Faith, 'Resistance: Lessons from Foucault and Feminism', in H. Lorraine Radtke and H. Stam, eds, *Power/Gender: Social Relations*

in Theory and Practice (London, 1994), 55. At the same time, this emphasis on the body risks 'retaining the emphasis on female corporeality that has been so prevalent in patriarchal culture'. Soper, 'Productive Contradictions', 35.

51. Foucault, *History of Sexuality*, 45.

52. Strange, *Toronto's Girl Problem*; Margaret Little, *'No Car, No Radio, No Liquor Permit': The Moral Regulation of Single Mothers in Ontario, 1920–97* (Toronto, 1998).

53. Foucault, *Discipline and Punish*, 22, 170, 222–3. Allan Hunt and Gary Wickam note that Foucault explores the interdependence of the law and the disciplines, but there is still a tendency for the disciplines to dominate the law. See Hunt and Wickam, *Foucault and Law* (London, 1994), 47, 49.

54. Jacques Donzelot, *The Policing of Families* (New York, 1979), 110.

55. Linda Mahood, *Policing Gender, Class and Family: Britain, 1850–1940* (London, 1995); Dorothy Chunn, *From Punishment to Doing Good: Family Courts and Socialized Justice in Ontario, 1880–1940* (Toronto, 1992).

56. Foucault, *The History of Sexuality*, 89.

57. Foucault, *Discipline and Punish*, 170.

58. Hunt, *Explorations*, ch. 12.

59. Smart, *Feminism and the Power of the Law*, 4.

60. Nikolas Rose and Mariana Valverde, 'Governed by Law?', *Social and Legal Studies* 7, 4 (1998): 542.

61. Graham Burchell and Colin Gordon, eds, *The Foucault Effect: Studies in Governmentality* (Hemel Hempstead, 1991), 2–3, 102–3.

62. David Garland, 'Governmentality and the Problem of Crime: Foucault, Criminology, Sociology', *Theoretical Criminology* 1, 2 (1997): 182.

63. As David Garland observes, governmentality theorists often conflate 'agency' with 'freedom'—two very different things. Ibid., 197.

64. Ibid., 204–5.

65. Hunt, *Explorations*, 288.

66. Nikolas Rose, 'Governing "Advanced" Liberal Democracies', in Andrew Barry, Thomas Osborne, and Nikolas Rose, eds, *Foucault and Political Reason* (Chicago, 1996), 42, 56, 60.

67. Boris Frankel criticizes the failure to discuss the role of globalized capitalist market values of individualism, competition, and consumerism in this turn of events. See Frankel, 'Confronting Neo-liberal Regimes: The Post-Marxist Embrace of Populism and Realpolitik', *New Left Review* 226 (1997): 57–92.

68. Nancy Hartstock, 'Foucault on Power: A Theory for Women?', in Linda Nicholson, ed., *Feminism/Postmodernism* (New York, 1990), 157–75; Hartstock, *The Feminist Standpoint Revisited* (Boulder, Colo., 1998),

205–27. See also Faith, 'Resistance: Lessons from Foucault and Feminism', 36–66.

69. Frankel, 'Confronting Neo-Liberal Regimes', 83–4.

70. For example, Nikolas Rose, *Governing the Soul: The Shaping of the Private Self* (New York, 1990).

71. Ebert, *Ludic Feminism and After*. Although some claim Foucault's projects are implicitly grounded in truth claims, they are not explicitly so. For the former, see Nancy Cook, 'The Thin Within the Thick: Social History, Postmodern Ethnography and Textual Practice', *Histoire sociale/Social History* 63 (May 1999): 98.

72. As Smart points out, 'work like [Judith] Butler's, should it be used in the legal forum, would almost certainly be treated as incomprehensible.' Carol Smart, 'Law, Feminism and Sexuality: From Essence to Ethics?', *Canadian Journal of Law and Society* 9, 1 (1994): 26.

73. Alcoff, 'Feminist Politics and Foucault': 'Since subjectivity is nothing but the product of discourses, there can be no autonomous agent who rebels against regulation or oppression.'

74. Smart, *Feminism and the Power of the Law*, 163–4.

75. Currie, 'Feminist Encounters with Postmodernism', 76, 82.

76. Colin Sumner, 'Introduction: Contemporary Socialist Criminology', in Gelsthorpe and Morris, eds, *Feminist Perspectives in Criminology*, 1–11.

77. Colin Sumner, 'Re-thinking Deviance: Towards a Sociology of Censure', in Gelsthorpe and Morris, eds, *Feminist Perspectives in Criminology*, 15–40. See also Sumner, 'Foucault, Gender and the Censure of Deviance', ibid.; Paul Roberts, 'Social Control and the Censure(s) of Sex', *Crime, Law and Social Change* 19 (1993): 171–86.

78. Sumner, 'Re-thinking Deviance', 28–9.

79. For a discussion of the evolution of materialist feminism, see Rosemary Hennessy and Chris Ingraham, 'Introduction: Reclaiming Anticapitalist Feminism', in Hennessy and Ingraham, eds, *Materialist Feminism: A Reader in Class, Difference and Women's Lives* (New York, 1997).

80. What Foucault thought about the 'extra-discursive' is open to contention. For one view, see Maureen Cain, 'Foucault, Feminism and Feeling: What Foucault Can and Cannot Contribute to Feminist Epistemology', in Ramazanoglu, ed., *Up Against Foucault*, 73–96.

81. Hay, 'Law's Violence'.

82. Engle, *Getting Justice and Getting Even*, 10, 180.

83. Eagleton, *The Illusions of Postmodernism*, 56.

84. Smart, 'Feminist Approaches to Criminology', 70.

85. Nikolas Rose and Peter Miller, 'Political Power Beyond the State: Problematics of Government', *British Journal of Sociology* 43, 2 (1992): 177: 'Our studies of government eschew sociological realism and its burdens

of explanation and causation. We do not try to characterize how social life really was.' For a defence of sociological 'realism', see Garland, 'Governmentality'.

86. Empirical inquiry can be differentiated from much maligned 'empiricism', or the idea there is a recoverable, exact truth. As Richard Price argues, the historical method, especially in social history, inevitably rubs up against some post-structuralist writing. See Price, 'Postmodernism as Theory and History', in John Belcham and Neville Kirk, eds, *Languages of Labour* (Aldershot, 1997), 11–43. For other materialist critiques, see Bryan Palmer, *Descent into Discourse: The Reification of Language and the Writing of Social History* (Philadelphia, 1990); Alex Callinicos, *Theories and Narratives: Reflections on the Philosophy of History* (Durham, NC, 1995); Neville Kirk, 'History, Language, Ideas and Postmodernism: A Materialist View', in Keith Jenkins, ed., *The Postmodern History Reader* (London, 1997). Feminist theorists have also argued for the radical potential of empiricism, as well as the continuing relevance of standpoint theory. See Hartstock, *The Feminist Standpoint Revisited*; Dorothy E. Smith, *Writing the Social: Critique, Theory and Investigations* (Toronto, 1989); Maureen Cain, 'Realism, Feminism, Methodology and Law', *International Journal of the Sociology of Law* 14 (1986).

87. Maureen Cain, 'Towards Transgression: New Directions in Feminist Criminology', *International Journal of the Sociology of Law* 18, 1 (1990): 1–18.

88. Richard Evans, *In Defence of History* (London, 1997), 98.

89. This issue is discussed in Ruth Roach Pierson, 'Experience, Difference, Dominance and Voice in Writing of Canadian Women's History', in Karen Offen, Ruth Pierson, and Jane Rendall, eds, *Writing Women's History: International Perspectives* (Bloomington, Ind., 1991), 79–106; Radha Jhappan, 'Post-Modern Race and Gender Essentialism or a Post-Mortem of Scholarship', *Studies in Political Economy* 51 (1996): 15–63.

90. I am not sure we need to make the polar distinctions that Tina Loo suggests: 'focusing on coercion can reduce subjects of regulation to objects or victims who possess little agency. . . . what little they do have is limited to . . . reacting to the actions and agenda of the powerful.' Loo, 'Dan Cranmer's Potlach: Law as Coercion, Symbol and Rhetoric in British Columbia, 1884–1951', *Canadian Historical Review* 73, 2 (1992): 125–65.

91. Susan F. Hirsch and Mindie Lazarus-Black, 'Performance and Paradox: Exploring Law's Role in Hegemony and Resistance', in Hirsch and Lazarus-Black, eds, *Contested States*, 1.

92. Walter Tarnopolsky, *Discrimination and the Law in Canada* (Toronto, 1982); James W. St G. Walker, *'Race' Rights and the Law in the Supreme Court of Canada* (Toronto, 1997), 12–50: Constance Backhouse, *Colour Coded: A Legal History of Racism in Canada, 1900–50* (Toronto, 1999); Constance Backhouse, 'White Female Help and Chinese Canadian Employers: Race, Class, Gender and Law in the Case of Yee Clung, 1924', *Canadian Ethnic Studies* 26, 3 (1994): 34–52; James W. St G. Walker, 'The Quong Wing Files', in Iacovetta and Mitchinson, eds, *On the Case*, 204–23. Sexuality and race also converged in eugenic discourse and legislation. See Angus McLaren, *Our Own Master Race: Eugenics in Canada, 1885–1945* (Toronto, 1990).

93. Peggy Pascoe, 'Miscegenation Law, Court Cases, and Ideologies of "Race" in Twentieth Century America', in Martha Hodes, ed., *Sex, Love, Race: Crossing Boundaries in North American History* (New York, 1999), 464–90.

94. On feminist critical race theory, see Sharene Razack, *Looking White People in the Eye: Gender, Race and Culture in Classrooms and Courtrooms* (Toronto, 1998); F. Anthais and N. Yuval-Davis, eds, *Racialized Boundaries: Race, Nation, Gender and Colour and Class and the Anti-Racist Struggle* (London, 1992); Rose Brewer, 'Theorizing Race, Class and Gender', in Stanlie James and A. Busia, eds, *Theorizing Black Feminisms: The Visionary Pragmatism of Black Women* (New York, 1993); Adrian K. Wing, ed., *Critical Race Feminism: A Reader* (New York, 1997).

95. Enakshi Dua, 'Beyond Diversity: Exploring the Ways in Which the Discourse of Race has Shaped the Institution of the Nuclear Family', in Dua and A. Robertson, eds, *Scratching the Surface: Canadian Anti-Racist Feminist Thought* (Toronto, 1999), 237–60.

96. Winona Stevenson, 'Colonialism and First Nations Women in Canada', in Dua and Robertson, eds, *Scratching the Surface*, 49–82.

97. For specific explications relating to women, see, e.g., Marlee Kline, 'Complicating the Ideology of Motherhood: Child Welfare Law and First Nation Women', in Martha A. Fineman and Isabel Karpin, eds, *Mothers in Law: Feminist Theory and the Legal Regulation of Motherhood* (New York, 1995), 118–41; Razack, *Looking White People in the Eye*.

98. Ian F. Haney Lopez, *White By Law: The Legal Construction of Race* (New York, 1996), 144.

99. Ibid.

100. Kimberlé Williams Crenshaw, 'Race, Reform and Retrenchment: Transformation and Legitimation in Antidiscrimination Law', *Harvard Law Review* 101 (1988): 1358.

101. Hennessy and Ingraham, 'Introduction', 4.

Chapter 2

1. The time period for this chapter differs slightly from the others, in part due to the availability and nature of sources (see Note on Sources). In Ontario, Criminal Assize indictments (CAI) are available from the 1880s to 1929, catalogued by charge and county, allowing for review of all incest cases coming to this upper court. After 1930, these categories of record retention were abandoned and court cases are extremely difficult to locate. Only one county (York) catalogued its CAI files after 1920 by charge. Two other (lower) criminal courts in York kept similar records, yielding cases for the 1930s, but not for the subsequent war years. Many cases were tried in lower and county courts for which we have no surviving records. I have also used case files of women and girls charged with juvenile offences but whose backgrounds included charges of incest.

2. Judith Herman and Lisa Hirschman, 'Father-Daughter Incest', *Signs* 4, 2 (1977): 735–56.

3. Linda Alcoff and Laura Gray, 'Survivor Discourse: Transgression or Recuperation?', *Signs* 18, 2 (1993): 260–90. The authors also show how survivor stories become part of commodity culture, marketed in the media within the dominant discourse, only allowed legitimacy if 'explained' by the experts.

4. Lynne Segal, *Why Feminism?* (New York, 1999), 127. Segal parts company with feminists who see Freud as complicit, if not worse, in the suppression of incest stories.

5. Diana Russell, *The Secret Trauma: Incest in the Lives of Girls and Women* (New York, 1999), 5–9.

6. Vikki Bell, *Interrogating Incest: Feminism, Foucault and Law* (London, 1993), 75.

7. Dean MacCannell and Juliet Flower MacCannell, 'Violence, Power and Pleasure: A Revisionist Reading of Foucault from the Victim Perspective', in Ramazanoglu, ed., *Up Against Foucault*, 203–38.

8. Bell, *Interrogating Incest*, 63–70.

9. Harriet Fraad, 'At Home with Incest', *Rethinking Marxism* 9, 4 (1996–7): 16–39.

10. Linda Martin Alcoff, 'Dangerous Pleasures: Foucault and the Politics of Pedophilia', in Hekman, ed., *Feminist Interpretations of Michel Foucault*, 123.

11. MacCannell and MacCannell, 'Violence, Power and Pleasure', 204–5.

12. Ibid., 230. The failure to analyse whether a child can really offer 'consent' is also a crucial blindspot in his writing.

13. W. Woodhull, 'Sexuality, Power and the Question of Rape', in Diamond and Quinby, eds, *Feminism and Foucault*, 167–76.

14. Bell, *Interrogating Incest*, 25.

15. Ian Hacking, 'The Making and Moulding of Child Abuse', *Critical Inquiry* 17 (Winter, 1991): 259.

16. Joan Scott, Review of *Heroes of Their Own Lives: The Politics and History of Family Violence*, and Linda Gordon, Reply, *Signs* 15, 4 (1990): 853.

17. There were earlier nineteenth-century laws in some provinces such as Nova Scotia, Prince Edward Island, and New Brunswick, but no law in the larger provinces of Ontario and Quebec.

18. Canada, *Statutes of Canada*, Criminal Code, 176, 1890.

19. Ibid., 1927, ch. 36, s. 213.

20. Tamara Myers, 'Qui t'a Débauchée?: Sexual Histories of Female Adolescents in the Montreal Juvenile Delinquents Court in the Early Twentieth Century', paper presented at the Carleton Conference on the History of the Family, May 1997, 2. For example, in the cases before the Ontario Criminal Assize Courts, only one man was previously charged with contributing to juvenile delinquency for an 'indecent assault' on his daughter before the incest charge was laid. In a Quebec appeal, the higher courts ruled against using the Juvenile Delinquents Act to prosecute a father for incest (probably under the 'contributing' clause) because this offence could not be tried summarily, even on consent of the accused. *Leroux v. the King* (1928), D.L.R. 299. See also W.L. Scott, *The Juvenile Court in Law* (Ottawa, 1941), 34–5. However, a case could be removed from the Juvenile Court to adult court, as described below.

21. MPs worried that 'designing women' might use seduction laws to 'blackmail them'. Canada, *House of Commons Debates*, 10 Apr. 1890, 3168, 3166. See Karen Dubinsky, ' "Maidenly Girls" or "Designing Women"? The Crime of Seduction in Turn-of-the-Century Ontario', in Franca Iacovetta and Mariana Valverde, eds, *Gender Conflicts: New Essays in Women's History* (Toronto, 1992), 27–66; Graham Parker, 'The Legal Regulation of Sexual Activity and the Protection of Females', *Osgoode Hall Law Journal* 21, 2 (1983): 187–244.

22. *House of Commons Debates*, 10 Apr. 1890, Sir John Thompson, 3162.

23. Ibid.

24. Ibid., Mr Casey, 3172.

25. Ibid., Mr Blake, 3172.

26. Ibid., Sir John Thompson, 3172.

27. This chapter is based primarily on incest charges, though some carnal knowledge cases involving close relations were taken into account. I do substitute the term 'sexual abuse' for incest, using it in its more modern sense as encompassing incest. For an excellent study of sexual assault in

general, see Karen Dubinsky, *Improper Advances: Rape and Heterosexual Conflict in Ontario, 1880–1929* (Chicago, 1993).

28. *Desellier v. R.,* 45 C.C.C. 246 (1925). As one appeal tried to argue, 'the purpose of the law is undoubtedly to prevent issue from such unnatural relations. Therefore the sexual relations must be such as may produce conception.' *R. v. Fournier*, 62 C.C.C. 397.

29. This was one of the issues in the Peterborough case discussed below. *R. v. Lindsay*, S.C.O. in 26 C.C.C. 163 and *R. v. Lindsay*, 3 Mar. 1916 in O.L.R. 171 (1916). See also AO, RG 22–476–1–14, Judge Mulock's Benchbooks, 18 Feb. 1916.

30. This came up more than once; proof of consanguinity, other than testimony, was sometimes demanded, sometimes not. Quebec laws made written proof (other than testimony) essential. See *Rex v. Smith*, 13 C.C.C. 403 (1908) and *Queen v. Garneau*, 4 C.C.C. 69 (1899) on the first issue; on Quebec, *R. v. Garneau*, 4 C.C.C. 69 (1899).

31. *R. v. Bloodworth*, 9 C.A.R. 80 (1913).

32. Supposedly, incest was not named in the Criminal Code as one of the offences requiring corroboration of other witnesses. *Crankshaw's Criminal Code of Canada* (1935), 181. However, this is not always what happened in practice.

33. The word 'accomplice' is repeatedly used. See, for example, *R. v. Bloodworth*; *R. v. Gordon*, 19 C.A.R. 20. On the issue of sisters being automatically guilty, see *R. v. Draker*, 21 C.A.R. 47 (1919) and *R. v. Gordon*.

34. *Rex v. Elzear Pailleur*, O.W.R. 15, 3, 73. The court convicted him under s. 570 of the Criminal Code, which stated that everyone is guilty of an indictable offence who attempts an indictable offence.

35. *R. v. Bloodworth*, 9 C.A.R. 80 (1913).

36. *R. v. Proteau*, 33 B.C.L.R. 39 (1923).

37. Ibid.

38. Canada, *Statistics of Criminal and Other Offenses*, 1922–45; Ontario, *Report of Prisons and Reformatories*, 1936–45.

39. Dubinsky, *Improper Advances*, 172. Of the 348 sexual violence cases in Ontario from 1880 to 1929 that she studied, 47 (13.5 per cent) were charges against family members, with a 49 per cent conviction rate. Of her total 665 cases (including seduction), only 18 were incest charges, also underlining the 'uncommon' nature of the charge.

40. Admittedly, those before the Assizes were highly contested to begin with. Of the 25 cases before the Criminal Assizes, 12 were not guilty, five were guilty of incest, four had no bills, one secured a rape charge, one an assault charge, one had an unknown verdict, and one case file was lost in the archives.

41. For other historical studies on incest, see Gordon, *Heroes of Their Own Lives*, ch. 7; Elizabeth Pleck, *Domestic Tyranny: The Making of American Social Policy against Family Violence from Colonial Times to the Present* (New York, 1987), 95–7, 156–7. On child abuse more generally, see Carol-Ann Hooper, 'Child Sexual Abuse and the Regulation of Women: Variations on a Theme', in Smart, ed., *Regulating Womanhood*, 53–77; Lela Costin, Howard Karger, and David Stoesz, *The Politics of Child Abuse in America* (New York, 1996).

42. For example, I found only one case of a male victim noted in the case law. Although it appears under incest cases, the charge was committing an act of gross indecency. An appeal was granted to the accused since he was convicted only on the testimony of the male 'accomplice' or victim. *R. v. Roynton* (1935), O.W.N. 11 (1934). Current research confirms the predominance of the sexual abuse of girls.

43. Fraad, 'At Home with Incest', 22.

44. This is based on 217 cases between 1858 and 1938. Marie-Aimée Cliche, 'Un secret bien gardé: L'inceste dans la société traditionnelle québécoise, 1858–1938', *Revue d'histoire amérique française* 50, 2 (automne 1996): 211.

45. Dorothy Chunn, 'Secrets and Lies: The Criminalization of Incest and the (Re)formation of the "Private" in British Columbia, Canada, 1890–1940', unpublished paper. My thanks to Dorothy for allowing me to read this work before publication.

46. *St Catharines Standard*, 6 Mar. 1923. The defendant was found not guilty.

47. AO, RG 4–392 (Attorney General: Criminal Assize Indictments), box 122, Perth County, 1929.

48. AO, RG 22–392, box 85, Lincoln County, 1895; box 85a, Lincoln County, 1902.

49. Ibid., box 167, Welland County, 1923; *St Catharines Standard*, 6 Mar. 1923.

50. AO, RG 22–392, box 167, Welland County, 1923. 'These people' would apply to the whole family, but clearly he was arguing for the father's respectability.

51. Moreover, the mother was quizzed on whether her daughter had a 'beau coming around', probably to cast doubt on the daughter's virginity. Ibid., box 26, Carleton County, 1927.

52. Ibid., box 56, Hastings County, 1909.

53. Karen Dubinsky gives one good example in *Improper Advances*, 60, for a carnal knowledge case involving a common-law stepfather. This did not come out in as many incest cases in this period, but it clearly was a subtext in other legal and medical commentary.

54. AO, RG 22–393, box 124, Peterborough County, 1913.

55. AO, RG 22–392, box 56, Hastings County, 1909. The lack of understanding by judges that incest may not leave 'visible' scars remains a problem in contemporary cases. See Judy Steed, *Our Little Secret: Confronting Child Sexual Abuse in Canada* (Toronto, 1994), 201.

56. AO, RG 22–392, box 124, Peterborough County, 1923.

57. Ibid., box 258, York County, 1895. The father was found not guilty on charges against the older sister but guilty on the charge of rape against the younger one, presumably because the case was subsequently tried without a jury.

58. Ibid., box 143 and box 144, Stormont and Dundas Counties, 1890 and 1892; *Cornwall Freeholder*, 11 Mar. 1892.

59. This is also true of carnal knowledge cases. See AO, RG 22–392, box 5, Algoma.

60. Because Karen Dubinsky has covered this case in some detail, I have not. See Dubinsky, *Improper Advances*, 60–1.

61. *Peterborough Daily Review*, 23–4 Sept. 1915.

62. AO, RG 23 (Ontario Provincial Police Records), E–10 (Criminal Investigations), box 1, file 1.6. All quotes from letters of Inspector Boyd to Superintendent Rogers, 4, 11, 15 Nov. 1915.

63. *Peterborough Daily Review*, 28 Oct. 1915.

64. AO, RG 22–476–1–14, Judge Mulock's Benchbooks, 18 Feb. 1916.

65. *Peterborough Examiner*, 26 Apr. 1916.

66. The second trial, presided over by Supreme Court Justice Glenholme Falconbridge, was not covered in his benchbooks.

67. *Peterborough Examiner*, 28 Apr. 1916.

68. *Peterborough Daily Review*, 12 Sept. 1915.

69. AO, RG 23, E–10, box 1, Constable Boyd Report, 21 Feb. 1916. Indeed, another woman in the berry patch claimed not to remember the scene of Sandford on top of his daughter being pointed out to her. AO, RG 22–476–1–14, Mulock Benchbooks, 17 Feb. 1916. Ten years later, Boyd repeated his claim that neighbours in the area were afraid to turn in 'low class' criminals to the Attorney General. AO, RG 4–32, file 509 (he is referring to another case involving violence against a child, the Dwyer case).

70. In another incest case in adjoining Hastings County, the justice of the peace noted: 'While his neighbours seem to think him guilty, they are unable to give material evidence.' AO, RG 22–392, box 56, Hastings County, 1910. This is also one of Cliche's conclusions.

71. Chunn, 'Secrets and Lies'.

72. AO, RG 4 (Attorney General's Records), series 32, file 2326A, G.W. Hatton to Attorney General, Jan. 1916.

73. T. Morrison, 'The Proper Sphere: Feminism, the Family and Child-Centred Reform in Ontario, 1875–1900', *Ontario History* 68, 1 (Mar. 1976), and 68, 2 (June 1976): 45–74; John Bullen, 'Hidden Workers: Child Labour in Late Nineteenth Century Urban Ontario', *Labour/Le Travail* 18 (Fall 1986): 163–88; Neil Sutherland, *Children in English Canadian Society: Framing the Twentieth Century Consensus* (Toronto, 1976).

74. W.R. Young, 'Conscription, Rural Depopulation and the Farmers of Ontario', *Canadian Historical Review* 53, 3 (1972): 289–320. See also Dubinsky, *Improper Advances*, 152–4.

75. AO, Royal Commission on the Feeble Minded, RG 8–5, container 56, Provincial Secretary's Correspondence, file 'Feeble Minded', Report for Mr Semple, 21 Jan. 1919, from J. Morgan Shaw for the Royal Commission. See also Mariana Valverde, *The Age of Light, Soap, and Water: Moral Reform in English Canada, 1885–1925* (Toronto, 1991), 94, 99.

76. In fact, this may have aided the claim of the Lindsays' lawyer that bias already existed towards them.

77. One silence, especially in contrast to more contemporary writing, was striking: only the opinions of local (male) notables and experts were secured, never those of complainants, victims, or survivors of violence.

78. *Globe and Mail*, 26 Mar. 1926.

79. Peterborough Museum and Archives, [uncatalogued] Report on Certain Conditions existing in a part of the Northern District of the County of Peterborough and Adjoining Lands, presented by the Grand Jury, Peterborough Assizes, 1916 (hereafter, Grand Jury Report), 14.

80. The idea that poverty and overcrowding were causes of incest had already been graphically illustrated in another Badlands incest trial a few years before. The Crown produced pictures showing the family's log shack, with many children outside it, and also photographed them inside, crowded onto a dirty bunk bed. AO, RG 4–392, box 56, Hastings County, 1909. Hastings County, just to the east of Peterborough County, was often included in the geography of the Badlands.

81. Grand Jury Report, 11.

82. Ibid., 10.

83. Ibid., 5.

84. Ibid., 7.

85. Ibid., 1, 9.

86. Dubinsky, *Improper Advances*, 62. In a comparable manner, wife-battering was attributed to immigrant and working-class men, but not to middle-class men. David Peterson del Mar, *What Troubles I Have Seen: A History of Violence against Wives* (Cambridge, Mass., 1996), ch. 3.

87. Rob Shields, *Places on the Margin: Alternative Geographies of Modernity* (London, 1991), 7.

88. Edward Soja, *Postmodern Geographies: The Reassertion of Space in Critical Social Theory* (London, 1989), 61. See also Shields, *Places on the Margin*, 255–6.

89. Matt Wray and Annalee Newitz, 'Introduction', in Wray and Newitz, eds, *White Trash: Race and Class in America* (New York, 1997), 2.

90. These were penned by an emerging class of experts whose use of eugenics reinforced their own professional importance and class position. (The same might be true of Canadians like Dr Helen MacMurchy.) Nicole Hann Rafter, 'Introduction', in Rafter, ed., *White Trash: The Eugenic Family Studies 1877–1919* (Boston, 1988), 13.

91. AO, RG 18–65, Royal Commission on the Feeble Minded and Venereal Disease, container 1, Report on the Care and Control of the Feeble Minded by Chief Justice Hodgins, 5.

92. Joan Sangster, 'Masking and Unmasking the Sexual Abuse of Children: Perceptions of Violence against Children in the "Badlands" of Ontario, 1916–26', *Journal of Family History* 25, 4 (Oct. 2000): 504–26.

93. AO, RG 22–5870, York County Court Judges Criminal Court (hereafter CCJCC), file 74–34 (1934).

94. *Bergeron v. the King*, 56 C.C.C. 62 (1930). The defence lawyers often called the girls 'accomplices', though the higher court rejected this language.

95. *Rex v. Pegelo*, 62 C.C.C. 78 (1934); *Rex v. Guilbault*, 72 C.C.C. 254 (1939). While these appeals failed, it is interesting that lawyers were still using these well-worn arguments. It is also possible that such arguments also swayed juries in lower courts.

96. AO, RG 22–5871, York County General Sessions (GS), file 34–39 (1939).

97. AO, RG 22–5870, CCJCC, 110–33 (1933). Since her statement was not in the file, we only have his interpretation for the court, which was designed to secure his acquittal.

98. AO, RG 22–5871, GS, file 35–31 (1931).

99. AO, Ontario Training School for Girls (OTSG) case file 275, 1930s.

100. AO, RG 22–5870, CCJCC, file 4–31 (1931).

101. AO, RG 22–5871, file 34–39 (1939). The father was also convicted of assault causing bodily harm.

102. AO, OTSG case file 75, 1930s.

103. AO, OTGS case file 275, 1930s.

104. AO, OTSG case file 1088, early 1940s.

105. AO, OTSG case file 250, 1930s.

106. Joan Sangster, 'Incarcerating "Bad Girls": The Regulation of Sexuality through the Female Refuges Act in Ontario, 1920–45', *Journal of the History of Sexuality* 7, 2 (Oct. 1996): 267–8.

107. AO, OTSG case files 1531 and 365, 1940s.

108. AO, OTSG case file 835, 1940s; emphasis added.

109. Ibid.

110. AO, RG 22–292, box 258, York County, 1892.

111. *St Catharines Standard*, 6 Mar. 1923.

112. AO, RG 22–392, box 143, 144, Stormont County, 1890, 1892.

113. AO, OTSG case file 853, 1940s.

114. The first two were articulated even within one file by different experts. See AO, OTSG case file 225, 1930s, and the latter, file 1651, 1950s.

115. AO, OTSG case files 835 and 225, 1940s, 1930s.

116. For example, see G. Devereux, 'Social and Cultural Implications of Incest Among the Mohave Indians', *Psychoanalytic Quarterly* 8 (Oct. 1939): 510–33.

117. L.S. Penrose, 'A Contribution to the Genetic Study of Mental Deficiency', *British Medical Journal* 1 (Jan. 1934): 10–11.

118. Eleanor Pavenstedt, 'Discussion' for Irving Kaufman, Alice Peck, and Consuelo Tagiuri, 'The Family Constellation and Overt Incestuous Relations between Father and Daughter', *American Journal of Orthopsychiatry* (Apr. 1954): 278.

119. Eva Karpinski and Paul Sloane, 'Incest: Effects on Participants', *American Journal of Orthopsychiatry* 12 (Oct. 1942): 666–73.

120. Ibid., 666.

121. L. Bender and A. Blau, 'The Reaction of Children to Sexual Relations with Adults', *Journal of American Orthopsychiatry* 7 (1937): 500–18.

122. It is important to note that this study was then drawn on by other researchers. J. Butler Tompkins, 'Penis Envy and Incest: A Case Report', *Psychoanalytic Review* (July 1940): 324.

123. Kaufman, Peck, and Tagiuri, 'The Family Constellation and Overt Incestuous Relations', 268.

124. Ibid., 271, 275.

125. Gordon, *Heroes of Their Own Lives*, 208.

126. Russell, *The Secret Trauma*, 5–8. See also Judith Herman, *Father-Daughter Incest* (Cambridge, Mass., 1981).

127. Janet Liebman Jacobs, 'Reassessing Mother Blame in Incest', *Signs* 15, 3 (1990): 500–15. Jacobs also explains the tendency for victims themselves to engage in mother-blaming.

128. Costin et al., *The Politics of Child Abuse*, 99. The authors noted other causes, such as disillusionment with Juvenile Courts, which would have been less important in Ontario, as widespread Juvenile Courts came somewhat later. See also Barbara Nelson, *Making an Issue of Child Abuse: Political Agenda Setting for Social Problems* (Chicago, 1994), 129. For brief comment on Britain, see George Behlmer, *Child Abuse and Moral Reform in England, 1870–1920* (Stanford, Calif., 1982),

225. On the negative influence of psychiatric thinking, see Pleck, *Domestic Tyranny*, 156–7.

129. Peterborough CAS Records, Minute Books, 9 Nov. 1926.

130. Ibid., Annual Report of the Superintendent, 27 Nov. 1928.

131. Canada, *Hansard*, 12 Feb. 1954, Mr Nowlan, 2037.

132. Ibid., Mr Diefenbaker, 2038.

133. Ibid., Mr Garson, 2038.

134. Canada, *Statutes of Canada*, 1954, Criminal Code, s. 131.

135. Recently, some have argued that the 'myth of classlessness' about abuse has been promoted to dissociate anti-abuse programs from more unpopular anti-poverty ones. As a result, material deprivation and the social causes of abuse are downplayed in favour of a 'medical' model of individual disease or deviance. See Nelson, *Child Abuse as Social Problem*, 13–14; Costin et al.; *The Politics of Child Abuse*.

136. Bell, *Interrogating Incest*, 95.

137. Alcoff, 'Dangerous Pleasures', 99–100.

Chapter 3

1. *Peterborough Examiner* (hereafter *Examiner*), 26 Jan. 1950.

2. Ibid., 15 Nov. 1928.

3. Canada, *Statutes of Canada*, 1927, Criminal Code, ch. 36, s. 292 (c). Family Courts did have jurisdiction for assault, but only between husbands and wives, parents and children.

4. There is some debate about the use of the term 'battered wife' as some feminists argue this implies victimhood. Given my emphasis also on women's resistance, this is clearly not my intent. I have used a number of interchangeable terms in this chapter, including wife assault, wife-beating, and wife-battering. 'Wife' includes both common-law and legally married partners. 'Spousal abuse' may refer to violence by male and female partners, but unless noted, it refers here to male violence against women.

5. The papers used for the Toronto Family Court directly overlap with York County (what is now Metro Toronto, the surrounding urban area). Originally collected under the auspices of York County, the papers were transferred to the Toronto location when the courts were amalgamated in 1953, and the files include ones from both locations. See Note on Sources.

6. Margo Wilson and Martin Daly, 'Till Death Do Us Part', in Jill Radford and Diana Russell, eds, *Femicide* (New York, 1992), 92.

7. Tracy Chapman, 'Till Death Do Us Part: Wife Beating in Alberta, 1905–20', *Alberta History* 36, 4 (1988): 13.

8. The former view is suggested by conservatives intent on creating a mythical view of familial happiness in the past. The latter has been suggested by others who recognize the continuities of violence but still see increases due to changing gender roles and anxieties on men's part. See, e.g., Peterson del Mar, *What Troubles I Have Seen*, 168–9.

9. Canadian research has focused on the late nineteenth century and very early twentieth century. See Katharine Harvey, 'To Love, Honour and Obey: Wife Battering in Working-Class Montreal, 1869–79', *Urban History Review* 19, 2 (Oct. 1990): 128–40; Harvey, 'Amazons and Victims: Resisting Wife Abuse in Working-Class Montreal, 1869–79', *Journal of the Canadian Historical Association* 2 (1991): 131–48; Judith Fingard, 'The Prevention of Cruelty, Marital Breakdown and the Rights of Wives, 1880–1920', *Acadiensis* 22, 2 (1993): 84–101; Chapman, 'Till Death Do Us Part', 13–22; Annalee Goltz, 'Uncovering and Reconstructing Family Violence: Ontario Criminal Case Files', in Iacovetta and Mitchinson, eds, *On the Case*, 289–311; Carolyn Strange, 'Historical Perspectives on Wife Assault', in Mariana Valverde, Linda MacLeod, and Kirsten Johnson, eds, *Wife Assault and the Canadian Criminal Justice System* (Toronto, 1995). For comparative studies on the US and Britain, see Pat Ayers and Jan Lambertz, 'Marriage Relations, Money and Domestic Violence in Working-Class Liverpool, 1919–39', in Jane Lewis, ed., *Labour of Love: Women's Experiences of Home and Family, 1850–1940* (Oxford, 1986), 195–219; Ellen Ross, 'Fierce Questions and Taunts: Married Life in Working Class London, 1870–1914', *Feminist Studies* 8, 3 (1982): 575–602; Nancy Tomes, 'A Torrent of Abuse: Crimes of Violence between Working-Class Men and Women in London, 1840–75', *Journal of Social History* 11, 3 (1978): 328–45; Gordon, *Heroes of Their Own Lives*; Pleck, *Domestic Tyranny*; Peterson del Mar, *What Troubles I Have Seen*.

10. Sharon Cook, *Through Sunshine and Shadow: The Woman's Christian Temperance Union, Evangelicalism and Reform in Ontario, 1874–1939* (Montreal, 1995). In temperance literature, working-class men were 'weak, selfish, irresponsible and violent' (86).

11. James Snell, 'Marriage Humour and Its Functions', *Atlantis* 11, 2 (1986): 70–85.

12. Gordon, *Heroes of Their Own Lives*, 22–3.

13. This assumption is implicit in many sociological studies, such as Gillian Walker's *Family Violence and the Women's Movement* (Toronto, 1990). Even the the Royal Commission on the Status of Women of 1967 did not champion the issue of domestic violence.

14. For an overview of feminist views on this issue, see Anne Edwards, 'Male Violence in Feminist Theory: An Analysis of the Changing

Conceptions of Sex/Gender Violence and Male Dominance', in Jalna Hanmer and M. Maynard, eds, *Women, Violence and Social Control* (London, 1987), 13–29.

15. Carole Yawney, 'From "Uncle Tom to Aunt Jemima": Towards a Global Perspective on Violence against Women', *Canadian Women's Studies* 6, 1 (1985): 13–15.

16. Dubinsky, *Improper Advances*, 32.

17. Lynne Segal, *Slow Motion: Changing Masculinities, Changing Men* (New Brunswick, NJ, 1990), 256.

18. Ibid.

19. Kathleen Ferraro, 'The Dance of Dependency: A Genealogy of Domestic Violence Discourse', *Hypatia* 11, 4 (1996): 77–91.

20. Russell Dobash and R. Amerson Dobash, 'The Context Specific Approach', in David Finkelhor et al., eds, *The Dark Side of Families: Current Family Violence Research* (London, 1983), 261–76. The authors refer to E.P. Thompson and M. Foucault in the same breath.

21. Donzelot, *The Policing of Families*, 103–4. This is also true of Christopher Lasch, *Haven in a Heartless World* (New York, 1979). For a critique, see Michele Barrett and Mary McIntosh, *The Anti-social Family* (London, 1982); Chunn, *From Punishment to Doing Good*.

22. MacCannell and MacCannell, 'Violence, Power and Pleasure', 205.

23. Andrea Westlund, 'Pre-Modern and Modern Power: Foucault and the Case of Domestic Violence', *Signs* 24, 4 (1999): 1045.

24. Ibid.

25. The number of official charges of 'assault on wife' in Ontario (which had the majority of Canadian charges) in these years was small: 56 in 1925; 103 in 1930; 171 in 1935; 184 in 1940; 288 in 1945. After 1950 the charge was listed as assault on wife and female, with 240 in 1950 and 179 in 1955. Even when conviction rates were high, the numbers convicted and jailed were always small. Canada, *Statistics of Criminal and Other Offences*, 1925–55.

26. See, e.g., the exposé of the family dispute occasioned when an Italian husband was 'wronged' by another 'Latin' boarder who 'ran off' with his wife. *Examiner*, 13 Jan. 1931.

27. Ibid., 23 Jan. 1926.

28. Ibid., 10 Apr. 1926.

29. AO, RG 4–32, Attorney General's Correspondence, file 509, Dwyer case. See also Sangster, 'Masking and Unmasking the Sexual Abuse of Children'; *Examiner*, 23 Jan. 1939.

30. There is some debate about the timing of secularization, especially vis-à-vis sociology and the social work profession. Some see it emerging in the post-World War I years, others by the later 1930s. For the former,

see Marlene Shore, *The Science of Social Redemption: McGill, the Chicago School, and the Origins of Social Research in Canada* (Toronto, 1987); Richard Allen, *The Social Passion: Religion and Social Reform in Canada* (Toronto, 1973). On the latter, Nancy Christie and Michael Gauvreau, *A Full-Orbed Christianity: The Protestant Churches and Social Welfare in Canada, 1900–40* (Montreal, 1996).

31. For a general view of family life, see Cynthia Comacchio, *The Infinite Bonds of Family: Domesticity in Canada, 1850–1940* (Toronto, 1999). On the Catholic Church and the family, see Jeffrey Burns, *American Catholics and the Family Crisis, 1930–62* (New York, 1988). Even more recent publications ignore the issue of family violence. For example, E.J. Sheridan, ed., *Do Justice! The Social Teachings of the Canadian Catholic Bishops, 1945–86* (Toronto, 1987); John Williams, *Canadian Churches and Social Justice* (Toronto, 1984).

32. *Examiner*, 25 May 1933.

33. Interview with J.F., 9 July 1991.

34. Rev. E.S. Lautenslater, 'A Minister's Frank Talk to Brides and Grooms', *Chatelaine* (May 1954): 97–8.

35. Christie and Gauvreau, *A Full-Orbed Christianity*, 120. These authors see this alliance as a positive one for women.

36. For example, Crown Attorney's files indicate that in the 1920s there were 11 cases that made it to the Peterborough County Court, in the 1930s, 35 cases, and in the 1940s, 66 cases. In the Toronto Family Court, during the 1930s assaults comprised only 4–11 per cent of all Family Court cases. Over 95 per cent of these assault charges were against males.

37. It is very difficult to ascertain accurate numbers, even of the women who went to court. Different names, for instance, appear in jail registers, Crown attorney files, and local newspapers for Peterborough County.

38. The second charge came under the federal Criminal Code, s. 215 (2), i.e., 'rendering the home unfit' for the child through habitual drunkenness, sexual immorality, or any 'other form of vice'. The third came under the 'contributing' clauses of the Juvenile Delinquents Act.

39. AO, Attorney General/Court Records, RG 22, Crown Attorney's Records, Peterborough, 1939, case 492 (hereafter CA Peterborough).

40. Conviction rates for the general category of assaults in the province, for instance, ranged from 55–75 per cent. Averages taken from Ontario, *Report of the Inspector of Prisons*, 1930–60, using five-year intervals.

41. The York Family Court was set up in 1931.

42. Judge Hosking, 'The Family Court', *Child and Family Welfare* 8, 3 (1932): 25.

43. NAC, Canadian Council on Social Development Papers (CCSD), MG 28 I 10, vol. 32, file 151, Judge Mott quoted in *Montreal Gazette*, 25 Jan. 1943.

44. Ibid.

45. Hosking, 'The Family Court', 24.

46. Complaints about sex generally involved men complaining about women's failure to live up to their marital 'duties' or women complaining about men's excessive, unwelcome demands. 'Eg. You asked me if my husband was oversexed and I should say very much so, that's all he lives for. . . . I only wish God would take me out of this world.' AO, RG 22, Attorney General/Court Records, York County Domestic and Occurrence Files (hereafter York Domestic Files), box 1602, anonymous file from the 1930s.

47. AO, York Domestic Files, box 190, file 32744.

48. Ibid., box 195, file 33992.

49. Chunn, *From Punishment to Doing Good*, 172.

50. For example, the Annual Report of the Peterborough Family Court in 1957 indicates that 44 cases of assault were dealt with; this same number cannot be found in the police complaint files or arrest statistics from the jail registers.

51. On the role of probation officers, see D. Mendes Da Costa, ed., *Studies in Canadian Family Law* (Toronto, 1972).

52. Judge Philp, *Examiner*, 25 Oct. 1946.

53. Brock University Special Collections, County of Welland, Municipal Council Papers, Proceedings of Council, Dec. 1945.

54. AO, Attorney General, RG 22, Welland Family Court, series 5532 (hereafter WFC), box 10, F986.

55. Ibid., box 11, F609.

56. Ibid., F726.

57. Ibid., F1049.

58. Ibid., box 9, F1210.

59. Ibid., box 10, F4002.

60. Ibid., box 11, F459.

61. Ibid., F1431.

62. The actual ethnic breakdown of clients in Crown attorney and Family Court files is sometimes difficult to ascertain. About one-quarter of the Welland clients were characterized as Italian-Canadian, German-Canadian, etc., which could mean they were recent immigrants or that they were second-generation immigrants who still spoke more than one language.

63. Franca Iacovetta, 'Making New Canadians: Social Workers, Women, and the Reshaping of Immigrant Families', in F. Iacovetta and

M. Valverde, eds, *Gender Conflicts: New Essays in Women's History* (Toronto, 1992), 261–303.

64. AO, CA Peterborough, box 1, 1921, case 553.

65. AO, York Domestic Files, box 1584, C file.

66. Ibid., box 190, file 32702.

67. Ibid., box 1586, B file.

68. AO, WFC, box 10, F334.

69. These women lived on farms or in villages and small towns. In 1931 and 1941, the population of the city was about one-half that of the entire county.

70. AO, CA Peterborough, 1923, file 29.

71. AO, WFC, box 10, F627. The same conclusion is true for many women, who may not have returned simply because the Family Court really could not help them.

72. Ibid., box 11, F858.

73. AO, York Domestic Files, box 81, F4031. Note that a lawyer was used in this case, which took place in the early 1960s. One of the man's major complaints was 'he had to do the shopping'; perhaps this 'feminine' task was taken as an affront to his masculinity.

74. In over 50 per cent of the Welland case files, women pointed to more than one incident of violence.

75. *Examiner*, 1 Oct. 1934.

76. AO, York Domestic Files, box 82, F4326.

77. AO, WFC, box 10, F1216.

78. Ibid., box 11, F1115.

79. *Examiner*, 7 Sept. 1939.

80. On the nineteenth-century court, see Chris Burr, 'Roping in the Wretched, the Reckless and the Wronged: Narratives of the Late Nineteenth Century Toronto Police Court', paper presented at the annual meeting of the Canadian Historical Association, Calgary, 1994. For cases where the image of rural backwardness is used, see those emanating from the 'Badlands' of Peterborough County, such as charges against an abusive husband, *Examiner*, 22 Aug. 1922.

81. *Examiner*, 4 July 1947.

82. AO, WFC, box 11, F1133.

83. AO, York Domestic Files, box 1585, B file.

84. Peterson del Mar, *What Troubles I Have Seen*, 6.

85. Lisa Freedman, 'Wife Assault', in Connie Guberman and Margie Wolfe, eds, *No Safe Place: Violence against Women and Children* (Toronto, 1985).

86. AO, CA Peterborough, 1924, case 6.

87. In some families, women who were assaulted were then also prosecuted for beating their children, and this discredited them.
88. *Examiner*, 19 Nov. 1936.
89. In 1951, one Peterborough woman was found not guilty after admitting that she shot her abusive husband; the judge's strong direction to the jury noted that the woman was trying to prevent her husband from 'breaking up' the family home. *Examiner*, 6, 9 Nov. 1951. On the way in which the law of self-defence has historically denied the experience of battered wives, see Cynthia Gillespie, *Justifiable Homicide: Battered Women, Self-Defence, and the Law* (Columbus, Ohio, 1989).
90. Some war brides organized to offer support. On one level, this is also a revealing story about the experience of war brides. See *Examiner*, 9, 10 Nov. 1948.
91. Ibid., 9 Nov. 1948.
92. Ibid., 14 Feb. 1943.
93. Ibid., 1 Mar. 1943. The fact that she shot him in the back was taken as premeditation. Current analysis of 'battered wife syndrome' might analyse this differently. See Elizabeth Comack, *Feminist Engagement with the Law: The Legal Recognition of the Battered Woman Syndrome* (Ottawa, 1994).
94. AO, WFC, box 11, F609.
95. AO, WFC, box 10, F849.
96. AO, York Domestic Files, box 1583, A file.
97. In some cases, husbands clearly tried to persuade wives that they would 'lose their job' if they persisted. AO, WFC, box 80, F3847.
98. Fingard, 'The Prevention of Cruelty'.
99. AO, York Domestic Files, box 194, F4129.
100. Gordon, *Heroes of Their Own Lives*, 146–50. I have found little discussion of the issue in Canada.
101. In the latter case, the husband's claim that there are two sides to any story did not please the magistrate, who ordered a jail sentence. *Examiner*, 26 May 1939.
102. AO, CA Peterborough, 1933, case 66. The records may not adequately relate women's complaints of sexual cruelty. As James Snell points out, the twentieth century saw an increase in these complaints in divorce cases, and by the 1930s, some courts showed sympathy. See James Snell, 'Marital Cruelty: Women and the Nova Scotia Divorce Court, 1900–39', *Acadiensis* 18 (Autumn 1988): 3–32.
103. AO, York Domestic Files, box 1519, B file.
104. Ibid., box 1584, A file.
105. Ibid., box 1586, B file.
106. AO, CA Peterborough, box 11, 1947, case 68, 69.

107. Ibid., box 1942, case 155.
108. *Examiner*, 19 Feb. 1926.
109. Ibid., 19 Aug. 1942. After a difficult non-support case, Gee urged one husband to 'take better care' of his wife as she was 'fine looking . . . better looking than you'. *Examiner*, 24 July 1944.
110. AO, WFC, box 9, FA707; box 10, F986.
111. AO, WFC, box 10, F887.
112. Attorneys sometimes made the argument in defence of men that some physical 'force' was allowed, as long as it was not extreme. In one case the attorney said the husband only 'shoved' the wife, and that was acceptable as 'they were married'. Ibid., box 9, F521.
113. AO, York Domestic Files, box 191, file 32970.
114. Ibid., box 1607, W file. The judge might refuse the request for a jury trial.
115. Ibid., box 1513, anonymous file.
116. *Examiner*, 22 Jan. 1940.
117. AO, York Domestic Files, box 1515, B file, box 195, file 34227.
118. Peterson del Mar, *What Troubles I Have Seen*, 125.
119. AO, WFC, box 11, F661.
120. AO, WFC, box 10, F1313.
121. Ibid.
122. AO, WFC, box 11, F661.
123. AO, WFC, box 10, F918.
124. AO, WFC, box 9, F140.
125. AO, WFC, box 11, F1390, F495.
126. AO, WFC, box 10, F425.
127. AO, WFC, box 9, F1160.
128. AO, WFC, box 10, F654.
129. AO, York Domestic Files, box 193, F33454, box 376, F67.
130. AO, WFC, box 80, F3990.
131. *St Catharines Standard*, 15 Jan., 10, 20–4 Feb. 1945.
132. It is interesting that this question was even asked of women. AO, WFC, box 10, F1301.
133. AO, WFC, box 10, F640.
134. AO, York Domestic Files, box 1602, anonymous file.
135. AO, WFC, box 12, F508.
136. AO, York Domestic Files, box 191, F32957.
137. Peterson del Mar argues that there was a noticeable increase in affective violence in the post-World War II period. He explains this as a result of an intensified culture of individualism and disregard for self-restraint. Peterson del Mar, *What Troubles I Have Seen*, 116–17, 168. While this appears to be true for my study, I also know my records are more

comprehensive for this period. The sheer quantity and detail of violence described may not be a simple reflection of reality.

138. Chunn, *From Punishment to Doing Good*, 167.

139. Juvenile and Family Court of the County of Peterborough, *Annual Report for the Year 1947*, 9.

140. Hugh Dobson, 'Whither—The Canadian Family?', *Canadian Welfare* 16 (1940): 2–6. This article was penned by the secretary of the Evangelism and Social Services Committee of the United Church.

141. Judge Lorne Stewart, 'Family Breakdown', *Canadian Welfare* 33, 2 (1957): 61. Stewart entertained his audience with a classic tale of 'bad motherhood' in which a mother wanted her children 'placed out' so she could go to work. He was scathing about her desire for a 'holiday from her kitchen' and desire to shed her 'parenting duties'.

142. AO, WFC, box 10, F147.

143. AO, WFC, box 10, F963.

144. AO, WFC, box 11, F1320.

145. Gordon, in *Heroes of Their Own Lives*, points out that nagging was barely an issue in her case files until after 1930.

146. AO, WFC, box 10, F338, F369, box 11, F640.

147. AO, WFC, box 12, F902.

148. AO, WFC, box 10, F765.

149. There is little evidence, however, that families were much worse at mediating than the court; moreover, families often provided financial support to women who had to leave their homes.

150. AO, WFC, box 10, F1529.

151. AO, WFC, box 11, F405.

152. AO, WFC, box 10, F993.

153. AO, RG 20, Mercer Reformatory Records, reel 14, #11001, 1949.

154. AO, York Domestic Files, box 189, file 32621.

155. Ibid., box 194, file 34125.

156. Ibid., box 1602, S file.

157. Dorothy Chunn, 'Boys Will Be Men and Girls Will Be Mothers: The Legal Regulation of Childhood in Toronto and Vancouver', *Sociological Studies of Child Development* 3 (1990): 99. From the 1920s to the 1950s, the number of probation officers in the court increased from four to 14 and the number of occurrences handled by the Probation Department increased by 900 per cent. See John Hagan and Jeffrey Lyon, 'Rediscovering Delinquency: Social History, Political Ideology and the Sociology of Law', *American Sociological Review* 42 (1977): 594.

158. Toronto Family Court, *Annual Report*, 1920–53.

159. Dorothy Chunn, 'Regulating the Poor in Ontario: From Police Courts to Family Courts', *Canadian Journal of Family Law* 6, 1 (1987): 85–102;

Chunn, 'Rehabilitating Deviant Families through Family Courts: The Birth of "Socialized Justice" in Ontario, 1920–40', *International Journal of the Sociology of Law* 16 (1988): 137–58.

160. Not only are statistics on wife assault flawed; they are often unavailable. The jail register for Peterborough County shows an increase in non-support charges, but almost nothing for wife assault. Each Family Court kept its own records, and in both of these counties, the courts claim they no longer have them. The Toronto Family Court annual reports from 1945 to 1952 indicate a decrease in the number of assault charges attended to over this period.

161. AO, WFC, box 11, F370.

162. This is based on a sample of 40 cases drawn from the larger WFC records used.

163. For example, in one 1940 Peterborough County case, the man was also being investigated by the RCMP for having a still in his house—not something that endeared him to the magistrate.

164. The notion of wife as property often comes through quite clearly in these files as well. AO, York Domestic Files, Box 1607, anonymous file.

165. On the evolution of this idea of protection for some women in nineteenth-century British law, see Maeve Doggett, *Marriage, Wife Beating and the Law in Victorian England* (New York, 1993).

166. Nor should we dismiss women's own investment in this ideology of protection: something 'real' in the ideology spoke to women's daily experiences with violence and their need for immediate physical protection from their husbands.

167. For example, in a rape case, a young mother's visit to a beverage room, her attendance at a party without her husband, and her willingness to go in the man's car all cast her as a 'dishonourable' if not unbelievable victim, undeserving of the law's protection. Her case was dismissed. *Examiner*, 26 Mar. 1952.

168. Smart, *Ties That Bind*, 96.

169. For example, in the 1950s Mother's Allowances were made available to unwed and divorced mothers.

170. On the whole ideology of family containment in the 1950s, see Elaine Tyler May, *Homeward Bound: American Families in the Cold War Era* (New York, 1988). On the assumptions of social scientists and social workers about gender roles and the family, see Pleck, *Domestic Tyranny*; Wini Breines, 'The 1950's: Gender and Some Social Science', *Sociological Inquiry* 56, 1 (1986): 69–92. On the defence of masculinity in this period, see Barbara Ehrenreich, *The Hearts of Men: American Dreams and the Flight from Commitment* (New York, 1984).

171. Pleck, *Domestic Tyranny*, 146.

172. Lorraine Snider, 'Feminism, Punishment and the Potential to Empower-
ment', in Valverde et al., eds, *Wife Assault*, 236–59.

Chapter 4

1. Frances Shaver, 'The Regulation of Prostitution: Avoiding the Morality
Traps', *Canadian Journal of Law and Society* 9, 1 (1994): 134. See also
Janice Dickin McGinnis, 'Whores and Worthies: Feminism and Prostitution', *Canadian Journal of Law and Society* 9, 1 (1994): 105–22. Current
feminist debates about prostitution are extensive. For those who stress
the construction of sex work as a social problem, see Debi Brock, *Making Work, Making Trouble: Prostitution as a Social Problem* (Toronto,
1998); for continuing stress on patriarchy as well, see Christine Overall,
'What's Wrong with Prostitution? Evaluating Sex Work', *Signs* 17, 4
(1992): 705–24. For discussion of different approaches, see Sherene
Razack, 'Race, Space and Prostitution: The Making of a Bourgeois Subject', *Canadian Journal of Women and the Law* 10, 2 (1998): 338–73.
2. Sandra Lee Bartky, *Femininity and Domination* (New York, 1990), 65.
3. Soper, 'Productive Contradictions', 33.
4. Foucault, *The History of Sexuality*, 127.
5. Timothy Gilfoyle, 'Prostitutes in History: From Parables of Pornogra-
phy to Metaphors of Modernity', *American Historical Review* 104, 1
(1999): 140. Two examples of such differing approaches might be
Judith Walkowitz, *Prostitution and Victorian Society: Women, Class and
the State* (Cambridge, 1980) and her later *City of Dreadful Delight:
Narratives of Sexual Danger in Late Victorian London* (Chicago, 1992).
6. Foucault, *The History of Sexuality*, 4–11.
7. Catharine Annau, 'Eager Eugenicists: A Reappraisal of the Birth Control Society of Hamilton', *Histoire sociale/Social History* 27, 53 (1994):
111–34; Angus McLaren and Arlene Tigar McLaren, *The Bedroom and
the State: The Changing Practices and Politics of Contraception and
Abortion in Canada, 1880–1997*, 2nd edn (Toronto, 1997); Little, *'No
Car, No Radio, No Liquor Permit'*.
8. Margaret Hobbs and Joan Sangster, eds, *The Woman Worker* (St John's,
1999).
9. On the Ontario Royal Commission, see Mary Louise Adams, 'In Sickness and in Health: State Formation, Moral Regulation, and Early VD
Initiatives in Ontario', *Journal of Canadian Studies* 28, 4 (Winter
1993–4): 117–31. See also Dorothy Chunn, 'A Little Sex Can Be a Dangerous Thing: Regulating Sexuality, Venereal Disease and Reproduction
in British Columbia, 1919–45', in Susan Boyd, ed., *Challenging the*

Public/Private Divide: Feminism, Law and Public Policy (Toronto, 1997), 62–86.

10. Her estimate could go as high as 97 per cent. 'She shared the opinion . . . that every mental defective is a potential criminal', a view she promoted throughout the 1930s. McLaren, *Our Own Master Race*, 40.

11. C.K. Clarke, 'A Study of 5600 Cases Passing through the Psychiatric Clinic', *Canadian Journal of Mental Hygiene* 3, 2 (July 1921): 12–19. His popular version was 'Occupational Wanderers', *Maclean's*, 13 Apr. 1922. For a detailed analysis of this survey, see Jennifer Stephen, 'The "Incorrigible", the "Bad" and the "Immoral": Toronto's Factory Girls and the Work of the Toronto Psychiatric Clinic', in Susan Binnie and Louis Knafla, eds, *Law, Society and the State: Essays in Modern Legal History* (Toronto, 1995), 405–42.

12. Robert Weitz and H L. Rachlin, 'The Mental Ability and Educational Attainment of Five Hundred Venereally Infected Females', *Journal of Social Hygiene* (hereafter *JSH*) 31 (1945): 300–2.

13. Under a 1917 Order-in-Council it was illegal for any woman infected with VD to have sexual intercourse with a member of the armed forces or to solicit a member of the armed forces. Women arrested under these provisions could also be subject to compulsory medical examination. In 1919 the federal Criminal Code was amended to make it an offence to communicate VD to another person.

14. 'Fallen Women as Constant Pathologic Danger', *Journal of the American Medical Association* 79, 15 (7 Oct. 1922): 209.

15. These were constant themes in the American *JSH*, which admittedly was preoccupied intensely with venereal disease and prostitution. See, e.g., William Snow, 'Relations of Police and Health Officials to the Problems of Prostitution and the Venereal Diseases', *JSH* 18 (1932): 340–4; Bascom Johnson, 'A Current View of Prostitution and Sex Delinquency', *JSH* 22, 9 (1936): 389–402; Johnson, 'We Need Not Tolerate Prostitution', *JSH* 27, 9 (1941): 421–7.

16. Marilyn E. Hegarty, 'Patriot or Prostitute? Sexual Discourses, Print Media, and American Women during World War II', *Journal of Women's History* 10, 2 (Summer 1998): 115. It is important to note that Hegarty shows a contradictory 'mobilization of women's sexuality for war' as well.

17. Jay Cassel, *The Secret Plague: Venereal Disease in Canada, 1838–1939* (Toronto, 1987); Suzanne Buckley and Janice Dickin McGinnis, 'Venereal Disease and Public Health Reform in Canada', *Canadian Historical Review* 63, 3 (1982): 337–54; Ruth Roach Pierson, *'They're Still Women After All': The Second World War and Canadian Womanhood* (Toronto, 1986).

18. Donald H. Williams, 'The Facilitation Process and Venereal Disease Control', *Canadian Journal of Public Health* 34, 8 (Sept. 1943): 397, 399. This campaign was supposedly imitated in a US city. See Mayor Harry Cain, 'Blitzing the Brothels', *JSH* 29 (1943): 594–600.

19. W.I. Thomas, *The Unadjusted Girl: With Cases and Standpoint for Behaviour Analysis* (Boston, 1923); Aida Bowler, 'Social Factors Promoting Prostitution', *JSH* 17 (1931): 478.

20. Sheldon and Eleanor Glueck, *Five Hundred Delinquent Women* (New York, 1934), 303.

21. J.W. Holloway, 'Social Workers and Prostitution', *JSH*, 10 (Apr. 1924): 197.

22. Johnson, 'We Need Not Tolerate Prostitution', 424.

23. J.J. Heagerty, 'Education in Relation to Prostitution', *JSH* 10 (Mar. 1924): 130–1.

24. Hobson, *Uneasy Virtue*, 199.

25. Cambridge City Archives, Grandview Clipping File, A988.1007.198, John Okeefe, 'Last Chance School for Girls', *c.* 1960s, emphasis added.

26. Carole Groneman, *Nymphomania: A History* (New York, 2000), 37, 75, emphasis added.

27. Harold Greenwald, *The Elegant Prostitute: A Social and Psychoanalytic Study* [the updated version of *The Call Girl*] (New York, 1970), 199, 187, 147.

28. Ibid., 169. Some patient life histories, including their descriptions of sexual abuse, are given. He places less stock in their emphasis on sexual abuse than the patients do (see 49–51). Also, his research base was only six women for the first book, 18 for the second!

29. John Murtagh and Sara Harris, *Cast the First Stone* (New York, 1957), 297. Murtagh was a magistrate and Sara Harris a social worker. The latter went on to do an exposé of prison life as well.

30. Gwenyth Barrington, 'This is a Prostitute', *Maclean's*, 1 Oct. 1948, 13–14, 50–3.

31. Sidney Katz, 'The sleazy, grey world of the call girl', *Maclean's*, 11 Apr. 1959, 15–24.

32. Some point to the important connection in Foucault's work 'between religion, culture and power'. Jeremy Carrett, *Religion and Culture: Michel Foucault* (New York, 1999), 33.

33. Cynthia Comacchio, *The Infinite Bonds of Family: Domesticity in Canada, 1850–1940* (Toronto, 1999). Her conclusions can be extended through the 1950s.

34. Lévesque, *Making and Breaking the Rules*.

35. Christina Simmons, 'Modern Sexuality and the Myth of Victorian Repression', in Kathy Peiss and Simmons, eds, *Passion and Power: Sexuality in History* (Philadelphia, 1989), 157–77.

36. Hobson, *Uneasy Virtue*, 186.

37. Johnson, 'A Current View of Prostitution', 401.

38. Cain, 'Blitzing the Brothels', 599.

39. Timothy Gilfoyle commenting on national studies of Brazil and Russia in 'Prostitutes in History', 122.

40. Strange, *Toronto's Girl Problem*, 7.

41. Gilfoyle, *City of Eros*, 157. This comparison, of course, is made in the light of the pre-World War I fixation with prostitution. See Valverde, *The Age of Light, Soap, and Water*; Andrée Lévesque, 'Éteindre le 'Red Light': Les reformateurs et la prostitution—Montréal, 1865–1925', *Urban History Review* 17 (1989): 191–201; Lori Rotenberg, 'The Wayward Worker: Toronto's Prostitute at the Turn of the Century', in Janice Acton et al., eds, *Women at Work: Ontario, 1850–1930* (Toronto, 1974), 33–69; Nilsen, 'The Social Evil: Prostitution in Vancouver, 1900–20'.

42. Helen Boritch, 'The Making of Toronto the Good: The Organization of Policing and the Production of Arrests, 1859–1955', Ph.D. thesis (University of Toronto, 1985), 129. While these conclusions apply to Toronto and Ontario, there is some evidence for a similar experience in Vancouver. See Greg Marquis, 'Vancouver Vice: The Police and the Negotiation of Morality, 1904–35', in Hamar Foster and John McLaren, eds, *Essays in the History of Canadian Law: British Columbia and the Yukon* (Toronto, 1995), 257. Until other research is done, it is not clear whether this was a 'national' pattern. In Montreal, in contrast, there is evidence of renewed state and police persecution in later years, probably because of the influence of a city vice commission. See Danielle Lacasse, *La Prostitution Féminine—Montréal, 1945–70* (Montréal, 1994).

43. On the nineteenth century, see Backhouse, 'Nineteenth Century Prostitution Laws', 387–423.

44. *Statutes of Canada*, 1953–4, s. 164(c). This is essentially the same as the earlier section of the vagrancy statute, and this 'Vag C' clause was finally changed in 1972.

45. John McLaren, 'Twentieth Century Judicial Attitudes Toward Prostitution', in Sheilah Martin and Kathleen Mahoney, eds, *Equality and Judicial Neutrality* (Toronto, 1987), 283.

46. John McLaren, 'White Slavers: The Reform of Canada's Prostitution Law and Patterns of Enforcement, 1900–1920', *Criminal Justice History* 8 (1987): 125–65; McLaren, 'Chasing the Social Evil: Moral Fervour and the Evolution of Canada's Prostitution Laws, 1867–1917', *Canadian*

Journal of Law and Society 1 (1986): 125–65. Helen Boritch also notes the very 'noticeable' decline over the twentieth century in prostitution arrests. See Boritch, 'The Making of Toronto the Good', 262.

47. McLaren, 'Twentieth Century Judicial Attitudes', 284.

48. E. Neil Larsen, 'Canadian Prostitution Control Between 1914 and 1970: An Exercise in Chauvinist Reasoning', *Canadian Journal of Law and Society* 7, 2 (Fall 1992): 147–8.

49. Lacasse, *La Prostitution Féminine—Montréal*. Other authors have argued that police harassment brought pimps and male dominance. See Ruth Rosen, *Lost Sisterhood: Prostitution in America, 1900–18* (Baltimore, 1982), 33. American studies also point to the increasing intrusion of organized crime by the 1930s.

50. See, for example, the 1935 case in which women cannot legally be defined as 'accomplices' to living off the avails of prostitution, and therefore their testimony was admissible as corroboration. The 'charge of living off the avails . . . can only be laid against a male person.' *Rex v. Williams* (1935), C.C.C. 1935, 361. See also *Rex v. Scott* (1931), C.C.C. 1932, 380, for a wide definition of procuring.

51. For example, when one prostitute paid the bail for her male lover, he was convicted of living off her earnings. *Rex v. Cavanaugh* (1941), C.C.C. 1942, 79–80. This decision reflected earlier amendments intended to police men more stringently.

52. *Rex v. Novasad* (1939), C.C.C. 27. See also *Regina v. Simpson* (1959), C.C.C. 317.

53. AO, RG 22–5869, York County Court General Sessions, file 71–37.

54. One major problem with Table 6 is that the streetwalking/vagrancy clause for prostitutes is rolled in with the overall vagrancy numbers. All we know, therefore, is that the vagrancy numbers for women included some prostitution arrests.

55. *Rex v. West* (1950) cited in *Martin's Criminal Code* (Toronto, 1955), 354.

56. The woman must be a prostitute, must be wandering in a public place, and must fail to give a satisfactory account of herself.

57. Clayton James Mosher, *Discrimination and Denial: Systemic Racism in Ontario's Legal and Criminal Justice Systems, 1892–1961* (Toronto, 1998), ch. 6.

58. Catharine Carstairs, 'Nefarious Traffickers: Illegal Drug Use in 1920s English Canada', *Journal of Canadian Studies* 33, 3 (Fall 1998): 148–9; Emily Murphy, *The Black Candle* (Toronto, 1922).

59. These women, she complained, were 'dumped' into Canada and were plying their trade in our cities and 'lumber camps'. NAC, Canadian Council on Social Development Papers (formerly Canadian Welfare

Council), MG 28 I 10 [hereafter CCSD Papers], vol. 129, file: League of Nations—Traffic in Women and Children', Charlotte Whitton to O.D. Skelton, 13 July 1938. My thanks to Marg Hobbs for these Whitton references.

60. NAC, CCSD Papers, vol. 129, file: 'League of Nations'.

61. Margaret Patterson, 'Bad Girl', *Chatelaine* (Oct. 1935): 8–9.

62. Helen Norsworthy Sangster, 'Women for Sale', *Chatelaine* (Apr. 1937), 105.

63. Margaret Hobbs, 'Gendering Work and Welfare: Women's Relationship to Wage Work and Social Policy During the Great Depression', Ph.D. thesis (University of Toronto, 1995). Quote from W. Hutchinson, 'Tentative Principles and Problems in the Care of Destitute Single Women', would suggest only 'abnormal' women became prostitutes.

64. Kathleen Derry, 'Women and the Unemployed', *Canadian Congress Journal* (Dec. 1931): 38–9.

65. NAC, MG 26K, Bennett Papers, vol. 790 (reel M1447), D.H. Mackay to Bennett, 24 Oct. 1934.

66. NAC, National Council of Women Papers, MG 28 I 25, vol. 71 (NCW Papers), Report of Dorothy Gregg, National Convenor of Moral Standards Committee, 31 Oct. 1936.

67. NAC, CCSD Papers, vol. 129, file 2348, D.C. Draper to C. Whitton, 25 Oct. 1935. The chief's concluding remark seems to indicate the recognition that incarceration was as much punishment as rehabilitation: if a 'prostitute is *unfortunate* enough to serve a term at Belmont or the Mercer, they are taught all kinds of housework.'

68. Ibid., Hilda Aldrige to Whitton, 28 Oct. 1935.

69. Ibid., Our Sisters of Charity to Provincial Secretary Neelands, 20 Sept. 1935.

70. Ibid., Aldrige to Whitton, 28 Oct. 1935.

71. Wendy Ruemper, 'Formal and Informal Social Control of Incarcerated Women in Ontario, 1857–1931', Ph.D. thesis (University of Toronto, 1994), 460.

72. In the 1920s, for instance, a sample of those incarcerated on prostitution charges indicated an average sentence of 14 months served. The majority were under 21, and they came from across Ontario. By the 1940s, sentences were about five months and there were more women in their twenties than their teens.

73. My calculations, based on a count from the Mercer register, show that this was true for 1942 as well, but the annual report of the Mercer superintendent shows more prostitution charges in 1942 than I counted in the register (another sign of the inaccuracies of quantitative data). However, both my examination of the register and the annual report

numbers indicate this was true of 1943–5. AO, RG 50–1, reel 3404 and 3405, Prison Registers, and Annual Report of Reformatories, 1942–5. The dramatic increase in VD incarcerations also indicates the difficulty of using statistics to gauge women's actual prostitute work.

74. Toronto VD arrests for men and women were as low as 14 a year in the mid-1930s. They began to rise after 1937, and in 1941 they hit a high of almost 1,000, only to fall precipitously again afterwards. For these numbers, and discussion of the concerted campaign against VD and the replacement of street prostitution with VD arrests, see City of Toronto, Annual Report of the Chief of Police (hereafter Annual Police Report), esp. 1944, 1945, and 1946.

75. Margaret A. Jackson and Curt Griffiths, eds, *Canadian Criminology: Perspectives on Crime and Criminality* (Toronto, 1991), 123. In Toronto, vice arrests peaked in 1912, remained high until 1925, then declined over the next 30 years. The 'most noticeable decline in arrests in the 20th century was for prostitution'. Boritch, 'The Making of Toronto the Good', 262.

76. Annual Police Report, 1941.

77. Annual Police Report, 1942.

78. *Examiner*, 18 Feb. 1930. Peterborough arrest statistics supported his claim, with Liquor Control Act charges far outstripping anything else in 1930s, and no bawdy-house charges at all.

79. AO, Mercer case 5382, 1920s. A letter was sent to a prominent citizen from the superintendent: 'I think you may be interested in hearing that Rose seems perfectly sincere in her statement regarding your accidental visit to her house, and is emphatic in saying it was your first and last visit there.'

80. AO, Mercer file 5383, 1920s.

81. Ontario, Royal Commission on Public Welfare, *Report* (Toronto, 1930). AO, Toronto Industrial Refuge, Annual Report of 1927–8, includes a history of the Refuge. For the situation before closing, see Annual Report, 1937–8.

82. John Graham, 'The Haven, 1878–1930: A Toronto Charity's Transition from a Religious to a Professional Ethos', *Histoire sociale/Social History* 25, 50 (Nov. 1992): 283–306.

83. AO, Mercer file 5000, 1920s.

84. AO, Mercer file 5735, 1920s.

85. AO, Mercer file 10005, 1940s.

86. AO, Mercer file 9970, 1940s.

87. AO, Mercer file 6681, 1930s.

88. AO, Mercer file 11454, 1950s.

89. AO, Mercer file 8349, 1940s.

90. AO, York Family Court Records, box 1602, anonymous case file.
91. AO, Mercer file 5826, 1920s.
92. AO, Mercer file 7833, 1930s.
93. AO, Mercer file 9909, 1940s.
94. AO, Mercer file 8612, 1940s.
95. AO, Mercer file 8553, 1940s.
96. AO, Mercer file 5724. In the 1920s, for instance, a doctor concluded this prostitute was a 'high grade mental defective' and thus her inherited traits were from her mother, a 'low intelligence type', rather than from other family members, 'superior types'.
97. AO, Mercer file 5055, 1920s.
98. AO, Mercer file 7226, 1930s.
99. AO, RG 20, 16–2, Dept. of Reform Institutions, container 45, Mercer file, 1956–7.
100. AO, RG 20, 16–2, container 47, File 'Female Refuges Act', memo from Director of Psychology and Neurology to minister, 11 Feb. 1958, and RG 20 16–2, container 45, Mercer file.
101. See Carolyn Strange, 'The Velvet Glove: Maternalistic Reform at the Andrew Mercer Ontario Reformatory for Females, 1874–1927', MA thesis (University of Ottawa, 1983).
102. AO, Mercer file 5699, 1920s.
103. AO, Mercer file 5788, 1920s.
104. *Rex v. Wright*; *Rex v. Parker*, Ontario Supreme Court appeal (1930) C.C.C., 1930, 311.
105. *Toronto Star*, 20 Apr. 1933.
106. AO, Mercer file 5822, 1920s.
107. *Toronto Star*, 17 Oct., 5 Nov. 1935; *Examiner*, 9 Nov. 1935, 25 Nov. 1940.
108. *Toronto Star*, 11 July 1935.
109. Kelly Pineault, 'The Mentally Weak or Inherently Bad?: The Regulation and Reform of Women "Criminals" at the Concord Industrial Farm for Women', Honours paper, Trent University, 18.
110. Ibid., 19.
111. AO, Mercer file 8610, 1940s.
112. AO, Mercer file 13782, 1950s. The authorities hoped to deport her but could not do so.
113. AO, Mercer file 9809, 1940s.
114. Katz, 'The sleazy, grey world of the call girl', 15–24.
115. Luise White quoted in Gilfoyle, 'Prostitutes in History', 124.
116. Men could also be deported for importing the women for immoral purposes.
117. During the 1930s, when Charlotte Whitton was bemoaning the weak Canadian RCMP response to these fallen women, she collected countless

cases of their cross-border dealings. NAC, CCSD Papers, vol. 129, file 'League of Nations 1936–9'.

118. AO, Mercer file 13734, 1950s. See also Joan Sangster, 'Criminalizing the Colonized: Ontario Native Women Confront the Criminal Justice System, 1920–60', *Canadian Historical Review* 80, 1 (Mar. 1999): 32–60.

119. AO, Mercer file 7485, 1930s.

120. Katz, 'The sleazy, grey world of the call girl'.

121. AO, Mercer file 5083, 1920s.

122. AO, Mercer file 5054, 1920s.

123. AO, Mercer file 8452, 1940s.

124. AO, Mercer file 10006, 1940s.

125. For an example of the former, see Clarke, 'A Study of 5600 Cases', 14. It was suggested these 'defectives' might be 'permanently deprived of their liberty', sent to 'colonies near the cities' where they could perform useful manual work. Ontario, Royal Commission on the Treatment of the Feeble Minded and Venereal Disease [Hodgins Commission], 1920, 65.

126. AO, Mercer file 9827, 1940s. This case shows some of the problems in using official statistics of any kind to measure sexual regulation.

127. There were so many 'immoral' men and women living in 'adultery' who were deported that the border seemed to represent a means of informal divorce to working-class couples. NAC, CCSD Papers, vol. 129, file 'League of Nations—Traffic in Women'.

128. A woman who was kept by one man as a mistress could not be convicted of vagrancy. She could be convicted when, for the most part, she supported herself through prostitution. *Bedard v. King* (1916), 26 C.C.C. 99: R.M. Catty, *Canadian Law Book* (Toronto, 1925), 809.

129. *Rex v. Davis* (1930), O.W.N. 99–100.

130. On Patterson, see Dorothy Chunn, 'Maternal Feminism, Legal Professionalism and Political Pragmatism: The Rise and Fall of Magistrate Margaret Patterson, 1922–34', in W. Wesley Pue and Barry Wright, eds, *Canadian Perspectives on the Law and Society: Issues in Legal History* (Ottawa, 1988), 91–118; Amanda Glasbeek, 'Maternalism Meets the Criminal Law: The Case of the Toronto Women's Court', *Canadian Journal of Women and the Law* 10, 2 (1998): 480–502.

131. Royal Statutes of Ontario (RSO), 1897, c. 311, An Act Respecting Houses of Refuge for Females; RSO, 1919, c. 84, An Act Respecting Industrial Refuges for Females (Female Refuges Act), see esp. s. 15; RSO, 1927, c. 347, s. 15, 16, 17, emphasis added. See Allan Dymond, *The Laws of Ontario Relating to Women and Children* (Toronto, 1923), ch. 9. Women could be put in a refuge for 'bad habits' like drunkenness if they were unable 'to protect themselves'.

132. This change came after an inquest into this suicide. *Globe and Mail*, 12 Apr. 1919.

133. This applied to daughters who were under 21. Using other laws, parents had essentially been able to do this before 1919.

134. Ontario, Legislative Assembly Debates, Mar. 1958, 742.

135. Some of the case files are incomplete in terms of such information. An immigrant was often noted if there was a possibility of deportation.

136. AO, Mercer file 9617, 1940s.

137. AO, Mercer file 10708, 1940s.

138. AO, Mercer file 8141, 1930s.

139. Foucault, *The History of Sexuality*, 61.

140. AO, Mercer file 8170, 1930s.

141. AO, Mercer file 8111, 1930s. The doctor who examined Kathleen at the Whitby hospital disagreed with the judge, noting Kathleen was 'restrained too much'. The judge ignored the assessment: 'a fine example of cooperation', he sarcastically commented. Although medical assessments were important, they could also be ignored by a judge.

142. Joy Danousi, 'Depravity and Disorder: The Sexuality of Convict Women', *Labour History* 68 (May 1995): 30–45. In a few cases, female social workers displayed the same voyeurism.

143. AO, Mercer file 9097, 1940s.

144. For discussion of homosexuality in American prisons, see Estelle Freedman, *Their Sisters' Keepers: Women's Prison Reform in America, 1830–1930* (Ann Arbor, Mich., 1981), 139–41.

145. AO, Mercer file 7733, 1930s.

146. AO, Mercer file 8989, 1940s.

147. AO, Mercer file 7616, 1930s.

148. Pineault, 'Mentally Weak or Inherently Bad?', 33.

149. It appears the baby was used in a war between penal staff and the inmate. AO, Mercer file 11929, 1950s.

150. AO, Mercer file 11730, 1950s.

151. Parental reaction depended on how marginalized or how respectable the working-class family was, with the latter far more upset by illegitimacy. On the US, see Kunzel, *Fallen Women, Problem Girls*, 73; on Canada, see Lori Chambers, 'Courtship, Condoms, and "Getting Caught": Working-Class Sexuality in Southern Ontario, 1930–60', paper presented at the annual meeting of the Canadian Historical Association, Montreal, Aug. 1995.

152. AO, Mercer file 6649, 1930s, emphasis added.

153. AO, Mercer file 8129, 1930s.

154. AO, Mercer file 6972, 1930s.

155. AO, Mercer file 8398, 1940s.

156. AO, Mercer file 9404, 1940s.
157. For related discussion, see Odem, *Delinquent Daughters*, 80–1; Strange, *Toronto's Girl Problem*, 155–6; Dubinsky, *Improper Advances*, 88–9.
158. Elizabeth Fry Society of Toronto Library, Jill Copeland, 'The Female Refuges Act', unpublished paper, 9.
159. Pineault, 'Mentally Weak or Inherently Bad?', 29.
160. AO, Mercer file 9332, 1940s.
161. Ibid.
162. AO, Mercer file 8123, 1930s.
163. AO, Mercer file 8109, 1930s.
164. AO, Mercer file 8153, 1930s.
165. AO, Mercer file 10637, 1940s.
166. AO, Mercer file 7147, 1930s.
167. AO, Mercer file 8115, 1930s.
168. AO, Mercer file 8110, 1930s.
169. Ibid.
170. Ibid. The parents also believed Evelyn was mentally retarded, and though the number of women deemed feeble-minded by the medical examiners was probably exaggerated, it is possible some women were mentally challenged or had other disabilities. Incarcerating them in a reformatory was, as superintendents noted, not a solution to their problems.
171. AO, Mercer file 7629, 1930s.
172. AO, Mercer file 10121, 1940s.
173. AO, Mercer file 8111, 1930s.
174. Kunzel, *Fallen Women, Problem Girls*, 105.
175. AO, Mercer file 8357, 1940s.
176. AO, Mercer file 8111, 1930s.
177. AO, Mercer file 8140, 1930s.
178. AO, Mercer file 7570, 1930s.
179. AO, Mercer file 7851, 1930s.
180. AO, Mercer file 9097, 1940s.
181. NAC, CCSD Papers, vol. 129, file 2348, J.E. Bailey, Superintendent, to C.F. Neelands, 14 Oct. 1935.
182. AO, Mercer file 9900, 1940s.
183. Kunzel, *Fallen Women, Problem Girls*, 103.
184. The sexual regulation of heterosexual men was also fractured by race and ethnicity: liaisons between white women and non-white men were condemned and sometimes were terminated by the incarceration of the women.
185. Colin Sumner, 'Foucault, Gender and the Censure of Deviance', in Sumner, ed., *Censure, Politics and Criminal Justice* (Philadelphia, 1990), 37.

186. Foucault, *History of Sexuality*, 121.
187. Brock, *Making Work, Making Trouble*.

Chapter 5

1. My use of the term 'delinquent' recognizes its historical and social construction and does not denote an embrace of the negative designation of these girls as 'deviant'. The same applies to words such as 'immorality' and 'promiscuity' used repeatedly to describe the girls.
2. Paul Tappan, *Delinquent Girls in Court* (New York, 1947), 59.
3. The Ontario Training School for Girls (OTSG), later known as Grandview, was established in 1933 as the first secular, provincially run training school for girls. (There was also a Catholic training school, St Mary's.) The files used here included girls transferred from the Alexandra Industrial School for Girls (1891–1936). See Note on Sources.
4. Other North American historical research has concentrated on the period up to the 1930s, while Canadian studies often focus on the broad contours of the JDA or specific case studies. The definitions of delinquency described here were created in a larger North American context, but until more regional research is done we will not know how common the Ontario experience of juvenile justice was. The situation in Quebec was distinct because of the role of the Catholic Church in rehabilitation efforts, although one comparative essay still suggests common experiences of girls in reform schools in Ontario and Quebec. See Tamara Myers, 'Criminal and Bad Girls: Regulation and Punishment in Montreal, 1910–1930', Ph.D. thesis (McGill University, 1996); Tamara Myers and Joan Sangster, 'Retorts, Runaways and Riots: Patterns of Resistance in Canadian Reform Schools, 1930–60', *Journal of Social History* (Spring 2001). Other useful comparative studies include Odem, *Delinquent Daughters*; Ruth Alexander, *The 'Girl Problem': Female Sexual Delinquency in New York, 1890–1930* (Ithaca, NY, 1995); Strange, *Toronto's Girl Problem*; Matters, 'Sinners or Sinned Against?', 265–77.
5. In Ontario, the 1893 Children's Protection Act had already established Children's Aid Societies and a federal Act of 1894 allowed separation of young offenders and their alternative placements in industrial schools. Until 1939, Ontario children placed in industrial schools were governed by the Industrial Schools Act, which was superseded by the Training School Act of 1931. On the early Juvenile Delinquents Act and child-saving, see Jean Trepanier, 'Origins of the Juvenile Delinquents Act of 1908: Controlling Delinquency through Seeking Its Causes and through Youth Protection', and Alison J. Hatch and Curt T. Griffiths, 'Child

Saving Postponed: The Impact of the Juvenile Delinquents Act on the Processing of Young Offenders in Vancouver', both in Russell Smandych, G. Dodds, and A. Esau, eds, *Dimensions of Childhood: Essays on the History of Children and Youth in Canada* (Winnipeg, 1991), 205–32 and 233–66; Rebecca Coulter, 'Not to Punish but to Reform': Juvenile Delinquency and the Children's Protection Act, 1909–29', in Raymond Blake and Jeffrey Keshen, eds, *Social Welfare Policy in Canada* (Toronto, 1995), 137–52; Marge Reitsma-Street, 'More Control than Care: A Critique of the Historical and Contemporary Laws for Delinquency and Neglect in Ontario', *Canadian Journal of Women and the Law* 3, 2 (1989–90): 510–30; Gloria Geller, 'Young Women in Conflict with the Law', in Adelberg and Currie, eds, *Too Few to Count*, 113–26; Canadian Welfare Council, *The Juvenile Court in Law* (Ottawa, 1941), 5–6; W.L. Scott, *The Genesis of the Juvenile Delinquents Act* (Ottawa, 1966); Sutherland, *Children in English Canadian Society*, 124–51; John Hagan and Jeffrey Long, 'Rediscovering Delinquency: Social History, Political Ideology and the Sociology of Law', *American Sociological Review* 42 (1977): 587–98.

6. Canada, *Statutes of Canada*, 1908, ch. 40, s. 31. This is an edited version of longer wording. Emphasis is mine to stress the immense latitude in the law. See also Canadian Welfare Council, *The Juvenile Court in Law*, 9–10.

7. Judges like H.S. Mott (Toronto) and Ethel MacLachlan (Regina) and others lobbied for this change specifically to widen their powers over girls. Bruno Theoret, 'Régulation juridique pénale des mineures et discrimination à l'égard des filles: la clause de 1924 amendment La Loi sur les jeunes délinquents', *Canadian Journal of Women and the Law* 4 (1990–1): 539–55. Other amendments were added in these years, and after a conference with child welfare officials in 1928 the minister introduced an amended Act in 1929 that remained largely unchanged for decades.

8. Earlier industrial schools, such as the Alexandra School for Girls and the Victoria School for Boys, were meant for neglected, destitute children as well as for children in conflict with the law; reformers assumed both were working-class and poor children in need of guidance. Earlier provincial legislation was sometimes specifically created for certain institutions; the 1931 (revised in 1939) Ontario Training School Act was more inclusive, preparing the way for the first provincially-run secular training school for girls, the OTSG, established in 1933 in Galt. On child-saving and delinquency in earlier years, see Carrigan, *Juvenile Delinquency in Canada*, 2; P. Rooke and R.S. Schnell, *Discarding the Asylum: From Child Rescue to the Welfare State in Canada, 1800–1950*

(Lanham, Md, 1983). On the provincial industrial school for boys, see Paul Bennett, 'Taming "Bad Boys" of the "Dangerous Class": Child Rescue and Restraint at the Victoria Industrial School, 1887–1935', *Histoire sociale/Social History* 21 (May 1988): 71–96.

9. AO, RG 60, Ontario Training School for Girls Ward Files (hereafter OTSG), case file 197. The judge had to ask the CAS official how many girls were in the OTSG, what their ages were, what it did.

10. During World War II, for instance, of the 19 Ontario Juvenile Courts, 12 were presided over by magistrates. On Family Courts, see Chunn, *From Punishment to Doing Good*, 167.

11. Ibid., 179–80.

12. Bernard Green, 'The Determination of Delinquency in the Juvenile Court of Metro Toronto', SJD thesis (University of Toronto, 1968); Green, 'Trumpets, Justice and Federalism: An Analysis of the Ontario Training Schools Act of 1965', *University of Toronto Law Journal* 16, (1966): 407–23. Green made his concerns public and his critique—especially after the Training Schools Act was amended in 1965—was met with rebuttals from those connected to the ministry, such as University of Toronto social work professor and researcher Tad Grygrier. See T. Grygrier, 'A Minor Note on Trumpet', *Canadian Journal of Corrections* 8, 3 (1966): 262–7.

13. Tappan, *Delinquent Girls in Court*, 65.

14. Paul Havemann, 'From Child Saving to Child Blaming: The Political Economy of the Young Offenders Act, 1908–84', in Stephen Brickey and Elizabeth Comack, eds, *The Social Basis of Law: Critical Readings in the Sociology of Law* (Toronto 1986), 226.

15. AO, RG 22, Attorney General, York County Family Court Files (hereafter York Court), box 1524, unnamed file, 1950s.

16. Psychoanalysis was influential in the sociology of 'deviance'. Colin Sumner, *The Sociology of Deviance: An Obituary* (New York, 1994), 76.

17. Fraser, 'Michel Foucault: A Young Conservative?', 26.

18. Psychologists were sometimes used to do the kind of assessments psychiatrists were supposed to do, presumably because they were cheaper and easier to hire. On the faith in psychiatry helping delinquent girls, see Margaret Gildea, 'Psychiatric Problems in Training School for Delinquent Girls', *American Journal of Orthopsychiatry* (Jan. 1944): 128–35.

19. Gloria Geller, 'The Streaming of Males and Females in the Juvenile Justice System', Ph.D. thesis (University of Toronto, 1981), 121. By the 1960s some did argue that psychiatry had too much 'permeated public [and social work] thinking on delinquency'. Michael Hakeem, 'A Critique of the Psychiatric Approach to the Prevention of Juvenile

Delinquency', in Rose Giallambardo, ed., *Juvenile Delinquency: A Book of Readings* (New York, 1966), 454.

20. Psychologists used the Simon-Binet test to assess mental age, which was equated with intelligence. Early mental hygienists classified these by class and ethnicity. See E.K. Clarke, 'A Survey of the Toronto Public Schools', *Canadian Journal of Mental Hygiene* 2, 2 (July 1920): 182–5. By the 1950s some psychologists and psychiatrists noted that the tests were shaped by 'socio-economic factors' (AO, OTSG case file 2353, 1950s), but they were seldom willing to abandon the tests.

21. Ontario, *The Report of the Royal Commission on Public Welfare* (Toronto, 1931), 9, 32. On the punitive consequences of mental hygienist thinking in this period, see Robert Menzies, 'Governing Mentalities: The Deportation of Insane and Feebleminded Immigrants out of B.C., from Confederation to World War II', *Canadian Journal of Law and Society* 13 (1998): 135–73.

22. W. Mitchell, 'Delinquency—A Psychiatric Viewpoint', *Mental Health* 7, 3 (Mar. 1932): 21. Calls were essentially being made for 'streaming', including special classes for the 'gifted'. *Mental Health* also had some pro-sterilization articles, e.g., D.M. Le Bourdais, 'Eugenical Sterilization in California', *Mental Health* 4, 1 (Jan. 1929): 7.

23. Margaret Reeves, *Training Schools for Delinquent Girls* (New York, 1929), 75, 343, 246.

24. Paul Tappan, 'The Nature of Juvenile Delinquency', in Giallambardo, ed., *Juvenile Delinquency: A Reader*, 9.

25. Clifford Shaw and Henry McKay, *Juvenile Delinquency and Urban Areas* (Chicago, 1942). A Canadian study drew on this method in the 1960s. See Barbara Nease, 'Measuring Juvenile Delinquency in Hamilton', *Canadian Journal of Corrections* 8 (1966): 133–45.

26. Albert Cohen, *Delinquent Boys* (New York, 1955). There was intense concern about male gangs in Canada as well, starting in the 1930s and especially in the post-World War II period. See Kenneth Rogers, *Street Gangs in Toronto: A Study of the Forgotten Boy* (Toronto, 1945); Michael Young, 'The History of Vancouver Youth Gangs, 1900–85', MA thesis (Simon Fraser University, 1993).

27. On the former, see Mary Louise Adams, *The Trouble with Normal: Postwar Youth and the Making of Heterosexuality* (Toronto, 1997), 58; on Peterborough, NAC, Canadian Council on Social Development Papers (CCSD Papers) [formerly Canadian Welfare Council], MG 28 I 10, vol. 87, file 1856, 'Delinquency: General', G.H. Naphtali, 'The Juvenile Delinquent and the Problem Boy of Peterborough', July 1941. Early mental hygiene studies did sort the results of children's intelligence tests by class and ethnicity. The strongest equation was the association

of low scores with the 'labouring classes' and high scores with the professional classes. See Clarke, 'A Survey of the Toronto Public Schools'.

28. Ngaire Naffine, *Female Crime: The Construction of the Female in Criminology* (Sydney, 1987); Anne Campbell, *Girl Delinquents* (Oxford, 1981); Carol Smart, *Women, Crime and Criminology* (London, 1976); Shelley Gavigan, 'Women's Crime: New Perspectives and Old Theories', in Adelberg and Currie, eds, *Too Few To Count.*

29. There were some exceptions, usually dealing with specific institutions. See A.G. Westman, 'Trends in the Care of Delinquent Girls', *Canadian Child and Family Welfare* 6, 3 (1930): 33–6; Sister Bernadette, 'Recreation as an Institution', *Canadian Welfare* 27 (Dec. 1951): 22–7.

30. Glueck and Glueck, *Five Hundred Delinquent Women.* See Chapter 4 for discussion of this book.

31. Dr Anderson and Dr Blatz, 'Report from the Psychiatric Department', in City of Toronto, Annual Report of the Toronto Family Court (hereafter Toronto Court Report), 1945, 31. Articles in Canadian social work journals also stressed the high correlation of delinquency and broken homes. See M. Moore, 'Treatment without Operating', *Child and Family Welfare* 9, 6 (1934): 43–7; Hugh Dobson, 'Whither the Canadian Family?', *Canadian Welfare* 16, 6 (1940): 2–10. As late as 1965, the federal government's Task Force on Juvenile Delinquency noted that the most common cause cited in all submissions was the 'family'. Canada, Dept. of Justice Committee, *Juvenile Delinquency in Canada* (Ottawa, 1965), 16.

32. Ontario, Dept. of Reform Institutions, Annual Report upon the Ontario Training Schools (hereafter Ontario Reports), 1935–59.

33. W.I. Thomas quoted in Sumner, *The Sociology of Deviance*, 81.

34. Augusta T. Jameson, 'Psychological Factors Contributing to the Delinquency of Girls', *Journal of Juvenile Research* (Jan. 1938): 25–32.

35. Hilary Allen, *Justice Unbalanced: Gender, Psychiatry and Judicial Decisions* (Philadelphia, 1987), 71, 39.

36. For a good example, see Kate Friedlander, *Psychoanalytic Approaches to Juvenile Delinquency: Theory: Case-Studies: Treatment* (London, 1947).

37. Elizabeth Lunbeck, *The Psychiatric Persuasion: Knowledge, Gender, and Power in Modern America* (Princeton, NJ, 1994), ch. 7.

38. Herbert Herskovitz, 'A Psychodynamic View of Sexual Promiscuity', and Peter Blos, 'Three Typical Constellations in Female Delinquency', both in Otto Pollock and A. Friedman, eds, *Family Dynamics and Female Sexual Delinquency* (Palo Alto, Calif., 1969), 93 and 103.

39. Ames Roby, 'The Runaway Girl', ibid., 127.

40. Halleck, *Psychiatry and the Dilemmas of Crime*, 141.

41. Herskovitz, 'A Psychodynamic View', 89.

42. AO, RG 20 (Dept. of Reform Institutions), 16–2, container J 21, Galt file, letter of OTSG Superintendent to Deputy Minister, 6 Nov. 1952. My conclusions about boys are drawn primarily from Family Court files, not training school ones, so it is possible they will be contradicted by future research. Exhibitionism and pedophilia, for example, were seen as problems, but not consensual sex with girls.

43. There is quite a vast literature on this. One of the best-known American scholars is Meda Chesney-Lind, 'Judicial Enforcement of the Female Sex Role, the Family Court and Female Delinquency', *Issues in Criminology* 8 (1973): 51–70; Chesney-Lind, 'Sexist Juvenile Justice: A Continuing International Problem', *Resources for Feminist Research* 13 (1985–6): 7–9. See also Smart, *Women, Crime and Criminology*; Dorie Klein, 'The Etiology of Women's Crime: A Review of the Literature', *Issues in Criminology* 8 (1973): 3–30; Geller, 'Young Women in Conflict with the Law', 113–26. Historical studies include Steven Schlossman and Stephanie Wallach, 'The Crime of Precocious Sexuality: Female Juvenile Delinquency in the Progressive Era', *Harvard Educational Review* 48 (Feb. 1978): 65–95; Tamara Myers, 'Qui t'a débauchée?: Female Adolescent Sexuality and the Juvenile Delinquents' Court in Early Twentieth-Century Montreal', in Ed Montigny and Lori Chambers, eds, *Family Matters: Papers in Post-Confederation Canadian Family History* (Toronto, 1998), 377–94; Matters, 'Sinners or Sinned Against?'.

44. Kerry Cannington, *Offending Girls: Sex, Youth and Justice* (Sydney, 1993).

45. Cynthia Comacchio, 'Dancing to Perdition: Adolescence and Leisure in Interwar English Canada', *Journal of Canadian Studies* 32, 3 (1997): 5–35.

46. The question of whether the Depression resulted in more delinquency occurrences and/or court appearances is complicated. The claim by 'power control' theory advocates McCarthy and Hagan that more fathers at home meant children (especially boys) were better controlled, and therefore there was less delinquency, is too simplistic. Bill McCarthy and John Hagan, 'Gender, Delinquency and the Great Depression: A Test of Power-Control Theory', *Canadian Review of Sociology and Anthropology* 24, 2 (1984): 153–77. Marcus Klee shows that incidence of juvenile crime rose in Toronto from 1933 to 1937 in 'Between the Scylla and Charybdis of Anarchy and Despotism: The State, Capital and the Working Class in the Great Depression, Toronto, 1929–40', Ph.D. thesis (Queen's University, 1998), 139–40. However, girls' occurrence rates did not change substantially, and social workers later commented that Toronto rates began to *fall* after 1938 and only

rose again with the war. Moreover, as other evidence indicates, Toronto is not the only measure of social trends vis-à-vis delinquency.

47. Jeffrey Keshen, 'Wartime Jitters over Juveniles: Canada's Delinquency Scare and Its Consequences, 1939–45', in Keshen, ed., *Age of Contention: Readings in Canadian Social History, 1900–45* (Toronto, 1997), 364–86.

48. NAC, CCSD Papers, MG 28 I 10, vol. 87, file 1856, address by Nora Lea to Regina Children's Aid and Calgary Family Welfare Bureau, May 1943; letter of Allan J. Fraser, Ottawa Family Court judge, to Milton Wieber, 26 Aug. 1943. An emphasis on irresponsible mothers did not disappear at war's end. See Judge Lorne Stewart's characterization of the bad mother in *Canadian Welfare* 33, 2 (1957): 61.

49. AO, RG 20, 16–2, container J 1, Juvenile Delinquency File, 1943–4.

50. Pierson, *'They're Still Women After All'*; Susan Prentice, 'Workers, Mothers, Reds: Toronto's Postwar Daycare Fight', *Studies in Political Economy* 30 (1989): 115–41; Mona Gleason, *Normalizing the Ideal: Psychology, Schooling, and the Family in Postwar Canada* (Toronto, 1999); Mariana Valverde, 'Building Anti-Delinquent Communities: Gender and Generation in the City', in Joy Parr, ed., *A Diversity of Women: Ontario, 1945–80* (Toronto, 1995), 19–45. On the US, see Elaine Tyler May, *Homeward Bound: American Families in the Cold War Era* (New York, 1988); Wini Breines, *Young, White and Miserable: Growing Up Female in the Fifties* (Boston, 1992); John d'Emilio, *Sexual Politics, Sexual Communities: The Making of a Homosexual Minority in the U.S., 1940–70* (Chicago, 1983).

51. Some MPPs on the committee wanted to ban common-law unions and one suggested sterilization of promiscuous women. See AO, RG 20, 16–2, container J 36, Select Committee on Reform Institutions, clipping file.

52. Mary Louise Adams, 'Youth, Corruptibility, and English-Canadian Postwar Campaigns Against Indecency, 1948–55', *Journal of the History of Sexuality* 6, 1 (1995): 89–117.

53. AO, RG 20, 16–2, container J 48, Mercer file, quoted in clipping, *Toronto Star*, 10 Sept. 1957.

54. Halleck, *Psychiatry and the Dilemmas of Crime*, 139. He admits that when the college girls he treated engaged in the same behaviour as working-class girls, the former tended to be seen as neurotic, the latter morally delinquent.

55. AO, RG 20, 16–2, container J 15, Superintendent of OTSG to Deputy Minister, 18 Nov. 1953.

56. Franca Iacovetta, 'Gossip, Contest, and Power in the Making of Suburban Bad Girls: Toronto, 1945–60', *Canadian Historical Review* 80, 4 (1999): 585–623.

57. AO, OTSG case file 131, 1930s.

58. AO, OTSG case file 2197, 1950s.

59. AO, OTSG case file 6, 1930s.

60. From 1920 to 1950, the increase in cases handled this way was 900 per cent, according to Hagan and Lyon, 'Rediscovering Delinquency', 594.

61. According to Dorothy Chunn, occurrences in Toronto Family Court out-ranked court appearances by a ratio of 3:2 in the 1930s and by 6:1 in 1945. These figures represented adults and children. In the late 1940s, when separate statistics were kept, the same trend existed, with children slightly *more* likely to face the court. See Chunn, 'Boys Will Be Men, Girls Will Be Mothers: The Legal Regulation of Childhood in Toronto and Vancouver', *Sociological Studies of Child Development* 3 (1990): 99; Toronto Court Report, 1948, 1950, and 1952. The ratio of juvenile court appearances to occurrences for these years are: 1:3; 1:3; 1:4.

62. Gerald Markowitz and David Rosner, *Children, Race and Power: Kenneth and Mamie Clark's Northside Centre* (Charlottesville, Va, 1966), 84.

63. AO, York Court, box 1598, anonymous file, 1944.

64. This lenience applied to boys as well. Note a case where boys charged with theft got a suspended sentence. The father, who had his own busi-ness, gave them part-time jobs. They also went to 'summer camp, con-tinued in high school, played hockey and went to church'. AO, York Court, box 1522, anonymous file, 1945.

65. AO, OTSG case file 890, 1940s.

66. They used such influence to get daughters into training school, or more often, to try to get them out. In one case, an MPP helped a middle-class mother get her daughter into the OTSG, overriding the TSAB decision. AO, OTSG case file 85, 1930s. However, when a working-class family dropped too many names and wrote too many letters, they were seen as overstepping their place by the authorities. OTSG case file 2261, 1950s.

67. AO, OTSG case file 140, 1930s.

68. AO, York Court, box 1600, anonymous file, 1940s.

69. AO, York court, box 1519, anonymous file, 1950s.

70. AO, OTSG case file 197, 1930s.

71. AO, OTSG case file 1440, 1950s.

72. AO, OTSG case file 340, 1940s.

73. AO, OTSG case file 905, 1940s.

74. AO, OTSG case file 725, 1940s.

75. AO, OTSG case file 2080, 1950s.

76. Carlen, *Women, Crime and Poverty*, 73–106.

77. AO, OTSG case file 2289, 1950s.

78. AO, OTSG case file 320, 1939.

79. AO, OTSG case file 925, 1940s.

80. AO, OTSG case file 920, 1940s.

81. AO, OTSG case file 2295, 1950s.

82. AO, OTSG case file 65, 1930s.

83. In this and another case, the OTSG admitted that without someone to teach lip reading, the girl was actually suffering at the school. AO, OTSG case file 853, 1940s. Also, some files describe 'bad behaviour', which the authorities did not relate to disabilities but today would suggest problems such as attention deficit disorder.

84. AO, OTSG case file 280, 1930s.

85. AO, York Court, box 1607, anonymous file.

86. AO, OTSG case file 270, 1930s.

87. AO, OTSG case file 340, 1930s.

88. AO, OTSG case file 2241, 1950s.

89. See Joan Sangster, 'She Is Hostile to Our Ways: Native Girls Sentenced to the Ontario Training School for Girls, 1933–60', *Law and History Review* (forthcoming).

90. AO, OTSG case file 430, 1940s.

91. Ontario Reports and Toronto, *Annual Report of the Family Court.*

92. Girls' problems may have been processed as occurrences until their situation was perceived to be critical, thus biasing these numbers.

93. AO, OTSG case file G1, 1930s.

94. AO, OTSG case file 205, 1930s.

95. AO, OTSG case file 193, 1930s.

96. AO, OTSG case file 480, 1940s.

97. AO, OTSG case file 460, 1940s.

98. AO, OTSG case file 1079, 1940s.

99. AO, OTSG case file 675, 1940s.

100. AO, OTSG case file 230, 1930s.

101. AO, OTSG case file 22, 1930s.

102. AO, OTSG case file 173, 1930s.

103. AO, OTSG case file 155, 1930s.

104. AO, OTSG case file 843, 1940s.

105. AO, OTSG case file 1579, 1950s.

106. AO, OTSG case file 1465, 1950s.

107. AO, OTSG case file 15, 1930s.

108. AO, OTSG case file 340, 1930s.

109. AO, OTSG case file 2289, 1950s; case file 365, 1940s.

110. AO, OTSG case file 2127, 1950s.

111. AO, OTSG case file 40, 1930s.

112. AO, OTSG case file 310, 1940s.

113. AO, OTSG case file 15, 1930s. Another mother blamed her daughter's physical appearance, especially failing eyesight, on masturbation. Case file 29, 1930s.

114. AO, OTSG case file 1419, 1950s.
115. AO, RG 20, 16–2, container J 76, file: 'Training Schools'. Statement from TSAB to the Child Welfare Council in 1961 suggested alternative care for unmarried mothers: 'training school is no place for a girl in this condition . . . [although] in a sense, all unmarried mothers have been delinquent.'
116. This was a complicated political issue that emerged after Judge Orde, in *King v. Vahey* (1931), rejected a common-law union as inevitably 'immoral' under s. 215 of the Code—but this had implications for the JDA as well. The CWC lobbied for amendments to the law to make the equation of adultery (which was sometimes just a common-law union) and immorality more clear-cut, but even after amendments were passed, judges' decisions persisted in the earlier vein—to the consternation of W.L. Scott and the CWC. For some discussion of this long process, see Scott, *The Juvenile Court in Law*, 30–2, and for Charlotte Whitton's lobbying of the government on behalf of the CWC, see NAC, CCSD Papers, vol. 31, file 151. Presumably, World War II marked a turning point on this issue because the CWC had dropped it by this point.
117. This is true of larger city courts. The change is especially noticeable by the early 1960s.
118. AO, OTSG case file 145, 1930s. Psychiatrists also sometimes employed biological metaphors, e.g., case file 197, 1940s: 'seems she has inherited her mother's personality'.
119. AO, OTSG case file 2011, 1950s.
120. Ontario, *Report of Select Committee on the Problems of Delinquent Individuals* (Toronto, 1954), 400.
121. AO, OTSG case file 104, 1930s.
122. Judges' decisions were shaped by advice from the experts around them and this differed in large and small courts, rural and urban areas. The CAS was often involved in smaller courts, while in large cities the probation department, the court clinic, or psychiatrists from local hospitals were used.
123. AO, OTSG case file 420, 1940s.
124. AO, OTSG case file 1651, 1950s.
125. AO, OTSG case file 2212, 1950s.
126. AO, OTSG case file 780, 1940s.
127. AO, OTSG case file 420, 1940s.
128. AO, OTSG case file 285, 1930s.
129. AO, OTSG case file 1525, 1940s.
130. AO, OTSG case file 2300, 1950s.
131. AO, OTSG case file 125, 1930s.
132. AO, OTSG case file 470, 1940s.

133. Bernard Green's study in the 1960s described the process for parents as one of 'status degradation' despite the fact they often felt they had a fair hearing. Green, 'The Determination of Delinquency', 75.

134. 'Perhaps you overdid it', remarked the judge wryly in the first case. AO, OTSG case file 430, 1940s; case file 2230, 1950s.

135. AO, OTSG case file 270, 1930s.

136. AO, OTSG case file 330, 1940s.

137. AO, York Court, box 1594, anonymous file, 1944.

138. AO, OTSG case files 2084, 2095, 1950s.

139. AO, OTSG case file 1555, 1950s.

140. Green, 'The Determination of Delinquency',76.

141. AO, OTSG case file 235, 1930s.

142. AO, OTSG case file 170, 1930s.

143. AO, OTSG case file 750, 1940s.

144. AO, OTSG case file 1500, 1950s.

145. AO, OTSG case file 2356, 1950s.

146. AO, OTSG case file 95, 1930s. For a similar case where the girl took some pleasure in shocking the court with the list of men involved, case file 1023, 1940s.

147. AO, OTSG case file 2095, 1950s.

148. AO, OTSG case file 1068, 1940s.

149. AO, OTSG case file 1565, 1950s.

150. June Callwood, 'The Most Heartbreaking Job in Canada', *Maclean's* 66 (Dec. 1953): 12–13, 90–2.

151. AO, OTSG case file 2241, 1940s.

152. AO, OTSG case file 22, 1930s.

153. One CAS worker noted a girl had been abused by her stepfather, then went on to say that he had generally been 'good to all the children'. AO, OTSG case file 2440, 1950s.

154. AO, RG 20, D–13, Ministry of Correctional Services, Mercer Reformatory for Women, case file 15918, 1950s.

155. AO, OTSG case file 1480, 1940s.

156. AO, OTSG case file 1167, 1950s.

157. AO, OTSG case file 1168, 1950s.

158. AO, OTSG case file 2040, 1950s.

159. AO, OTSG case file 1495, 1950s.

160. AO, OTSG case file 1050, 1940s.

161. AO, OTSG case file 769, 1940s.

162. AO, RG 20, 16–2, container J 21, Galt inmate file, Memo on Detention from Isabel MacNeil, 1953, and container 54, Galt file, clipping of speech, 20 Jan. 1959, from Ruth Bentley, who resigned (probably with some pressure) as superintendent in 1959.

163. A tentative parallel is noted by Danielle Lacasse in her study of a Catholic reform school for boys. Although the Brothers adopted the trappings of social science 'professional' ideas in the post-World War II period, she notes that much of the disciplinary content of the program remained unchanged. Lacasse, 'Du délinquent à ouvrier qualifé: Le Mont-Saint-Antoine, 1945–64', *Histoire sociale/Social History* 22, 44 (1989): 287–316.

Chapter 6

1. AO, RG 20, Mercer Reformatory Records (hereafter Mercer), file 7057, 1930s.

2. For contemporary analyses of Native women's overincarceration, see Ontario Advisory Council on Women's Issues, *Native Women and the Law* (Ottawa, 1989); Carol LaPrairie, 'Selected Criminal Justice and Socio-demographic Data on Native Women', *Canadian Journal of Criminology* 24 (1982): 161–9. For a historical view, see Sangster, 'Criminalizing the Colonized', 32–60.

3. On political 'acculturation', see Anthony Boldt, *Surviving as Indians: The Challenge of Self-Government* (Toronto, 1993), ch. 3.

4. The rhetoric of citizenship was often used by the Training School Advisory Board, as well as by some judges. See also Police Chief Draper: 'the family is the fountain of all morality for the nation'. Toronto City Archives, Annual Report of the Chief of Police, 1944. On family, race, and nation, see Dua, 'Beyond Diversity: Exploring the Ways in Which the Discourse of Race has Shaped the Institution of the Nuclear Family', 237–60; Himani Bannerji, *The Dark Side of the Nation: Essays on Multiculturalism, Nationalism and Gender* (Toronto, 2000), esp. ch. 3.

5. Tarnopolsky, *Discrimination and the Law in Canada*; Walker, *'Race' Rights and the Law in the Supreme Court of Canada*; Backhouse, *Colour Coded*.

6. This is drawn from Lopez, *White By Law: The Legal Construction of Race*. On critical race theory and feminism, see also Razack, *Looking White People in the Eye*; Carol Aylward, *Canadian Critical Race Theory: Racism and Law* (Halifax, 1999); Crenshaw, 'Race, Reform and Retrenchment', 1331–87.

7. I have been influenced by theories of 'intersectionality', i.e., the need to look at the intersection of class, race, and gender, rather than fixing on a single axis of oppression. See Kimberlé Crenshaw, 'Demarginalizing the Intersection of Race and Class', *Chicago Legal Forum* (1989): 139–68; Crenshaw, 'Intersectionality, Identity Politics and Violence against Women of Colour', *Stanford Law Review* 43 (1991): 1241–99;

Brewer, 'Theorizing Race, Class and Gender'; Patricia Williams, 'It's All in the Family: Intersections of Gender, Race, and Nation', *Hypatia* 13, 3 (1998): 62–82.

8. Sangster, 'She Is Hostile to Our Ways'.

9. The 'primitive and the pauper' were overlapping projects of colonialism and working-class reform, parallel projects for bourgeois reformers intent on reconstructing their home lives by inculcating the values of 'modern domesticity'. Comaroff and Comaroff, *Ethnography and the Historical Imagination*, 289.

10. Martin Chanock, *Law, Custom and Social Order: The Colonial Experience in Malawi and Zambia* (Cambridge, 1985), 4.

11. Peter Fitzpatrick, 'Custom as Imperialism', in Jamil M. Abun-Nasr et al., eds, *Law, Society and National Identity in Africa* (Hamburg, 1990), 22–3.

12. Foucault, *Discipline and Punish*, 82.

13. Sharon Tiffany and Kathleen Adams, *The Wild Woman: An Inquiry into the Anthropology of an Idea* (Cambridge, 1985).

14. James Frideres, *Native Peoples in Canada* (Scarborough, Ont., 1983), 295–6.

15. For a review of some of this literature, see Ann Stoler, 'Making Empire Respectable: The Politics of Race and Sexual Morality in 20th Century Colonial Cultures', *American Ethnologist* 16, 4 (1989): 634–59.

16. John Comaroff and Jean Comaroff, *Of Revelation and Revolution: Christianity, Colonialism and Consciousness in Southern Africa* (Chicago, 1991), 13–14.

17. Anne Hellum, 'Actor Perspectives on Gender and Legal Pluralism in Africa', in Hanne Petersen and Henrik Zahle, eds, *Legal Polycentricity: Consequences of Pluralism in Law* (Aldershot, Hants, 1995), 13. Hellum is drawing on the work of anthropologist Sally Falk Moore.

18. Comaroff and Comaroff, *Ethnography and the Historical Imagination*, 28–9.

19. Ann Laura Stoler, *Race and the Education of Desire: Foucault's History of Sexuality and the Colonial Order of Things* (Durham, NC, 1995); Anne McClintock, *Imperial Leather: Race, Gender and Sexuality in the Colonial Contest* (London, 1995).

20. Stoler argues for addition of 'race' and Europeans' obsession with interracial sex as the fifth of Foucault's 'strategic unities' (i.e., the Malthusian couple, the masturbating child, the perverse adult, and the hysterical woman).

21. Ann Laura Stoler and Frederick Cooper, 'Introduction', in Stoler and Cooper, eds, *Tensions of Empire: Colonial Cultures in a Bourgeois World* (Berkeley, 1997), 19.

22. Laura Tabili, review of *Imperial Leather, Victorian Studies* 40, 3 (1997): 497. For another critical review of this book, see Tamara Jakubowska, *Race and Class* 38, 2 (1996): 89–92.

23. Definitions of customary law vary. Martin Chanock's work makes a useful distinction between custom, a set of values and social practices maintaining order in pre-colonial times, and customary law, the product of interaction between missionaries, courts, administrators, and indigenous people in the post-contact period. A general definition is: a set of common practices, traditions, and norms accepted by the community, accompanied by moral pressure or other means of social control to maintain these practices. For definitions in Canada, see Scott Clark, 'Aboriginal Customary Law Literature Review', paper for Manitoba, Public Inquiry into the Administration of Justice for Aboriginal Peoples (Winnipeg, 1990), 5–9.

24. The revelations of racism exposed by the Donald Marshall, Betty Osborne, and J.J. Harper cases, and subsequent inquiries, hastened this search. Manitoba, *Report of the Aboriginal Justice Inquiry*, 1991; Nova Scotia, Royal Commission on the Donald Marshall Prosecution, 1989; Canada, Royal Commission on Aboriginal Peoples, report on *Aboriginal Peoples and the Justice System*, 1993; Law Reform Commission of Canada, *Report on Aboriginal Peoples and Criminal Justice*. See also Bryan A. Keon-Cohen, 'Native Justice in Australia, Canada, and the U.S.A.: A Comparative Analysis', in Canadian Legal Aid Bulletin, ed., *Native People and Justice in Canada*, part 2 (1982), 187–258. Despite its proximity to the US, Canada never imitated the establishment of Indian tribal courts. See Bradford Morse, *Indian Tribal Courts in the United States: A Model for Canada?* (Regina, 1980); Morse, 'Indigenous Law and State Legal Systems: Conflict and Compatibility', in Harold Finkler, ed., *Commission on Folk Law and Legal Pluralism*, vol. 1 (Ottawa, 1983).

25. On oral sources, see Julie Cruikshank, *Life Lived Like a Story: Life Stories of Three Yukon Native Elders* (Vancouver, 1990). The classic case of oral traditions being denigrated is *Delgamuukw v. The Queen*. See Dara Culhane, *The Pleasure of the Crown: Anthropology, Law and First Nations* (Burnaby, BC, 1998).

26. 'There is white man's law, traditional law and bullshit law. The latter is the distortion of traditional law by the legal system to justify violence against women.' Sharon Payne, 'Aboriginal Women and the Law', in Chris Cunneen, ed., *Aboriginal Perspectives in Criminal Justice* (Sydney, 1992), 37. For Canada, see Teressa Nahanee, 'Dancing with a Gorilla: Aboriginal Women, Justice and the Charter', in Royal Commission on Aboriginal Peoples, *Aboriginal Peoples and the Justice System*

(Ottawa, 1993), 359–82; Nahanee, 'Sexual Assault of Inuit Females: A Comment on Cultural Bias', in Julian Roberts and Renate Mohr, eds, *Confronting Sexual Assault: A Decade of Legal and Social Change* (Toronto, 1994), 192–204; Margo Nightingale, 'Judicial Attitudes and Differential Treatment: Native Women in Sexual Assault Cases', *Ottawa Law Review* 23, 2 (1991): 71–98.

27. Jo-Anne Fiske, 'The Supreme Law and the Grand Law', *B.C. Studies* 105–6 (1995): 193.

28. Deborah Posel, 'State Power and Gender Conflict over the Registration of Customary Marriages in South Africa, 1910–70', *Journal of Historical Sociology* 8, 3 (1995): 223–56; Robert Gordon, 'The White Man's Burden: Ersatz Customary Law and Internal Pacification in South Africa', *Journal of Historical Sociology* 2, 1 (1989): 41–65.

29. Jo-Anne Fiske, 'From Customary Law to Oral Traditions', *B.C. Studies* 115–16 (1997–8): 208.

30. Some of these gloss over differences between Aboriginal cultures, others are more specific. Michael Coyle sees similarities between Iroquois and Ojibwa laws in 'Traditional Indian Justice in Ontario: A Role for the Present?', *Osgoode Hall Law Journal* 24, 2 (1986): 607–29. See also Patricia Monture-Angus, *Thunder in My Soul: A Mohawk Woman Speaks* (Halifax, 1995); Rupert Ross, 'Leaving Our White Eyes Behind: The Sentencing of Native Accused', *Canadian Native Law Reporter* 3 (1989): 1–15; Ross, *Dancing with a Ghost: Exploring Indian Reality* (Markham, Ont., 1992); Ross, *Returning to the Teachings: Exploring Aboriginal Justice* (Toronto, 1996); Kjikeptin Alex Denny, 'Beyond the Marshall Inquiry: An Alternative Mi'kmaq Worldview and Justice System', in Joy Mannett, ed., *Elusive Justice: Beyond the Marshall Inquiry* (Halifax, 1992), 103–8; Russell Smandych and Gloria Lee, 'Women, Colonization and Resistance: Elements of an Amerindian Autohistorical Approach to the Study of Law and Colonialism', *Native Studies Review* 10, 1 (1995): 21–46; Marianne Nielsen, 'Criminal Justice and Self-Government', in Silverman and Nielsen, eds, *Aboriginal Peoples and Canadian Criminal Justice*, 243–58; *Canadian Journal of Criminology* special issue on Aboriginal crime and justice (July-Oct. 1992).

31. In Native societies 'all were equal . . . irrespective of handicap, age, sex'. Eileen Couchene, 'Aboriginal Women's Perspective of the Justice System in Manitoba', paper for Manitoba, Public Inquiry into the Administration of Justice for Aboriginal Peoples (Winnipeg, 1990), 18. Though many scholars stress the egalitarian nature of Iroquois and Algonquin societies, few designate these as 'matriarchal' or female-dominated. This also seems to ignore evidence of more 'male-centred' Plains societies. See Laura Peers, *The Ojibwa of Western Canada,*

1780–1870 (Winnipeg, 1994); John Milloy, *The Plains Cree: Trade, Diplomacy and War, 1790–1870* (Winnipeg, 1988). A recent examination of Dogrib (Dene) customary law points to traditions that include some patterns of male dominance and physical punishment of women—how much these are true 'customs', how much customary law, is unclear. Joan Ryan, *Doing Things the Right Way: Dene Traditional Justice in Lac La Martre, NWT* (Calgary, 1995). For a recent overview exploring status in relation to patrilineal, matrilineal, and bilateral societies, see Ramona Ford, 'Native American Women: Changing Statuses, Changing Interpretations', in Elizabeth Jameson and Susan Armitage, eds, *Writing the Range: Race, Class and Culture in the Women's West* (Norman, Okla., 1997), 42–69.

32. Jo-Anne Fiske, 'The Womb is to the Nation as the Heart is to the Body: Ethnopolitical Discourses of the Canadian Indigenous Women's Movement', *Studies in Political Economy* 51 (1996): 65–95.

33. Vic Satzewich, 'Where's the Beef?: Cattle Killing, Rations Policy and First Nations "Criminality" in Southern Alberta, 1892–1895', *Journal of Historical Sociology* 9, 2 (1996): 188–212; R.C. Macleod and Heather Rollason, ' "Restrain the Lawless Savage": Native Defendants in Criminal Courts of the North West Territories', *Journal of Historical Sociology* 10, 2 (1997): 157–83; Tina Loo, 'Tonto's Due: Law, Culture and Colonization in British Columbia', in H. Foster and J. McLaren, eds, *Essays in the History of Canadian Law: British Columbia and the Yukon* (Toronto, 1995), 128–70.

34. Chanock, *Law, Custom and Social Order*, argues that once custom was codified by the colonizers as a text, customary law became *less* flexible than custom. See also Gordon Woodman, ed., *African Law and Legal Theory* (New York, 1995); Emmet Mittlebeller, *African Custom and Western Law: The Development of Rhodesian Criminal Law for Africans* (New York,1976); Sally Faulk Moore, *Social Facts and Fabrications: Customary Law on Kilimanjaro, 1880–1980* (Cambridge, 1986); Engle, 'Law and Colonialism', *Law and Society Review* 25 (1991): 889–922; Douglas Hay and Frances Snyder, eds, *Law, Labour and Crime in Historical Perspective* (New York, 1987); Mindie Lazarus-Black, *Legitimate Acts and Illegal Encounters: Law and Society in Antigua and Barbuda* (Washington, 1994).

35. Customary law in Africa was 'the most far reaching invention of tradition'. Terence Ranger, 'The Invention of Tradition in Colonial Africa', in Ranger and E. Hobsbawm, eds, *The Invention of Tradition* (Cambridge, 1983), 250. The invention of tradition may be taken for granted, for the debate concerns its usefulness for the present community, argues E.J. Dickson-Gilmore, in 'Finding the Ways of the Ancestors: Cultural

Change and the Invention of Tradition in the Development of Separate Legal Systems', *Canadian Journal of Criminology* (July-Oct. 1992): 479–502. Monture-Angus, *Thunder in My Soul*, 242.

36. See, e.g., Karen Anderson, *Chain Her by One Foot: The Subjugation of Women in Seventeenth Century New France* (New York, 1991); Sylvia Van Kirk, *Many Tender Ties: Women in Fur Trade* Society (Winnipeg, 1979); Jennifer Brown, *Strangers in Blood: Fur Trade Company Families in Indian Country* (Vancouver, 1980); Carol Devens, *Countering Colonization: Native American Women and Great Lakes Missions, 1630–1900* (Berkeley, 1992); Diane Rothenberg, 'The Mothers of the Nation: Seneca Resistance to Quaker Intervention', in E. Leacock and Mona Etienne, eds, *Women and Colonization: Anthropological Perspectives* (New York, 1980); Carol Cooper, 'Native Women of the Northern Pacific Coast: An Historical Perspective, 1830–1900', *Journal of Canadian Studies* 27, 4 (1992–3): 44–75; Jo-Anne Fiske, 'Colonization and the Decline of Women's Status: The Tsimshian Case', *Feminist Studies* 17, 3 (Fall 1991): 509–36; Sally Roesch Wagner, 'The Iroquois Confederacy: A Native American Model for Non-sexist Men', in W. Spittal, ed., *Iroquois Women: An Anthology* (Ohsweken, 1990), 217–22; Elizabeth Tooker, 'Women in Iroquois Society', in Spittal, ed., *Iroquois Women*, 199–216; Patricia Buffalohead, 'Farmers, Warriors, Traders: A Fresh Look at Ojibwa Women', *Minnesota History* 48 (1983): 236–44. On residential schools, Assembly of First Nations, *Breaking the Silence: An Interpretive Study of Residential School Impact and Healing as Illustrated by the Stories of First Nations Individuals* (Ottawa, 1994); J.R. Miller, *Shingwauk's Vision: A History of Native Residential Schools* (Toronto, 1996); Jo-Anne Fiske, 'Gender and the Paradox of Residential Education in Carrier Society', in Jane Gaskell and Arlene Tigar McLaren, eds, *Women and Education*, 2nd edn (Calgary, 1991), 131–46. On the home and family, see Pamela White, 'Restructuring the Domestic Sphere—Prairie Indian Women on Reserves: Image, Ideology and State Policy, 1880–1930', Ph.D. thesis (McGill University, 1987).

37. Anderson, *Chain Her by One Foot*.

38. Nancy Shoemaker, 'The Rise or Fall of Iroquois Women', *Journal of Women's History* 2 (1991): 39–57, and her introduction to Nancy Shoemaker, ed., *Negotiators of Change: Historical Perspectives on Native American Women* (New York, 1995); Jo-Anne Fiske, 'Fishing is a Woman's Business: Changing Economic Roles of Carrier Women and Men', in Bruce Alden Cox, ed., *Native People/Native Lands: Canadian Indian, Inuit and Metis* (Ottawa, 1988), 186–98.

39. Kathleen Jamieson, *Indian Women and the Law in Canada: Citizens Minus* (Ottawa, 1978); Janet Silman, ed., *Enough is Enough: Aboriginal*

Women Speak Out (Toronto, 1987); Susan Hynds, 'In a Circle Everybody is Equal: Aboriginal Women and Self-Government in Canada', MA thesis (Trent University, 1996); Katherine Beatty Chiste, 'Aboriginal Women and Self-Government: Challenging Leviathan', *American Indian Culture and Research Journal* 188, 3 (1994): 19–43.

40. More rapid urbanization occurred after the 1960s. Some Native peoples still officially living on reserves were looking for work in nearby communities.

41. Peter Schmaltz, *The Ojibwa of Southern Ontario* (Toronto, 1996), 10; Robin Brownlie, 'A Fatherly Eye: Two Indian Agents on Georgian Bay, 1918–1939', Ph.D. thesis (University of Toronto, 1996), ch. 2; Sally Weaver, 'The Iroquois: The Consolidation of the Grand River Reserve in the Mid-Nineteenth Century, 1847–1875', in Edward Rogers and Donald Smith, eds, *Aboriginal Ontario: Historical Perspectives on the First Nations* (Toronto, 1994), 213–57. On the west coast as well, argues Jean Barman with reference to sexual codes, 'Aboriginal societies did come to mimic their colonial counterparts', which is not surprising, given the advantages of doing so. Jean Barman, 'Taming Aboriginal Sexuality: Gender, Power and Race in British Columbia, 1850–1900', *B.C. Studies* 115–16 (1997–8): 263.

42. Brownlie, 'A Fatherly Eye'. On the history of the Act, see Jim Miller, *Skyscrapers Hide the Heavens: A History of Indian-White Relations in Canada* (Toronto, 1989); John Tobias, 'Protection, Civilization and Assimilation: An Outline History of Canada's Indian Policy', *Western Canadian Journal of Anthropology* 6, 2 (1976): 13–30; Brian Titley, *A Narrow Vision: Duncan Campbell Scott and the Administration of Indian Affairs in Canada* (Vancouver, 1986); Noel Dyck, *What Is This 'Indian' Problem? Tutelage and Resistance in Canadian Indian Administration* (St John's, 1991). On its uneven application, see Ken Coates, *Best Left as Indians: Native-White Relations in the Yukon Territory, 1840–1971* (Montreal, 1991); Sarah Carter, *Lost Harvests: Prairie Indian Reserve Farmers and Government Policy* (Montreal, 1990).

43. NAC, Dept. of Indian Affairs, RG 10, vol. 7978, file 1–18–26, Dept. of Justice to Indian Affairs, quoted to Kenora agent, 8 July 1944. Emphasis added.

44. NAC, RG 10, vol. 7978, file 1–18–26, 'Indian Marriage'. Letters between Dept. of National Defence and Indian Affairs discuss this issue during the war.

45. NAC, RG 10, vol. 3990, file 180/636, 'Policy re: Marriage', 1908.

46. Ibid.

47. NAC, RG 10, vol. 8869, file 487, 'Immorality in Kenora', Indian agent to Dept. of Indian Affairs, 19 Aug. 1919.

48. NAC, RG 10, vol. 2991, file 216/447, circular to all agents, n.d. (*c.* 1908).

49. NAC, RG 10, vol. 7978, file 1–18–26, Manitoba Inspector of Agencies to Ottawa, 4 Dec 1944.

50. NAC, RG 10, vol. 7978, file 11–18–26, Blackfoot Agent Gooderham to Dept. of Indian Affairs, Feb. 1944. Although my sources and examples focus on Ontario, I have drawn on Indian Affairs files from other areas of Canada to indicate views that had some broad acceptance among Indian agents.

51. NAC, RG 10, vol. 8869, file 487, 18–6, letter of N. Patterson to Ottawa, 8 July 1944.

52. This was not an isolated case—that is, of a principal in a residential school warning the agent of immorality. Ibid., 'Report of Agent to Ottawa', 18 Sept. 1930.

53. AO, Cape Croker Reserve Records, Diary of Jesuit Priests, reel 3. These cases took place just before World War I, but there is evidence that the priest continued to pressure for similar outcomes after the 1920s. Often, though, his primary concern seemed to be baptizing Native children before a Protestant minister could.

54. NAC, RG 10, vol. 8869, file 487, 18–6, 'RCMP Report', 14 Aug. 1933.

55. Ibid., 30 June 1933.

56. NAC, RG 10, vol. 2991, file 216/447, 18 Apr. 1943.

57. NAC, RG 10, vol. 8869, file 487, 18–6, Agent Edwards to Dept. of Indian Affairs, 25 Sept. 1941.

58. NAC, RG 10, vol. 9173, file B64, 19 Oct. 1927. This letter actually came from a western agent.

59. Posel, 'State Power and Gender Conflict', 241.

60. See discussion in Chapter 5 and note 116 to that chapter.

61. AO, Mercer case file 7644, 1930s. The case file is incomplete, but her father objected to her claims she could be paroled to 'an aunt in Parry Sound' as he said she didn't have an aunt in Parry Sound! 'She should serve her whole term. It is better for her to be in there', he wrote. Although more than one Native woman was imprisoned for bigamy, it is not clear whether they were in customary marriages or not.

62. NAC, RG 10, vol. 8869, file 487, 18–6, letter from Ottawa to Ontario Indian agent, *c.* 1920.

63. NAC, RG 10, vol. 11346, file 13, and 18–16, *c.* 1956.

64. NAC, RG 10, vol. 9744, file 487, Resolution of Whitefish Bay Council, sent to Dept. of Indian Affairs, Jan. 1939.

65. NAC, RG 10, vol. 7978, file 1–18–26, letter of Ontario agent to Dept. of Indian Affairs, 22 Feb. 1943.

66. The term was used by an agent from western Canada, but the paternalism was widely shared. NAC, RG 10, vol. 11415, file 984, 18–16, Agent

Perry to Dept. of Indian Affairs, 31 May 1920. It was often articulated by magistrates in court cases as well. See AO, Mercer case file 9393: 'she [a young Native woman] is easy victim for unprincipled Indian and white men.'

67. NAC, RG 10, vol. 10721, file 484, 18–16, letter of Chapleau agent, 19 Nov. 1956.

68. NAC, RG 10, vol. 8869, file 487, 18–6, report of 16 June 1933.

69. Brownlie, 'A Fatherly Eye', 67.

70. NAC, RG 10, vol. 8869, file 487, letter of councillor to Ottawa, 7 Feb. 1936.

71. AO, Parry Island Reserve Records, MS 137, reel 2, minutes of 1922. The same council worried that year that young people were going into Parry Sound and keeping late hours. 'Young girls must go with their parents if they want to go', said the resolution, which was passed. Reel 1, minutes of Dec. 1920.

72. Anastasia Shkilnyk, *A Poison Stronger Than Love: The Destruction of an Ojibwa Community* (New Haven, 1985), 89–90. Some oral accounts, it is suggested, may 'idealize older versions of social control in contrast to current crises they face'. J.C. Yerbury and C.T. Griffiths, 'Conflict and Compromise: Canadian Indigenous Peoples and the Law', in Finkler, ed., *Commission on Folk Law and Legal Pluralism*, 983. See also Lillian Ackerman, 'Marital Instability and Juvenile Delinquency Among the Nez Perces', *American Anthropologist* 73 (1971): 595–603.

73. NAC, RG 10, vol. 10721, file 484, 18–16, letter to Indian agent, May 1955.

74. NAC, RG 10, vol. 19680, file 43, 18–28, part 1, letter to agent, 13 Feb. 1958.

75. AO, Cape Croker Council, reel 1, minutes, 1 Mar. 1920. There was also an account of parents refusing to take in their daughter and her illegitimate child. The priest tried to intervene in this case. AO, Cape Croker Diary of Mission Priest, reel 3, 1933. See also R.W. Dunning, *Social and Economic Change among the Northern Ojibwa* (Toronto, 1959), for discussion of an Ojibwa community's antipathy to illegitimacy, though not necessarily to premarital sex.

76. NAC, RG 10, vol. 2075, file 964, 'Immorality in West Bay Area', circular from Indian Affairs.

77. AO, Mercer case file 11232, 1950s.

78. While many early accounts stress the ease with which all children were adopted into Native societies, constricted economic conditions probably made it more difficult to take in extended family members. Also, the context in which the illegitimacy occurred related to acceptance of children. Children conceived when couples planned marriage were

accepted more than children whose parentage was unknown or whose mothers had numerous illegitimate children.

79. NAC, vol. 8869, 1–18–16–2, part 1, 'Illegitimacy', Nov. 1958. There was a long debate about this issue because Indian Affairs pointed out that the child's name had to be posted for the band to see if she/he was to have status.

80. AO, Mercer case file 9004, 1940s.

81. AO, Mercer case file 12813 and 14305, 1950s.

82. AO, Mercer case file 11089, 1940s.

83. AO, Mercer case file 8552, 1940s.

84. AO, Mercer case file 9434, 1940s. This description was for a woman living off the reserve. For discussion of the overlapping projects of sexual reform, see Joan Sangster, 'Defining Sexual "Promiscuity": "Race", Gender and Class in the Operation of Ontario's Female Refuges Act, 1930–60', in Wendy Chan and Kiran Mirandanchi, eds, *Crimes of Colour* (Peterborough, Ont., 2001).

85. For images of Native women, see Daniel Francis, *The Imaginary Indian: The Image of the Indian in Canadian Culture* (Vancouver, 1992); Sarah Carter, 'Categories and Terrains of Exclusion: Constructing the "Indian Woman" in the Early Settlement Era in Western Canada', in Joy Parr and Mark Rosenfeld, eds, *Gender and History in Canada* (Toronto, 1996), 1–40. On the earlier period, see David Smits, ' "The Squaw Drudge": A Prime Index of Savagism', *Ethnohistory* 29, 4 (1982): 281–306.

86. Barman, 'Taming Aboriginal Sexuality', 237–67. On the US, see Katharine Osburn, 'To Build Up the Morals of the Tribe: Southern Ute Women's Sexual Behaviour and the Office of Indian Affairs, 1895–1932', *Journal of Women's History* 9, 3 (1997): 10–27. It is important to distinguish, historically, between a colonial period when miscegenation was a primary anxiety of church and colonial officials, and the later twentieth century, when the 'segregation' of the reserve system made this a less potent anxiety for white officials and, indeed, for society.

87. AO, Mercer case file 9332, 1940s.

88. AO, Mercer case file 9955, 1940s.

89. AO, Mercer case file 10279, 1940s.

90. NAC, vol. 19680, file 43, 18–28, letter to Indian agent, *c*. 1950.

91. AO, Mercer case file 9318, 1940s.

92. AO, Mercer case file 15182, 1950s.

93. Foucault, *Discipline and Punish*, 104–31.

94. Brownlie, 'A Fatherly Eye', 152.

95. Tiffany and Adams, *The Wild Woman*, 79.

96. It is also important to distinguish between persisting ideals and actual practices. One American anthropological study claims that 'stable marriages' were first described as the normal practice, but on close questioning other practices, including 'husband stealing' and 'marital instability', were recounted. Ackerman, 'Marital Instability and Juvenile Delinquency among the Nez Perces'.

97. Sally Weaver, 'The Iroquois: The Grand River Reserve, 1875–1945', in Rogers and Smith, eds, *Aboriginal Ontario*.

98. Shkilnyk, *A Poison Stronger than Love*; Regina Flannery, *Ellen Smallboy, Glimpses of a Cree's Woman's Life* (Montreal, 1995).

99. Irving Hallowell, *Culture and Experience* (Philadelphia, 1955); Hallowell, 'Sin, Sex and Sickness in Saulteaux Belief', *British Journal of Medical Psychology* 18 (1939): 191–7; Schmaltz, *The Ojibwa of Southern Ontario;* Edward Rogers, *The Round Lake Ojibwa* (Toronto, 1962).

100. Rogers, *The Round Lake Ojibwa*, B91.

101. Ibid., B47.

102. Hallowell, *Culture and Experience*, 304–5. Hallowell was looking at transplanted Ojibwa in Manitoba. See also Peers, *The Ojibwa of Western Canada*, who argues that after migration, Ojibwa women might have seen a decline in status due to absorption of values from the more male-oriented Plains cultures. Ojibwa elders in twentieth-century Ontario were also divided over whether to oppose the 'marrying out' clause. Schmaltz, *The Ojibwa of Southern Ontario*, 199.

103. Ruth Landes, *Ojibwa Woman* (New York, 1938). As Carol Devens points out, Landes describes a culture of separate and unequal spheres of men and women that was a product of colonization. See Devens, *Countering Colonization*, 124–5.

104. Sally Cole, 'Women's Stories and Boasian Texts: The Ojibwa Ethnography of Ruth Landes and Maggie Wilson', *Anthropologica* 37 (1995): 3–25. Wilson told her stories to convey images of resourceful women overcoming their hardship and silencing, and Landes's background as a working-class Jewish outsider in male academe may have attuned her ears to hearing an 'outsider's' story.

105. Ibid., 16.

106. Loo, 'Tonto's Due', 129.

107. Sangster, 'Criminalizing the Colonized'.

108. Frederick Hoxie, 'Towards a "New" North American Indian Legal History', *Symposium on Contemporary and Historical Issues in Legal Pluralism: Prairie and Northern Canada* (Winnipeg, 1992), 7.

109. 'The art of punishing, then, must rest on the technologies of representation.' Foucault, *Discipline and Punish*, 104.

110. Carol LaPrairie, 'Community Justice or Just Communities? Aboriginal Communities in Search of Justice', *Canadian Journal of Criminology* 37, 4 (1995): 521–45.

111. Sally Merry Engle, 'Popular Justice and the Ideology of Social Transformation', *Social and Legal Studies* 1 (1992): 161–76, esp. 171: 'popular justice is often colonized by state law.'

Chapter 7

1. Allan Hunt, 'Foucault's Expulsion of Law: Toward a Retrieval', *Law and Social Inquiry* (1992): 1–38.

2. For a critical feminist discussion of resistance and Foucault, see Linda Alcoff, 'Feminist Politics and Foucault: The Limits to Collaboration', in Arleen Dallery, ed., *Crises in Continental Philosophy* (Albany, NY, 1990), 69–88.

3. Michael Ignatieff, 'The State, Civil Society and Total Institutions: A Critique of Recent Social Histories of Punishment', in Cohen and Scull, eds, *Social Control and the State*, 93.

4. Palmer and F. Pearce quoted in A. Woodiwiss, *Social Theory After Postmodernism: Rethinking Production, Law and Class* (London, 1990), 113.

5. As Terry Eagleton points out, however, seeing the conditions of possibility did not necessarily mean viewing discourses in a material context with the assumption of a causal relationship between the two. I clearly favour Eagleton's sympathy for some measure of historical determination. Terry Eagleton, 'Frère Jacques: The Politics of Deconstruction', in Eagleton, *Against the Grain: Selected Essays* (London, 1990), 85.

6. Smart, *Feminism and the Power of the Law*, 6.

Index

THE CANADIAN SOCIAL HISTORY SERIES

Terry Copp,
The Anatomy of Poverty:
The Condition of the Working Class
in Montreal, 1897–1929, 1974.
ISBN 0–7710–2252–2

Alison Prentice,
The School Promoters:
Education and Social Class in
Mid-Nineteenth Century
Upper Canada, 1977.
ISBN 0–7710–7181–7

John Herd Thompson,
The Harvests of War:
The Prairie West, 1914–1918, 1978.
ISBN 0–19–541402–0

Joy Parr, Editor,
Childhood and Family in Canadian His-
tory, 1982.
ISBN 0–7710–6938–3

Alison Prentice and
Susan Mann Trofimenkoff, Editors,
The Neglected Majority:
Essays in Canadian Women's History,
Volume 2, 1985.
ISBN 0–7710–8583–4

Ruth Roach Pierson,
'They're Still Women After All':
The Second World War and
Canadian Womanhood, 1986.
ISBN 0–7710–6958–8

Bryan D. Palmer,
The Character of Class Struggle:
Essays in Canadian Working-Class
History, 1850–1985, 1986.
ISBN 0–7710–6946–4

Alan Metcalfe,
Canada Learns to Play:
The Emergence of Organized Sport,
1807–1914, 1987.
ISBN 0–19–541304–0

Marta Danylewycz,
Taking the Veil:
An Alternative to Marriage,
Motherhood, and Spinsterhood in
Quebec, 1840–1920, 1987.
ISBN 0–19–541472–1

Craig Heron,
Working in Steel: The Early Years in
Canada, 1883–1935, 1988.
ISBN 0–7710–4086–5

Wendy Mitchinson and
Janice Dickin McGinnis, Editors,
Essays in the History of
Canadian Medicine, 1988.
ISBN 0–7710–6063–7

Joan Sangster,
Dreams of Equality: Women on the
Canadian Left, 1920–1950, 1989.
ISBN 0–7710–7946–X

Angus McLaren,
Our Own Master Race: Eugenics in
Canada, 1885–1945, 1990.
ISBN 0–19–541365–2

Bruno Ramirez,
On the Move:
French-Canadian and Italian Migrants
in the North Atlantic Economy,
1860–1914, 1991.
ISBN 0–19–541419–5

Mariana Valverde,
The Age of Light, Soap, and Water:
Moral Reform in English Canada,
1885–1925, 1991.
ISBN 0–7710–8689–X

Bettina Bradbury,
Working Families:
Age, Gender, and Daily Survival in
Industrializing Montreal, 1993.
ISBN 0–19–541211–7

Andrée Lévesque,
Making and Breaking the Rules:
Women in Quebec, 1919–1939, 1994.
ISBN 0–7710–5283–9

Cecilia Danysk,
Hired Hands: Labour and the
Development of Prairie Agriculture,
1880–1930, 1995.
ISBN 0–7710–2552–1

Kathryn McPherson,
Bedside Matters: The Transformation
of Canadian Nursing, 1900–1990, 1996.
ISBN 0–19–541219–2

Edith Burley,
Servants of the Honourable Company:
Work, Discipline, and Conflict in the
Hudson's Bay Company, 1770–1870,
1997.
ISBN 0–19–541296–6

Mercedes Steedman,
Angels of the Workplace: Women and the
Construction of Gender Relations in the
Canadian Clothing Industry, 1890–1940,
1997.
ISBN 0–19–541308–3

Angus McLaren and
Arlene Tigar McLaren,
The Bedroom and the State: The Chang-
ing Practices and Politics of Contracep-
tion and Abortion in Canada,
1880–1997, 1997.
ISBN 0–19–541318–0

Kathryn McPherson, Cecilia Morgan,
and Nancy M. Forestell, Editors,
Gendered Pasts: Historical Essays in
Femininity and Masculinity in Canada,
1999.
ISBN 0–19–541449–7

Gillian Creese,
Contracting Masculinity: Gender, Class,
and Race in a White-Collar Union,
1944–1994, 1999.
ISBN 0–19–541454–3

Geoffrey Reaume,
Remembrance of Patients Past: Patient
Life at the Toronto Hospital for the
Insane, 1870–1940, 2000.
ISBN 0–19–541538–8

Miriam Wright,
A Fishery for Modern Times: The State
and the Industrialization of the New-
foundland Fishery, 1934–1968, 2001.
ISBN 0–19–541620–1

Judy Fudge and Eric Tucker,
Labour Before the Law: The Regulation
of Workers' Collective Action in Canada,
1900–1948, 2001.
ISBN 0–19–541633–3

Mark Moss,
Manliness and Militarism: Educating
Young Boys in Ontario for War, 2001.
ISBN 0–19–541549–9

Joan Sangster,
Regulating Girls and Women: Sexuality,
Family, and the Law in Ontario,
1920–1960, 2001.
ISBN 0–19–541663–5